The Management of Meaning in Organizations

The Management of Meaning in Organizations

Sławomir Magala

Professor in Organization Theory and HRM, Erasmus University, The Netherlands

palgrave
macmillan

First published 2009 by
PALGRAVE MACMILLAN

Palgrave Macmillan in the UK is an imprint of Macmillan Publishers Limited,
registered in England, company number 785998, of Houndmills, Basingstoke,
Hampshire RG21 6XS.

Palgrave Macmillan in the US is a division of St Martin's Press LLC,
175 Fifth Avenue, New York, NY 10010.

Palgrave Macmillan is the global academic imprint of the above companies
and has companies and representatives throughout the world.

Palgrave® and Macmillan® are registered trademarks in the United States,
the United Kingdom, Europe and other countries.

ISBN-13: 978–0–230–01361–2   hardback
ISBN-10: 0–230–01361–9   hardback

This book is printed on paper suitable for recycling and made from fully
managed and sustained forest sources. Logging, pulping and manufacturing
processes are expected to conform to the environmental regulations of the
country of origin.

A catalogue record for this book is available from the British Library.

Library of Congress Cataloging-in-Publication Data

Magala, Slawomir.
  The management of meaning in organizations / by Magala, Slawomir.
    p. cm.
  Includes bibliographical references and index.
    ISBN 978–0–230–01361–2
  1. Organizational behavior. 2. Interorganizational relations. 3.
    Knowledge management. 4. Organizational change. I. Title.
  HD58.7.M3233 2009
  302.3'5—dc22

                                                          2008050875

10 9 8 7 6 5 4 3 2 1
18 17 16 15 14 13 12 11 10 09

Printed and bound in Great Britain by
CPI Antony Rowe, Chippenham and Eastbourne

Contents

List of Illustrations

Preface

What do we mean when we mean something? What do we make when we make sense? We manage to answer these questions because we live in an organized world. We learn who to ask for advice – a philosopher, a medical doctor, a certified accountant or a creative artist. All of them practise their skills and serve the broader public. Both the 'content' of their professional service (knowledge, wisdom, competence) and 'form' of its delivery (organization, institution, network) change. Looking 'back' we can trace some of the changes – and their influence upon the contemporary production of 'meaningful' knowledge. Looking 'down', beneath the level of official exchanges between knowledge producers we can trace some of the overlaps and borrowings. Some of the latter may be tacit, implicit, subconscious. Professionals interact and communicate. Researchers talk to managers (say, biochemists and medical doctors). Researchers talk to researchers (say, social psychologists and theoreticians of organization). Managers talk to managers (say, politicians and priests, corporate executives and NGO activists).

Looking back we discover some skeletons in the house of scientifically legitimized knowledge. How come we learned to be ignorant about the role of non-western contributors to the European Renaissance from Arabia, Persia, Syria, India or China? Why do we insist that our elites speak Latin and Greek, sometimes Hebrew, but not Arabic? Does it influence our contemporary bias in dealing with the 'near' and 'far' orient?

Looking down we discover a lively underground traffic in meanings and sensemaking, most of it either illegal or semi-legal. Are we aware that the 'charisma' we discover in a politician was purchased on the black market of meanings? It was smuggled into the languages of social sciences and political PR from Byzantine iconic wars in early Christianity. Does it still mean the same to us?

These questions may sound abstract and remote to a busy professional. I have tried to demonstrate their empirical relevance and emotional appeal. Most of our lives are spent in professional bureaucracies, which outsource meanings and recycle values. Understanding what makes them (and 'us' in 'them') tick cannot be just another esoteric exercise. It can be relevant, salient and appropriate. Can it? Can we? Yes, we can.

SŁAWOMIR MAGALA
KRIMPEN A/D IJSSEL/POZNAN, NOVEMBER 2008

1

Introduction: Can Values and Meanings be Outsourced and, if so, to Whom?

Finding a hidden 'plot' in history has tempted artists, scientists, scholars, philosophers, politicians, ideologues and religious leaders. Hegel tried to glimpse the cunning of Spirit manifesting itself through the material events of the history of human societies. Poets and religious leaders wanted to become – acknowledged or unacknowledged – legislators of mankind. Many of them tried to fathom secret ways, trace underground passages or envision 'invisible hands'. Many of them borrowed metaphors from one another. T.S. Eliot might have been making an erudite reference to G.W.F. Hegel's famous observation on the cunning of reason in history, when speaking of 'cunning passages'. Hegel, the philosopher, referred to the irony of historical fate, which has mounted 'reason' on a horse. Historical events gave a gifted general of the French revolution, Napoleon Bonaparte, imperial power to spread revolutionary ideals of liberty, equality and brotherhood at the point of the bayonets of his victorious armies. His Blitzkriegs were cruel to monarchies and kind to republics. Ironic twists of fate suggesting unseen deals between personal ambitions and public causes have been noted in metaphors used by numerous scientists and philosophers. Adam Smith, an economist and a philosopher, did not comment on cunning passages between moral sentiments and the wealth of nations, but he duly commented on the invisible hand dealing historical cards to human agents linked by their ability to experience the presence and needs of others. Karl Marx, a philosopher and a political scientist, persuaded social scientists, politicians and trade unionists that under the surface of ideological clashes there was a throbbing heart of class struggle that dictated the rhythm of economic and political change and melted everything that had been solid into thin air. Our contemporaries, for instance Fernand Braudel, a historian, and Immanuel Wallerstein, a historian and a sociologist, traced long processes of the emergence of continental civilizations and global world-systems, the rise and fall of trade routes, colonial empires and decolonized globalizations. They and many other researchers and thinkers, have been digging under the visible, empirically observable, recorded processes of social, political, economic and cultural exchanges. They surfaced with critical theoretical reflections on the management and change of complex organizations and societies. Before they surfaced, they had to descend below the level of observable phenomena, record-able data, 'speakable' acts. Tracing and reconstructing historical flows of trade, industry, and commerce on a global scale, they emerged with theories of civilizations and world-systems as reconstructions of (and perhaps blueprints for) large-scale transformations of complex societies. We are slowly beginning to glimpse the hidden messages in their work:

> If it is true that the views of society offered by the sociologists of the social were mainly a way of insuring civil peace when modernism was under way, what sort of collective life and what sort of knowledge is to be gathered by sociologists of association once modernizing has been thrown into doubt while the task of finding the ways to cohabit remains more important than ever?
>
> (Latour, 2005, p. 16)

Both Braudel and Wallerstein are prominent members of the academic community, but they do not capture a broader public's imagination, in spite of the fact that they are well known outside their original disciplines. Our imagination is captured much more readily by artists, among them poets and film-makers. The 'cunning of reason' and 'ironies of historical fate' remain abstract formulae if deprived of the emotional temperature of a work of art. Ideas have to be translated and drama-tized if they are to move – in more senses than one. Thinking about history's cunning, secret passages, one may, for instance, evoke a recent Balkan masterpiece. In one of the visionary scenes from a movie on civil war in former Yugoslavia two characters descend to Berlin's under-ground right in front of the old Reichstag building. Instead of finding the maze of sewers, wiring and pipes that form a large city's soft under-belly, they find themselves at a busy underground crossroads. Trucks with UN soldiers and refugees, smuggled and legal cargo, buses, cars and carts rush by. One of the road signs tells them how far they are from Athens.[1] The artist makes us reflect on how far we have strayed from the path to democracy symbolized by the name of the ancient Greek city-state. Looking at this scene we wonder about the democratic deficit of contemporary, complex, networked and overlapping, bureaucratically managed and professionally staffed organizations and societies. Road signs hidden in Europe's underground point towards Athens, but aren't our societies heading towards clashes of civilizations outside our continent and towards civil wars within it? Aren't the organizations in which we spend our working lives barely able to tame power struggles in bureaucratic fiefs? Cannot we manage ourselves better? Prevent outbreaks of hostilities? Stimulate and encourage creativity? Take democracy more seriously in formal organizations, including professional bureaucracies thriving on knowledge? Our organizations structure us as agents and imprint their matrixes upon our lives, but they fail to endow us with meaning as definitely as we imagine Greek urban communities or Italian city-states once did. Our organizations socialize us into professions and guide us into career paths, but they do not prevent either domestic, intra-organizational intrigues or disruptions of social interactions; outbreaks of hostilities, ethnic cleansings, religious clashes, civil wars. Shouldn't we be able to do more about it? Charity, after all, begins at our bureaucratically managed, organizational homes.

The European film-maker's vision of the powerful underground flows evokes other associations, too. We are also reminded of the underground traffic in smuggled goods, some of them highly illicit, illegal and clandestine, which goes on beneath the surface of the cities and provinces of our complex cultures and societies. Social, cultural and organizational evolution – as a result of the ever present contemporary media and the growth of knowledge – has gone public and is much more traceable than ever before. Much more became – at least potentially – transparent and accessible to educated, informed and curious individual citizens. We have, indeed, become societies of the spectacle, and we rewrite the scripts, modify plots, recast and redirect the actors and generally speaking scrutinize ourselves much more frequently than ever before. Novels of the nineteenth century were supposed to be mirrors on life. Contemporary media are more than mirrors. They are scanners which accompany us everywhere – to our offices and workshops, bedrooms and sitting-rooms, native villages and foreign metropolises, individual retreats and collective assemblies. As we go on writing and reading novels, taking and reviewing photographs, making and watching TV programmes, conducting research and learning about everything we can, composing songs and symphonies or listening to them, as we continue praying, teaching, learning, designing – we are but imperfectly, dimly aware of an enormous virtual bazaar of ideas and values, an enormous flow of material imports and exports, borrowings and thefts, translations and imitations, waste dumping and retrievals, recycling and re-branding.

The ground beneath our feet trembles, tectonic shifts and paradigmatic earthquakes never cease. All of it happens just under the surface of official announcements, formally endorsed documents, legal explanations, approved expressions, legitimate interpretations, acceptable justifications, copyrighted publications, online appearances in virtual cyberspace.

This fascinating underground of our symbolic culture's domains merits closer inspection. If traffic is as lively as we imagine, perhaps borrowed and lent meanings play a much more significant role in the outsourcing of interpretations and understandings. After all, values and beliefs have a very busy social life and they are notorious for masks, which they don on various occasions, as they slip out of their safe deposit boxes. In religious dogma or secular 'value' banks they can become 'virtues' or 'targets', 'principles', 'constitutions' or 'criteria' for choice or items on checklists for benchmarking. 'Objectives don't get you there', as Jack Welch famously remarked, 'values do' (General Electric, 1992) They inspire our actions, legitimize our pursuits, power our beliefs or decorate our self-justifications. Occasionally, they can be planted like explosives under our interactions and lead to transformations, which had barely been deemed possible before. This is, for instance, what happened to the value of respect for the individual re-packaged as 'human rights' and inserted into the political discourse of the late twentieth century, still within the context of the Cold War. The re-insertion had been prompted by the contempt of the communist elites for the enslaved masses expressed in Majakovski's (1925) famous exclamation that an individual is a zero and a nothing since he cannot lift a heavy log of wood on his own. Soviet communist leaders accepted this insertion of human rights into public discourse considering it a minor and easily manipulated ideological catchphrase and were surprised when some of their disenfranchised citizens took it seriously. Such and many other forms of recycling, re-branding and repackaging of values and ideas never stop, since this is what our culture (and increasingly many other cultures) is (are) mostly about.

The socially managed gardens of our culture, with carefully fenced and marked domains of various arts, sciences, moralities or religions are being subverted, undermined, corrupted and transgressed every day. Under schools of thought, styles of art, trends of morality, fashions of communicating and religious traditions there are unknown tunnels, secret pipelines, cunning passages, illegal trading rooms, clandestine networks. This is the impression we get from looking at the levels of cross-fertilization, hybridization or 'creolization' of cultural forms.

This is the impression we get when admiring cross-cultural translations and regretting intercultural clashes.

Suspected 'underground' or 'under-cultural' mazes of connections, labyrinths of communications, networks of contacts merit a more systematic study and a more focused reflection. After all, in dreams begin responsibilities, and dreams (or nightmares) expressed by our filmmakers can be read as warning signs, as signals of today's invisible outsourcing, the results of which may surprise us tomorrow. Perhaps it is worth looking at influences, changes, evolutionary and revolutionary mergers of ideas and ideals? Do we understand how religious or artistic values invade politics, prompting politicians and their PR experts to announce crusades or to market self-images in media-saturated environments? How do our political and economic values subvert or promote art, by exposing it in galleries and museums, by evaluating, pricing, praising, criticizing and selling it on the market? How does science, in its quest for truth, fall prey to religion, repeating its past dogmatic and institutional struggles in new guises? How does 'science' (networked individuals under organizational flags) succumb to the 'politics' (networked individuals under other organizational flags) of peer pressure and generational purges, trading truth for power and influence?

There is nothing terribly new in the suggestion that we should look beneath the surface of 'official' exchanges between domains of our culture, beneath official interactions between formal organizations producing and disseminating cultural content. Social scientists and humanists are familiar with long-standing discussions, arguments and quarrels about the partitioning of topics, objects, areas and events between various scholarly and scientific disciplines, different methodological paradigms, research programmes and schools. Cultural anthropologists, social psychologists, economists, philosophers of science, sociologists and historians all claim to have valid passports, enabling them to describe and explain the domain of, say, organizational culture or change, managers' success or failure, institutions' survival and development or decline and disappearance. Recent interest in knowledge management prompted another look at the 'input' of managerial insights from a broad range of academic disciplines and a new reshuffling of topics formulated as tasks and handed down to the researchers and experts. But even without this reshuffling we would be tempted to look at the management of meanings, since we cannot coexist, cooperate, act ('meaningfully', 'making sense', 'rationally') without them. Moreover, in social sciences, much more than in the natural ones, submerged links to the past are more systematically, antagonistically and clearly signalled in attempts to revise our knowledge, to construct a critical theory, to question the past outsourcing of the management of meaning and to propose new ways of doing it.

Clandestine, underlying, supporting influence of this cultural underground can clearly be detected in Freud's attempt to explain the unconscious by illustrating his theoretical views with a new interpretation of the drama of Oedipus Rex by the ancient Greek dramatist, Sophocles. No Freud without Sophocles? Tracing the link between the two would take us to the road sign in the European cultural underground pointing to Athens. We would have to look at the classicist education of European bourgeois, middle-class elites in fin-de-siècle Vienna in order to explain why Freud, trained to be a medical doctor, associated the tragic adventures of a fictitious character from ancient Greece with the struggle of partly blind forces for control of the individual within the personality of a non-fictional contemporary man or woman. Management of meaning by Freud had been co-shaped and 'framed' by a managed public education, with specially designed curriculae, which encouraged the search for analogies and lessons to be drawn from ancient Greek authors. But underground connections do not only run diachronically from the Greek philosophers, the Roman legislators and early Christian bishops to contemporary academic networks, parliaments or churchgoers. They crisscross each other in synchronic spaces as well. Marx dedicated his *magnum opus* on 'Capital' to Charles Darwin (who politely declined the honour, shocked by his German admirer's atheism), thus firmly testifying to his belief in the 'consilience' of human knowledge about biological and social developments. He had no doubts about the legitimacy of importing a theory of biological evolution and natural selection to the realm of social sciences and socio-cultural evolutionary and revolutionary processes. No Marx without Darwin? Indeed, no Marx, and subsequently no Lenin, Mao or Pol Pot. The intellectual debt had been clearly and duly acknowledged, as was the case with Freud and Sophocles. But this does not need to be the case.

Not all borrowings and inspirations are acknowledged. Let us, for instance, look at the domain of visual arts and cultural criticism. One might say from today's critical perspective that there would be no Picasso without Daguerre. Photographs played a major role in Picasso's artistic choices and procedures. Many famous paintings, including 'Les Demoiselles d'Avignon' can be traced back to the Spanish master's shrewd use of photography. However, Picasso was not keen on admitting that he had relied on photographs and his reluctance to acknowledge any debt to photography or reliance on photographers in the search for visual 'clues' would not have become known without critical 'archaeological' research after his death (Baldassari, 1997). Likewise, no Susan Sontag without Roland Barthes. However, she would not have admitted it herself. There is no detailed discussion of Barthes's ideas in her *magnum opus*, *On Photography*, nor even in the much later *Regarding the Pain of Others*. Only critical comparative studies can uncover the underground links between the American public intellectual and one of the most famous French structuralist philosophers of generalized, applied, extended cultural semiotics. If – as Serge Guilbaut (1983) famously stated – New York 'stole' the idea of modern art from Paris in the first years of the Cold War, then a study of Sontag's complex relationship to Barthes could help us understand the US-French intellectual traffic in the 1960s.

Generally speaking, academic intellectuals are more scrupulous in taking care of references and footnotes than artists and critics, media wizards and advertising agents. No Levi-Strauss or Chomsky without de Saussure (and linguistic structuralism). No Habermas without the Frankfurt School (Habermas had been Adorno's assistant at the university of Frankfurt am Main). No Popper without the Viennese neopositivists. No Feyerabend, no Lakatos without Popper. No Kuhn without Feyerabend and Lakatos. Without Kuhn the idea that management of meaning should rely on a reconstruction of 'underground' traffic in ideas and values from which generational and institutional groups emerge competing for the status of preferred supplier of meaning would still be dormant. It would be buried under cover of Popper's belief that there is a continuity in 'the logic of scientific discovery', which runs through natural, biological and social sciences. Popper, himself a rebel against the neopositivist illusions of the Vienna circle, could not accept further 'loss of control' over meaning, which is being managed by successive representatives of victorious paradigms. The idea that researchers cluster around emergent paradigms or rally to the defence of the established ones, supporting them while they are more or less openly polished, diversified, replaced and modified, franchised and disenfranchised under the same surface label; this idea, this vision, this philosophy of science would not have been voiced. The idea that traffic in ideas includes not only legitimate deals but also illegal transfers and intensive lobbying would be further away. Because of Kuhn's immense popularity, it is not only pragmatists and relativists who now reject the view that: 'there are firm, unchangeable foundations to knowledge . . . that philosophical insight would carve a secret path that ultimately leads to these foundations' (Baert, 2005, p. 147).

In contrast to Popper's expectations and fears, giving up foundationalism (even if this foundationalism is not ontological but epistemological, as in the logic of scientific discovery) does not mean that researchers will find themselves at the mercy of the collective fads and foibles of postmodernist gurus subjecting them to changeable criteria of evaluation at very short notice. Academic intellectuals have been more scrupulous than artists and critics in keeping track of their predecessors and of acknowledging borrowed theoretical scaffolding because their professional production of socially acceptable knowledge (that which is labelled as 'legitimate', 'state of the art', 'expert' and the like) *requires* them to duly acknowledge all relevant outsourcing events. However, even they can fail to notice the fact of their socialization into the tacit knowledge of their professional community. Even they can fail to notice that a subcultural, professional software – which is taken for granted – has been subtly installed in their minds by gradual acculturation and updated by professional training. They can be swept along by a fashion, carried away by a style and a mood, hijacked by a broader cultural or political movement. They are bound to follow a 'cultural logic of selfhood'[2] in practising their trade, when socialized into their profession. Uncovering, reconstructing, explaining and interpreting these hidden liaisons between branches of science, domains of culture or areas of social interaction is crucial to our understanding of ourselves as professionals, citizens and individuals. Magali Sarfatti Larson has phrased it very elegantly in her study of the transformation of the architects' profession:

> Architecture must have some purpose and meaning for people who devote their lives to it. The point is that even Richard Meier, an architect known for his uncompromising aestheticism, attributes to architecture the power to create and convey meaning for society *in general*. 'I am not sure [that architecture] shapes or reorders society, but I think it gives some focus, some sense of purpose or meaning that otherwise might not be there in the chaos of our time'. 'Meaning' has become an essential ideological justification of postmodern revisionism. Having retreated by will or force from exalting architecture as an agent of social reform to exalting its single products as works of art, their authors must still insist on making them 'speak'.
>
> (Larson, 1993, p. 149; emphasis in original)

They do so, by outsourcing the management of meaning to critics, who, in turn, look towards an academic or artistic pedigree. Again, Larson's comments illustrate some of this outsourcing of the production of meaning, understood as legitimization of professional activities, very well indeed:

> In the second half of the twentieth century, the advance of academicization has changed the substance of architectural criticism and

extended its public. Criticism uncovers methods of composition and spatial results that are not only difficult to interpret but even to see by untrained eyes. Yet academicization also promotes the continuing search for external theoretical legitimacy: it goes on, looking to science and ideology or, on the aesthetic side, to philosophy and literary theory.

(Ibid.)

Having interviewed many contemporary architects, Larson was able to identify the main suppliers of meaning managed by professional communities of architects; academic researchers and humanists, artists and critics, creative writers and literary scholars. And yet, this work of uncovering, digging up, recovering, reconstructing, explaining and interpreting of partly hidden, 'underground' traffic in meanings and in values attached to individuals and their work, has barely begun. Let us, for instance, consider one of the most important socio-cultural-political-economic processes of large-scale transformation of societies and interactions in the last two decades of the twentieth century, namely the breakup of the Soviet Union and the end of the Cold War. Not many researchers have been interested in tracing the links between the last phase of the Cold War (1968–89) and the emergence of such politicians as Margaret Thatcher and Ronald Reagan. One may claim, however, that these conservative politicians had at least been perceived by many political scientists as linked to surprisingly successful foreign policies in the bi-polar world. These policies accelerated the dismantling of the 'evil empire' and contributed to further weakening of the communist brand of totalitarian social organization. One may reasonably hope that perhaps a time will come when researchers will also start tracing their emergence (as neoconservative politicians) to the dynamics of the Cold War. Would there be Thatcher without Churchill's Fulton speech about the 'iron curtain'? Would there be Reagan without Kennedy's 'Ich bin ein Berliner'? Perhaps we will come closer to demonstrating that they were as much the late products of Cold War as they were the actors contributing to this war's unexpectedly sudden and relatively peaceful end. Policies and politicians of the Cold War – especially since the Cuban missile crisis – are systematically investigated by political scientists, historians, psychologists and sociologists, and a more balanced and profound reflection may soon be coming.

No such luck, however, with other, less prominent political and socio-cultural actors, who must also have been influenced and constrained by the Cold War, but in ways that at times appear as unpredictable as the *deus ex machina* intervention of a deity on a theatre stage. For instance, the fact that one group of cultural producers of the Cold War period, namely the abstract impressionist painters of New York, were singled out at the expense of the more realist visual artists – was a coincidence. Realists, even if 'magical', like Hopper or Rockwell, suited the tastes of top US politicians and businessmen much better. They were realistic and figurative. What you got was what you saw. However, the same could be said of the monumental sculptures and heroic paintings of the 'socialist realist' school in the Soviet Union. Thus Hoppers and Rockwells did not stand out against the compulsory socialist realist art style imposed on communist-dominated societies.[3] What mattered more than anything else was to be as different as possible. In the context of the Cold War such standing out was necessary to the 'war of images'. Thus abstract impressionists became symbols of the 'creative freedom' allowed to artists in democratic societies. They emerged from a fairly unusual clustering of circumstances, triggering events and negotiated compromises between partly secret CIA Cold War propaganda operations and the CIA's cultural 'cover' organizations (of which the Congress for Cultural Freedom was the best known). The 'decision' to support abstract impressionism rather than either geometrically abstract or socially engaged, realistic, figurative art must have come as a surprise to many, although artists themselves had contributed to this turn in cultural policies. Guilbaut quotes a critical introduction to the catalogue of an exhibition by the Polish artist, Teresa Zarnover, held in April 1946 in the Art of this Century Gallery in New York. The introduction had been written by Barnett Newman, one of the American avant-garde artists from New York City, associated with Pollock, Rothko and Gottlieb. Newman wrote his introduction to Zarnover's catalogue in April, after Churchill's Fulton speech on 5 March 1946 in which the term 'iron curtain' had first been used to describe the divisive nature of the aggressive policies of Stalin's Soviet Union in eastern and central Europe (and an anti-communist alliance was postulated):

> In this situation the work of the Polish artist took on a new signifi-
> cance, which Barnett Newman recognized ... For Newman, purist,
> abstract art was an illusion, a kind of totalitarianism. In contrast to
> geometric abstraction, expressionist fluidity was freedom: the free-
> dom to speak and to act. In Zarnover's rejection of the purist style
> Newman saw proof that his theories were in step with the march of
> history.
>   The art practiced by Newman and the avant-garde was one of a
> range of possible painting styles then being discussed in the press.

In 1946 the art world was in ferment. It was a moment of euphoria when everything seemed possible. If people were right that New York was going to take the place of Paris, then it was important to find the right image for America and its culture. This image would have to allow for the ideological requirements of both New York and the United States as well as take account of the international situation.

(Gilbaut, 1983, p. 114)

Why abstract impressionism? Gilbaut thinks that this is so because:

By 1948 their once disturbing vision could be integrated into the new anti-Communist rhetoric. Avant-garde radicalism did not really 'sell out', it was 'borrowed' for the anti-Communist cause. Indeed, the avant-garde even became a protégé of the new liberalism, a symbol of the fragility of freedom in the battle waged by the liberals to protect the vital center from the authoritarianism of the left and the right.

(Gilbaut, 1983, p. 202)[4]

Reconstructing the 'underground', clandestine, secret, covert activities as moves in the Cold War enables us to understand the logic of this choice, which ran contrary to the prevailing elite tastes, and its consequences for the subsequent development of visual and other arts and multimedia. Another case in point is provided by the apparently unpredictable rise to power of neoconservative think-tanks. With the arrival of the administration of George W. Bush these institutions became dominant in framing political discourse in the USA and in the EU. The emergence of the neoconservatives as the chief ideologues of the US ruling classes has not yet been fully traced to their professional careers anchored in Cold War contexts. No systematic study of neocons' embedding in Cold War-tainted organizations, institutions and networks has followed their appearance on a political stage. It is as if a collective organized amnesia has been agreed: the end of the Cold War is being studied, but mostly in connection with events east of the Elbe, not to the west of it. The end of the Cold War is being studied as a historical case: as the end of the communist utopia, not as a part of the dramatic change in global checks and balances that influenced the western, 'victorious' part as much as the eastern 'losers'.[5]

The absence of theoretical studies is intriguing as a 'black hole' in a model of outer space showing the evolutionary possibilities of social change.[6] The shortage of research reports is intriguing as a 'white spot' on a historically reconstructed map of the political and cultural history of the past quarter of a century. How is the meaning of the Cold War managed now that it is over but its consequences are still very much with us? Organized 'forgetting' of the Cold War has already started. The end of the Cold War has been overshadowed by ideological fads and foibles, none of them as crucial or as stabilizing for the world order as the Cold War had once been ('the end of history' or the 'clash of civilizations', 'globalization' or 'war on terror'). Initial attempts to tuck the end of the Cold War away under the label of 'return of post-socialist societies to the safe fold of the capitalist market' fizzled out with the drying up of the first generation of EU and government funds for joint research projects connecting EU and US researchers with their eastern, postcommunist colleagues. A more systematic reassessment and re-evaluation of both the Cold War and its end still looms large somewhere, ahead of research plans and public debates. After all, the extraordinary overturning of a large, militaristic system took place with the loss of very few lives. From the victory of the Polish trade union 'Solidarity' over the communist party in August 1980 to the 'orange revolution' in Ukraine in December 2004, with the fall of the Berlin Wall tucked between in November 1989, a quarter of a century witnessed major readjustments, changes, transformations and reversals in the management of meaning both in the 'old' member countries of the European Union and in its 'new' central European arrivals. It would be intriguing to trace fearful symmetries between 'decontamination' procedures east and west of the Elbe and to detect the consequences of learned ignorance on recent attitudes towards 'the Ossies'[7] in theoretical and political thinking.

It is intriguing to note that in spite of the end of the Cold War numerous western European theoreticians and politicians assume that having been on the capitalist side of the barricade somehow bestows theoretical and managerial superiority over 'helpless', 'orphaned' new Europeans, who have to start getting 'civilized' under the benevolent tutelage of their patronizing western counterparts. This aspect of the management of meaning of post-communist activities among western academic researchers, politicians, journalists and media specialists requires particular attention, because it promises to generate new insights into the historical continuity of bias, prejudice and stereotyping that accompany long-standing and highly politically and ideologically charged differences. In a sense, the well-known mechanism of blaming the victim has been put to a new use. Past communist constraints are forgotten and on the focus moves to differences in income levels and the sophistication of infrastructure, explaining them with reference to the inherent characteristics of those who are poorer and whose infrastructure is weaker (ignorance, laziness, backwardness, corruption, fundamentalism and so on are cited either openly or tacitly). Recent studies of changing stereotypes held by Poles of Germans and by Germans of their Polish neighbours in the years before Poland's access to the European Union seem to suggest that although this has, indeed, been the case, the reality of close contacts and interactions between groups may start to change even the most stubbornly held prejudices (although only very slowly). Any acceleration of such change remains impossible without corresponding change to the heavy filter of unexamined prejudice that is still detectible in the media of EU member countries (which still report on the former communist countries as if these consisted of the smoking ruins of abandoned army barracks). The enduring systematic bias against 'Ossies' in spite of the end of the Cold War and the preservation of the invisible 'iron curtain' of prejudice bring us to the second focal point of our investigations of 'underground' connections. Who, and which groups, networks, professional communities and institutional agencies are 'whitewashing' the meanings acquired in other domains of culture?

Isn't it intriguing, this relative neglect of potentially 'reconstructible' links between networks of 'culture workers' – producers, critics, mediators, educators, journalists, media people, curators, developers, managers of cultural institutions, experts from political think-tanks – and their role in co-determining the 'cultural content' that is being formed by the networks in which they participate? The internal division of labour between those creators of cultural content in the media should be reconstructed more frequently. One would see the connection between Fukuyama's 'end of history' thesis and Koyre's view of Hegelian destiny more clearly. The outsourcing of meaning maintenance can and should be traced to the mutually reinforcing exchanges between journalists and researchers, politicians and media owners, critics and artists, tourists and ideologues, pilgrims and religious leaders, advertisers and philosophers, sponsors and public intellectuals. Some of the links between them would lead to the analysis of censorship in the McCarthy era, to the outsourcing of the management of meaning activities to a CIA-sponsored Congress of Intellectual Freedom. Needless to say, the other side of the Cold War coin looks equally promising to an ambitious researcher, especially for the one willing to make use of newly open archives (although some of them were shut down again in Russia under Putin many more were opened up in Poland, Hungary, former East Germany and the Czech Republic).

First, the Comintern's notorious propaganda machinery has yet to be analysed together with its synchronized secret part run by the Soviet NKVD and western communist parties with their ring of non-party sympathizers ('useful idiots' in the parlance of communist masterminds). Second, the degrees of control and resistance on the part of the professionals involved in meaning maintenance and management have varied from one communist-dominated country to another. Criticism of McCarthy in the USA (as exemplified by a recent George Clooney movie, *Good Night and Good Luck*, 2005) had its eastern counterparts. In Poland, for instance, a wave of critical anti-communist works of art emerged during and after the 1956 'thaw' that followed the icy Stalinist phase of the Cold War. One is reminded, for instance, of Andrzej Munk's film *Eroica* from 1959, and Polański's *Bad Luck* from 1960 (Polański grew up as an artist in a Łódź film school, where Munk's artistic personality had been felt). Novels, poems, paintings, jazz, all broke with the 'social realist' canon of propaganda. Some of these critics, for example, the Polish Nobel Prize-winning poet, Czesław Miłosz, emerge as lucid analysts investigating the effects of totalitarian policies on intellectual elites early on in the course of the Cold War. Miłosz's study of the processes of individual adjustment made by Polish writers and philosophers to the new regime, *The Captive Mind*, first published in 1953, has become recognized as a classic case study of the attempts of creative intellectuals to come to terms with the management of meaning that had been outsourced to a totalitarian propaganda machine. What compromises are possible? Which are desirable? What will they bring about?

What do we learn from the answers given to such questions by intellectuals, including academic professionals, from *The Captive Mind*? When the book first appeared, it included detailed studies of prominent Polish intellectuals who had designed elaborate strategies for appeasing the new communist rulers and simultaneously preserving some degree of dignity and independence in an increasingly totalitarian society. Paying homage to the Polish Nobel laureate in the obituary published in *The New Criterion*, Hilton Kramer (2004) described Miłosz as a 'prophet of liberation for whom the individual exercise of disabused memory came to constitute a spiritual vocation'. Miłosz noticed that these intellectuals, brought up on western literature and educated in western universities, had started to display the kind of behaviour that had previously been observed among their eastern, Russian neighbours, subjected to totalitarian control. They had agreed to perform in an ongoing spectacle, for which their personal and private actions and utterances had been enlisted, filtered and drilled:

> It is hard to define the type of relationship that prevails between people in the East otherwise than as acting, with the exception that one does not perform on a theater stage but in the street, office,

factory, meeting hall, or even the room one lives in. Such acting is a highly developed craft that places premium upon mental alertness. Before it leaves the lips, every word must be evaluated as to its consequences. A smile that appears at the wrong moment, a glance that is not all it should be can occasion dangerous suspicions and accusations. Even one's gestures, tone of voice, or preference for certain kinds of neckties are interpreted as signs of one's political tendencies.

... To forestall doubt, the Party fights any tendency to delve into the depths of human being, especially in literature and art. Whoever reflects on 'man' in general, on his inner needs and longings, is accused of bourgeois sentimentality. Nothing must ever go beyond the description of man's behavior as a member of a social group. This is necessary because the Party, treating man exclusively as the by-product of social forces, believes that he becomes the type of being he pictures himself to be. He is a social monkey. What is not expressed does not exist.

(Miłosz, 1953, pp. 54–5)

As Christopher Hitchens duly noted, writing his own obituary of Miłosz, the Polish poet had explained the mechanism of self-protective and self-legitimizing behaviour under the most aggressively implemented communist regime in postwar Polish history (1949–56) with the aid of the Persian concept of 'ketman'. 'Ketman' referred to a style of cultural performance worked out by Persian dissident intellectuals learning how to survive a theocratic tyranny. These clandestine dissidents, studied by the French diplomat, Arthur Gobineau, in the mid-nineteenth century, were able to deceive the most vigilant censors and the most orthodox rulers, at the same time avoiding repression and preserving – if only for their own, private, domestic use – some degree of moral and professional autonomy. Hitchens also noted a quote from Miłosz in Azar Nafisi's *Reading Lolita in Tehran* and her ample use of the idea of 'ketman'.[8]

Incidentally, *The Captive Mind* was originally prevented from reaching a broader public in the west by hostile leftist intellectuals eager to sustain their illusions about Stalin's system. Many prominent western intellectuals were among those recruited to silence the anti-communist voices of Miłosz and other critical representatives of central European societies occupied by the Russians. These prominent intellectuals were often invited to royal tours of the Soviet Union, where carefully orchestrated visits enabled them to return to the west and claim that 'they have seen the future and it worked' – without noticing either the abject poverty of the masses or the camps of the Gulag behind the façades of

'Potemkin villages' erected especially for them. There was, for instance, a Nobel Prize-winning French philosopher and novelist, Jean-Paul Sartre. He had regularly served his communist masters throughout the Cold War, both by defending the Soviet Union and by criticizing the United States. There was, for instance, at least until 1956, Kingsley Amis, the novelist and a leftist, whose problems with understanding the role written for him by the Soviet communists eager to utilize *agents d'influence* among western intellectual elites has only recently been analysed by his son Martin (Amis, 2002).

Both Miłosz's decision to leave the ranks of state propagandists and Sartre's decision to serve them belong to the 'underground' history of the Cold War and their reconstruction sheds light on some of the changes in the ideological and scholarly climate after the wall came down. Understanding such individuals' political, philosophical and artistic choices requires an examination of the underbelly of Cold War politics. It requires a historical reconstruction of individual adjustments to the overall management of meaning by the institutionalized protagonists of the Second World War. It requires a reflection on the reasons and causes that made this Cold War, which had been one of the longest surviving patterns for generating meanings, one of the least studied and understood 'matrixes' of postmodernity.

However, while it may have taken time to get under way, the descent of social researchers to the underground of the Cold War has already begun. We learn, for instance, about the illusory – therapeutic – nature of civil defence programmes initiated by governments of both NATO and Warsaw Pact countries (Oakes, 2004; Sojak, 2005). The politicians and experts who had designed them were perfectly aware of the fact that these programmes would have failed to protect most of the civilian population in case of full-scale nuclear war. However, they would also have been aware of the fact that taking active part in civil defence preparations and exercises would reduce the level of fear. Scientific knowledge, political control and multimedia communications were linked in a unique historical project for 'civil defence', undertaken with fearful symmetry on both sides of the Elbe. Training all men and women in basic civil defence would – it was assumed – help discipline them by reducing the risk of panic and by getting the masses 'used' to the idea of 'mutually assured destruction', rapid political mobilization, prolonged hostilities, reduced citizenship. One is tempted to call this policy a project for a peaceful, civilian domestication of military nuclear threat with therapeutic consequences. This aspect of learning how to cope with the threat was well captured in the black comedy of, among others, the title of

Stanley Kubrick's *Dr Strangelove: Or How I Stopped Worrying and Learned to Love the Bomb* (1964). Another appropriate title might have been formulated as follows: 'How we learned to live with the bomb by acting in collectively staged and ritualized dress rehearsals of civil defence.'

On the eastern, for instance, the Polish side of the iron curtain researchers have also been trying to analyse the language of propaganda and the actions of civil defence specialists encouraging individuals to prepare for a potential nuclear confrontation with the capitalist 'enemy'. They have also tried to extend reflections started by Miłosz in 1951 and detect traces of communist distortion of political imagination and national memory (Śpiewak, 2005).

Researchers are slowly beginning to reconstruct the management of meaning on both sides of the iron curtain and to trace the consequences of the outsourcing of some of its operations to secret services and propaganda machines (Caute, 2003). Needless to say, academic and artistic, critical and literary establishments have not been immune to these operations (as the involvement of some artists, critics and scholars makes abundantly clear). And this rings true on both sides of the potential conflict between the world capitalist and global socialist systems. The rapid conquest of academic, research and think-tank networks by the representatives of the neopositivist methodology and the equally swift academic rise of rational choice theory to its dominant position in academic embedding of social sciences (especially in the period between the outbreak of the Korean war and the Cuban missile crisis and again in the period of student unrest 1966–72) can at least partly be explained by the Cold War focus of political decision-makers and by the secretive, confidential procedures of the selection of individuals to the top positions in research organizations and institutions (Amadae, 2003). Interestingly enough, as the consolidation of paradigmatic power in the hands of the RAND-like academic professionals was taking place, theoretical self-reflection of the entire academic profession moved away from the traditional neopositivist philosophy of the Vienna circle. Reflexive self-definition has acquired a momentum of its own, following the cultural logic of the Cold War only to a limited extent. What limited this influence? Perhaps, for example, generational struggles resulting from the expansion of educational bureaucracies (first, after the Second World War and then when the 'baby boom' generation arrived in late 1960s). Academic professionals were still influenced by Cold War traces, but there were more of them.

Initially, and predominantly in Europe, the professional articulation of academic identity moved towards the Popperian philosophy of science ('falsificationism') as a leading doctrine on how to manage meaning in professional academic institutions. Later on, and first in the United States, it moved towards the Kuhnian philosophy of scientific revolutions ('paradigmatic shifts') marking the transition between not very peaceful coexistence of dominant and minor paradigms and the subsequent enforced 'uneasy' postmodernist paradigmatic truce. The later shift (from the Popperian to the Kuhnian view of the growth of scientific knowledge) has been caused as much by the conservative as by the radical academic professionals, both of whom thought to have found a useful instrument for the management of meaning in the Kuhnian reconstruction of the history of science as a sequence of paradigms and revolutions. Why could parties that differed in all other respects agree on Kuhn's vision of the growth of knowledge as a sequence of long periods of routine research projects ('normal science') punctuated by sudden, short and violent mobilizations of revolutionary peers pushing a new paradigm through to the top of their ranking lists (under the pretext of solving accumulating anomalies, which the older paradigm did not allow to remove)? The answer is not self-evident. This is why the Kuhnian vision requires closer inspection. Some attempts have already surfaced.

Steven Fuller's (2000) attempts to explain the sources, the impact and the position of Thomas Kuhn in the contemporary philosophy of science, in the American academic establishment and in the post-Cold War cultural climate, are a case in point. In the case of Kuhn, the underground links to the Cold War are particularly intriguing, as the individual responsible for one of the most momentous encounters in contemporary philosophy of science, namely the Popper-Kuhn debate, came in from the communist cold, from behind the iron curtain. Imre Lakatos, who engineered the Popper-Kuhn debate in Great Britain and immortalized it by editing – together with Alan Musgrave – proceedings from this meeting,[9] was a Hungarian refugee, who left Hungary after the Russians brutally suppressed the Budapest uprising in 1956 (though it would be hard to count him among the victims of the regime, which he actively served and supported, while still in Hungary). Popper stood for the management of meaning by independent academic professionals, legitimizing their management with a foundationalist philosophy of science. The Popperian philosophy of science, from *Logic of Scientific Discovery* to *Objective Knowledge* stressed continuity (communities of practice were presented as competent professionals trying to falsify their hypotheses in a fair and peer-controlled way). It proposed the concept of rationality measured by inter-subjectively controlled standards. These standards evolved, but not without preserving a sufficient degree of continuity. Kuhn stood for a more mutable, discontinuous, generational and paradigmatic flexibility of the same professional community and replaced Popper's liberal belief in an open society (in which research communities were simply allowed to make free use of rationality) with a more pragmatic vision of the growth of science. The Kuhnian history of science allows us to see less continuity and greater socio-political dynamics in the working of academic communities. A few revolutions are always in the wind, ready to break the continuity of the evolution of scientific knowledge. The history of science is reconstructed as a series of generational power struggles around paradigmatic 'embodiments' of rationality. Why did this vision become so attractive as to turn Kuhn's technical study in the philosophy of science into a popular bestseller? Part of the explanation is in the book's generational appeal to representatives of the 1968 generation who were facing a long march through institutions and establishments. Part of the explanation lies in the simultaneous appeal of the vision of power struggles to the ideologues of the Cold War. They wanted to legitimize the visible hand of a political alliance between academic communities and the US political establishment as the core economic and military superpower of the democratic west. Citizens of 'free societies' had to be persuaded that this visible hand was needed if communities pursuing the production of knowledge were to survive under the protective umbrella of affluent market economies. Rationality could not be a dogma and had to be subjected to democratic negotiations (for instance, generational ones), thus sustaining democracy and contrasting it with the dead one-dimensionality of Soviet-controlled societies, where such negotiations were forbidden and rationality was firmly embedded in a single theoretical doctrine, namely Marxism-Leninism.

Lakatos had tried to come up with the compromise that would have helped him to capitalize on Popper's standing in the international academic rankings and at the same time to make ample use of Kuhn's support by the managerial elites of the US academic establishment (which is why he had convened the meeting in the first place). However, Lakatosian politics misfired and he never obtained the position he craved. He never replaced Popper as the crown prince of the academic philosophy of science, with the privilege of deciding which research paradigms are robust and 'progressive' and which are 'degenerative'.

However, the meeting he engineered turned out to be significant for both European and US intellectual history in the last three decades of the twentieth century, because the positions of both Popper and Kuhn and the echoes of their debate throughout academic communities had been influenced by the duality of hot World War II and the Cold War. Popper had been forced by the Nazis to emigrate to New Zealand, where he wrote *The Open Society and its Enemies*. Popper blamed Plato, Hegel and Marx for promoting a vision of a 'closed', totalitarian society in which a small, privileged elite had a monopoly on knowledge and imposed an absolute rule and a single ideology on its subjects. Since Popper observed analogies between Nazi Germany and Soviet Russia (other thinkers, writers and political experts – Arendt, Talmon, Friedrich, Brzezinski, Orwell had also stressed this similarity during the Second World War and the Cold War) his treatise, along with a later study, *The Poverty of Historicism* (1957) (in which he criticized the Marxist attempt to 'deduce' the logic of history from an analysis of past events and ridiculed the reduction of their explanation to the discovery of a single universal mechanism, for instance a 'class struggle') became one of the cornerstones of the liberal ideology of the west with which the communist propaganda of the east had been confronted (Popper, 2002).

Kuhn's was the more pragmatic approach: when he spoke of Galileo, he knew that a reconstruction of Galileo's famous dispute with cardinal Bellarmine and numerous other public experiments and speeches allowed one to notice games and tricks that undermined trust in Galileo's views. Therefore in *The Structure of Scientific Revolutions* (1962) Kuhn limited himself to the sociological and demographic arguments that the young and the networked shall eventually inherit top positions in academic research communities and occupy the best slots in organizational structures. His study became the cornerstone of the flexible rationalization and legitimization of scientific pursuits, the fundamental manifestation of the post-Fordist phase in the production of scientific knowledge (Kuhn, 1996).

The victory of Kuhn and the academic, professional 'masses' had to be justified. This justification was facilitated by the increasing numbers of members of 'elitist masses', of the best and the brightest. All those new professionals with their higher educational backgrounds were inclined to a tacit acceptance of the Kuhnian vision of the growth of scientific knowledge. The defenders of the earlier Popperian paradigm felt as Bellarmine's allies might have felt after Galileo's victory in the Renaissance. Both sides agreed that ultimate victory could only be claimed ex post facto. It could only be validated by the subsequent growth of knowledge and the desirable, positively evaluated – though often unintended – consequences. Voting for Galileo and against Bellarmine, historians of science tend to mention the scientific revolution of the European Renaissance and the Baroque, the knowledge production and creative management of the meaning of history in the Enlightenment project as among the most significant consequences of Galileo's victory. They also admit that less desirable consequences include the injustices of colonial expansion abroad and sharp inequalities and violent class struggles inside the countries undergoing the industrial revolution. Which desirable consequences of accepting the theory of scientific revolutions as paradigmatic shifts are being quoted by the 'Kuhnians' today? Are thirty-odd years enough to point them out? Are the proliferation of paradigms, interdisciplinary research projects, pragmatic networks with public authorities and private investors, interparadigmatic armistices and parallel methodological developments, cloned animals and genetically modified food to be regarded as a 'profit' or as a 'loss' compared to the consequences of knowledge production under the previous, neopositivist 'dictatorship'? Numerous researchers claim that a careful audit reveals a net profit: we are increasingly aware of the fact that researchers who create a theoretical 'frame' also enable individuals and groups to reflect upon themselves and their new relations and possibilities in the 'mirror' of newly won knowledge, which opens 'windows' of opportunity for new, previously unthought of actions:

> Each discipline is at once extending the range of entities at work in the world and actively participating in transforming some of them into faithful and stable intermediaries. Thus economists, for instance, are not simply describing some economic infrastructure which has always been there since the beginning of time. They are also revealing calculative abilities in actors who did not know before they had them and making sure that some of these new competences are sunk into common sense through the many practical tools of bank accounts, property rights, cash register slips, and other plug-ins. Sociologists of the social ... have done much more than 'discover' what a society is. They have always actively engaged in multiplying the connections among actors who did not know before they were related by 'social forces' and they have also offered the actors many ways to be grouped together ... Just as [a] spider casts a web, *economization* is what is crafted by economists, *socialization* by sociology, *psychologization* by psychology, *spatialization* by geography.
>
> (Latour, 2005, p. 257; emphasis in the original)

In other words, the fact that a majority of researchers chose to portray themselves in a theoretical framework provided by Kuhn rather than by Popper was linked to the growing awareness of the constructivist nature of the flexible accumulation of knowledge in professional academic bureaucracies. For a researcher investigating the 'switch' from Popper to Kuhn among representatives of academic research communities, the switch, which happened in the last three decades of the twentieth century, running parallel to the end of the Cold War, poses a truly mysterious and obscure object of theoretical desire. One should try to explain and understand this switch and one should attempt to trace it in one's own community of practice. A replacement of the logic of scientific discovery with the political sensitivity to the up and coming generational paradigm (in order to recognize the paradigm with a promise of progressive development) means a major, though rarely noticed, shift in contemporary management of meaning. Does it have anything to do with the parallel shift from the Cold War to the post-Cold War mode of management of meaning in societies in general and in academic communities in particular? In order to investigate it, we have to take account of another peculiarity of the management of meaning in formal organizations of professional communities.

First, most managers of meaning agree with another of Hegel's dictums, namely that the owl of Minerva flies at dusk, that is, that generals always fight past wars and that we respond to situations and contexts according to what we have learned by retrospective analysis of past actions – although circumstances and contexts might have changed by the time we respond to them, and so might the meaning we had once detected and created. Reflection and understanding always follow the problem and the action. This phenomenon has repeatedly been observed by social scientists reflecting on their own (mis)management of meaning and has contributed to the ultimate victory of Kuhn over Popper:

> During the 1960s, both as political radicals and as participants in the counterculture, we enthusiastically attempted to deny, by our willful actions, some of the oppressive determinisms of the corporate social order. And when, a few years or a decade later, we revolted against the positivist research strategies of social history and undertook studies of the cultural construction of the social world, I think we obscurely felt ourselves to be freeing historical scholarship ... But in retrospect our efforts seem to have been out of phase with socioeconomic realities. Our attack on the latent Fordism of social history was launched only at the time when the Fordist system of social regulation was itself entering a deep and final crisis ... Thus, cultural historians were kicking down the door of Fordist social determinisms at the moment when such determinisms – Habermas's systematic 'administration of human beings and their relations to each other by means of social

organization' – were collapsing. In the far more anarchic social world that was emerging, relations between human beings were increasingly determined by market forces rather than by systematic administration; social organization of the Fordist sort was being restructured into networks of entrepreneurial actors; and economic production – given the growing significance of design, advertising, and the entertainment industry – itself was increasingly becoming a play of signifiers (although decidedly not a free play).

(Sewell, 2005, pp. 60–1)

Isn't it possible that there is an analogy between 'delay' as described above (academic professionals criticizing the system that is about to dissolve) and a 'delay' in embracing a philosophy of science (academic professionals choosing Kuhn over Popper) at the moment when the professional autonomy of researchers enabling them to mobilize for a paradigmatic shift is already eroding under the influence of the new powerful shifts emerging from under and behind the postmodern façade? Isn't the fact that Kuhn's concept of scientific revolution as a paradigm shift fuelled by socio-demographic factors had been embraced by both political right and political left in itself intriguing? Kuhn had become popular both among the architects of the Cold War desiring to broaden the scope of their control of research communities as indispensable elements of defence networks (which is why James B. Conant supported him and made sure that he had been accepted at Harvard in spite of initial rejections) and among former student activists and radical faculty members trying to translate their countercultural ideals into the long march through the academic institutions. Thus, both those firmly embedded in the academic establishments and those firmly committed to the countercultural and critical reform of its institutions agreed on the same sensemaking proposal, in spite of different positions, interests and world outlooks. Paradigm became a household word, while falsificationism went into early retirement. Perhaps the popularity in question, the facility of dissemination of the concept of scientific revolutions reflected instant recognition of 'past wars', while in reality the processes of academic knowledge production had already dissolved not only the 'universalist' model of Popper, but also the 'relativist' model of Kuhn? Is the theory of a long march of scientific rationality through evolutionary normality and revolutionary changes of paradigms as obsolete as the theory of the logic of scientific inquiry? If so, can our analyses of contemporary management of meaning help us understand who and where we are right now?

If we are to understand how the idea of paradigmatic shifts linked to generational changes of the guard won the hearts and minds of academic professionals, we should devote some attention to the processes of organizational sensemaking and evaluation performed in the shadow of organizational power politics. Three approaches which come to an organizational scientist's mind are the Hofstedian theory of culture's consequences, the Weickian theory of organizational sensemaking and the most general theory of justifying/legitimizing ('economies of worth') by Boltanski and Thévenot.

All three tackle the link between values 'imprinted' in collective cultural 'softwares' customized by individual users and patterned, socially organized actions. None shies away from the problems of power struggles in human interactions. The problem of the uses of power in regular organizational interactions has often been conceptualized, with organizational scientists classifying the sources of organizational power, but relatively rarely inquiring into the exact composition of power elites (with the single exception of the critique of glass ceilings slowing down an overall upward mobility of female employees as compared to their male counterparts). Attempts to explain the different rhythms of power struggles within private companies and public offices are usually linked to individual and collective 'softwares' acquired during socialization in families, schools and organizations and 'customized' in group-specific and individual ways.

Two of the dimensions introduced by Geert Hofstede, namely 'power distance; low vs. high' and the 'masculinity-femininity continuum' are of particular importance from the point of view of organizational sensemaking in the shadow of power and emotions (Hofstede, 1980). Hofstede's model of culture's consequences allows us to measure the willingness of members of formal organizations to tolerate asymmetries of prestige, income and domination (power distance). It allows us also to measure the limits of members' readiness to tolerate these inequalities and the intensity of their desire to soften the impact of competitive struggles for the underdogs (the femininity end of the masculinity-femininity dimension). The robustness of Hofstede's model, in spite of growing criticism (compare Magala, 2005, pp. 70–85) is being acknowledged far beyond the academic world. The concept of the dimensions of culture is grounded in Hofstede's recognition of some of the 'underground' borrowings, which can be traced through various 'national' and 'organizational' cultural softwares. Tracing them we arrive in such domains of culture as religious doctrines. For instance, religious differences between Catholics and Protestants have resurfaced in – respectively – lower power distance in northern European countries, predominantly Protestant, and higher power distance in southern ones, mainly Catholic. Tracing them we arrive in such domains of culture as political ideologies. For instance, the size of the population of landed gentry as opposed to town burghers may matter for the course of democratic enfranchisement. Hofstede approvingly quotes d'Iribarne's distinction between 'the logic of honour' and the 'logic of contract' in explaining differences in preferred modes of organizing mutual obligations between interacting individuals. Hofstede links differences in the level of tolerance for inequality and its consequences to individual socialization. What are we socialized into as our socialization extends from family to school and to the workplace? We are being socialized into tacit acceptance of some forms of the exercise and manifestation of power and equally tacit reluctance to accept others. We are prone to rejecting or resisting those inequalities, which strike us as 'excessive', 'superfluous', 'unjustified'. Hofstede assumes that core values 'implanted' in the course of institutionalized socialization are relatively stable over time and thus can be identified and used to explain some preferences, choices and behaviours throughout individual lives and in a variety of situational contexts. Family, school, workplace are assumed to demonstrate a degree of stability as major socializing agencies that 'process' individuals and 'imprint' cultural 'softwares' with a certain degree of 'compatibility' in their ways of thinking, feeling and acting. However, this assumed stability has become a target of a growing number of critics, including Brendan McSweeney, who analysed statistics on industrial disputes and strikes in various European countries differentiated by their national culture's position on the masculinity-femininity dimension. McSweeney empirically demonstrated that predictions based on Hofstede's dimensions were not reliable, because it was not possible to use the relative position of a national culture (he chose the masculinity-femininity dimension) in order to predict frequency of strikes (or of consensus-building measures, if the country's culture had been diagnosed as 'feminine') in a business opened in a particular country. McSweeney concluded:

> Social phenomena are complex not merely because they are almost always the outcome of multiple variables but also because those variables can combine in a variety of ways and at different times. The combinatorial, and often complexly so, nature of social causation makes identification of causation highly challenging and far beyond the capability of unilevel analysis even when the latter is well executed.
>
> (McSweeney, 2007, p. 28)

There is a possibility of 'experimentum crucis' in this case: if challenges become more frequent and empirically grounded, the Hofstedian model could be defended on empirical grounds as well. His adherents might defend it as robust enough in spite of individual 'deviations' and 'anomalies'.[10] These latter difficulties become even more challenging if an objective analysis of the phenomenon in question is itself linked to social and organizational taboos and restrictions, which shape agendas and prefabricate the issues for public discussion. Among them power looms large. Power is also studied along with other factors that are suspected of influencing the 'structuration' of social environments for individual and collective actors and of dominating their communications. Most concepts of 'dominant ideology' or of 'managerialism' identify power struggles and their winners as important sources of hierarchies in organizations. However, as numerous authors (see, for instance, Pfeffer, 1997) have repeatedly observed, analysis of the research output of the representatives of organizational sciences points up an astonishing deficit; namely a distinct shortage, a significant scarcity of research projects devoted to the problems of power, power struggles, individual passion and interest devoted to the attempts to acquire or maintain power at the expense of the other members of formal organizations. While most of the readers of theoretical studies of contemporary management are familiar with the philosophy of management and of the corporate culture of General Electric expressed by Jack Welch, the exact nature of the power struggles that brought him to the top of this corporation and then enabled him to stay and even delay his final retirement in spite of illness remains mostly unresearched, unreported and unreflected upon. To cut a long story short: ritual references to Machiavelli notwithstanding (and despite something of a resurgence of interest in the 'Machiavellian intelligence' of some animal 'societies'; Byrne and Whiten, 1989), the processes of power are more often defined, reported, interpreted and made sense of in informal chats between friends and fellow-employees, in cynical comments on corporate politics and in 'gossip' than in formal research reports and serious interpretative studies. Isn't this an astonishing revelation as far as real taboos in open, liberal societies go?

Some of the 'power effects' fare a bit better. Concepts such as 'dominant discourse', 'hegemonic ideology' and the like usually refer a reader to the 'corporate' (or 'national', or 'religious') 'mission' and 'corporate culture' (powerful stakeholders and managers legitimizing their power and its exercise) or to privileged actors, for instance, the 'elite connection' (members of powerful teams and groups are then described as elite of some merit). If we choose to investigate the elite connections or the circulation of elites, our research is usually limited. Scarcity of data and the reluctance of the actual power elites to conduct their business of exercising power in as transparent a mode as possible force us to focus more on data linked to the elite's legitimizing of its actions than on understanding actual, empirically confirmed means and goals, and interpreting real alliances and careers or on checking the undemocratic excesses recorded in the conduct of members of power elites. Concepts of ideological control of communication by organizational elites are used in order to signal the relative power of some groups or individuals to influence organizational communications and to manifest and justify 'elite identities'. Studies conducted by Mats Alvesson and his collaborators in knowledge-intensive organizations (high-tech consulting companies) allowed him to isolate some criteria for legitimizing individuals' elite status:

> In some contexts, the construction and reinforcement of elite identity may draw upon fairly well recognized criteria for success and superiority (e.g. size, profit, wage level, growth, export rankings, etc.). In the context of consulting firms, however, these are not necessarily sufficient, as commercial success is not the same as 'intra-professional' criteria for excellence ... What are also required are criteria that emphasize distinctiveness and these are often less publicly recognized and frequently less obvious.
>
> (Alvesson and Robertson, 2006, p. 201)

The concept of elite identities could be useful in investigating an intriguing problem posed by parties of all political, ideological, methodological and social hues embracing the same, Kuhnian, philosophy of science. Could we try to see why groups so different with respect to their position in the power hierarchy – as, for example, the established ('modernist', 'neopositivist') elites controlling universities and research institutes and the counter-elites ('postmodernist', 'constructionist', 'interpretivist') trying to unseat them – have both embraced this brand of the philosophy of science? Could the analysis of power struggles in academic institutions help us understand why and how the philosophy of science formulated by Thomas Kuhn in *The Structure of Scientific Revolutions* has come to be seen as a valuable resource in academic power struggles no matter what one's methodological and ideological, scientific and political colours? Could we understand why both groups have managed to put this philosophy in a frame of their planned action and their ideological discourse, that is, to enclose it seamlessly in their elite and counter-elite identities? And what should we analyse if we want to understand which role was designed and justified for the concept of 'paradigmatic shift' within two different ideological discourses in academic research communities?

Perhaps we can attempt to understand this sudden and massive victory if we examine closely a process of transition and translation that took place in the late eighteenth and mid-nineteenth-century phases of industrialization. The process in question consisted of a shift between two opposing interpretations of exactly the same developments, which had originally been welcomed and praised and were subsequently re-assessed and critically condemned. Originally, as in the writings of Scottish moral philosophers, of whom Adam Smith is one of the most influential representatives, the emergence of a capitalist market economy had been greeted with moral approval. Moral virtues of prudence, frugality and the like, were assumed to bring a measure of rationality into previously unpredictable human actions. The primacy of profit should make the motivation of our contemporaries more transparent, providing a safer ground for predicting their future conduct, based on rational planning. *Enrichissez vous, messieurs!* – Get rich, gentlemen! (And let the history of human societies make more sense than ever before.) Those moral arguments that had been raised in praise of emergent capitalism were subsequently taken over, almost unchanged, by the socialist critics of capitalist exploitation and the market economy's sinister shadow of avarice and greed. Look at the consequences of the industrial revolution and capitalist entrepreneurs' search for profit; a rich fabric of human society, a perfumed garden of human history where a thousand flowers bloomed and many goals used to be pursued – all these goals and pursuits had been reduced to a single race-track, a single calculation, a sole motive for action. Capital has to circulate and multiply itself, individuals must try to get rich, and meanwhile the exploited masses must pay for the star status of the happy few millionaires. Critics agreed that the capitalist economy rationalized societies and simplified choices allowing for a more precise understanding and plotting of actions. However, they saw this as an impoverishment, a contamination and a curse, not as a blessing. What was greeted as a blessing (history simplified, developmental goals clear) came to be regarded as a curse disguised as a blessing, a fake (simplification means impoverishment, clarity of goals removes constraints on greed and ruthless competition, crowding other goals out). It took almost a century for this shift, this retranslation of ideological praise into a critique, to run the full circle. As Hirschman puts it, looking from a longer perspective (he writes in the 1970s and the shift in question took place between roughly 1750 and 1950), the cultural contradictions of capitalism are ideologically exaggerated by the radical left:

> Capitalist market society, suitably modified by Keynesianism, planning and welfare reforms, seemed to have escaped from its self-destructive proclivities and to generate, once again, if not douceur, at least considerable confidence in its ability to solve problems that it would encounter along its way. But the sense of pervasive crisis that had characterized it in the 1930s and 1940s reappeared in the 1970s, in part as an after-effect of the still poorly understood mass movements of the late 1960s and in part as an immediate reaction to contemporary shocks and disarray.
>
> (Hirschman, 1992, pp. 116–17)[11]

The reasons for this change of mind and heart (from apology to condemnation) are not entirely clear. Some economic historians blame the anti-bourgeois bohemian intellectuals of the mid-nineteenth century, from Baudelaire to Marx, from Proudhon to Nietzsche and from Rimbaud to Kropotkin, for setting the tone and throwing bourgeois virtues away (see McCloskey, 2006). Underground influences, transfers and borrowings united the prosperous middle class (which profited from capitalist and colonial growth) with a still poor and under-represented, but up and coming working class. Both embraced the view of capitalism's paradigmatic shift, differing only in the political choices they made. The middle classes were choosing mostly liberal remedies. The working classes chose socialist remedies (some chose more extreme forms – anarchist, communist, syndicalist, terrorist). Both the emergent elites of trade unions and workers' parties and the established elites of the middle class embraced critical diagnosis. They differed with respect to remedies. Their cultural content producers (whom Marx called 'literary representatives of social classes') – artists, critics, teachers, journalists and the like – helped to set the tone. A similar situation occurred after the mass movements of the 1966–74 period subsided. Among academic professionals, the new working classes of the knowledge economy, a period of conservative backlash started to take shape. Around 1970–74, the choice of a positive or negative view of the process of knowledge production made everybody aware of the historical mutability of 'the logic of scientific discovery' and 'the logic of collective action'. Changes in criteria of rationality were most successfully phrased as shifts of paradigms. Paradigms were used to legitimize methodologies defended as legitimate once articulated and embraced. Kuhn's book was an entry into a much broader public discussion than any of its participants realized at the time. He came first in what – retrospectively – can be called a race for a 'decision' or a 'choice' for a majority of academic professionals. This choice, as opposed to the choices described by Hirschman, was made almost instantaneously. Academics agreed that Kuhn had captured the spirit of the times; though some of them deplored the loss of universalist logic (which would have enabled them to legitimize their power much more authoritatively), others rejoiced in what they considered the first shot in their struggle to let a thousand paradigms bloom and enable them to move upwards in academic hierarchies without serving the establishment. Hirschman describes a process of ideological 'revisionism', which took a hundred years. Investigating Kuhn's rise to fame we observe that adjustments and reassessments started arriving only a quarter of a century later (three-quarters of a century sooner than in the case of arguments in favour of or against the capitalist rationalization of social life). Does this mean that history has accelerated and we are both four times quicker in running a re-evaluation of all values and more pragmatic and flexible in making our paradigmatic choices (even at the price of a tacit complicity with our professional 'enemies')? Are our managed health-care and streamlined public management campaigns and projects manifestations of this forthcoming re-evaluation?

Growing interest in the Kuhn-Popper debate testifies to the need to tackle the problem of a shadow cast by power struggles on organizational sensemaking or on the way in which individuals try to cope with understanding and legitimizing their and others' behaviour in formal organizations. Making sense of choices is a significant, relevant, salient aspect of an ongoing negotiation about legitimate courses of action in professional communities. We owe this concept to Karl Weick (1995, 2001), a social psychologist, who has recently redrawn his concept of organizational sensemaking in trying to account for organizational sentiments and power struggles,[12] which had been largely left out of his original study. Weick attempts to get back to the manageable level of organizational outsourcing of meaning labelled as 'organizational sensemaking' and has postulated a theoretical 'frame' of seven dimensions to identify, plot and interpret it:

> To shape hearts and minds is to influence at least seven dimensions of sensemaking; the social relations that are encouraged and discouraged, the identities that are valued or derogated, the retrospective meanings that are accepted or discredited, the cues that are highlighted or suppressed, the updating that is encouraged or discouraged, the standard of accuracy or plausibility to which conjectures are held,

and the approval of proactive or reactive action as the preferred mode of coping.

(Weick et al., 2005, p. 418)

When looking at professional organizations, especially academic institutions, whose dense and increasingly complex networks of communications accelerate multiple and overlapping processes, we can see that these dimensions allow us to analyse the triple role of sensemaking that can be attributed to academic professionals busy with accepting and disseminating a Kuhnian philosophy of science. The triple role in question consists of :

- *framing* (of the issue to be discussed and negotiated, for instance peaceful coexistence of hostile methodological research programmes),
- *mirror*-like reflecting (of individual and group situational preferences and underlying values, often abbreviated into 'identities')
- opening *windows* of opportunity (for future actions, often articulated as 'visions').

It is my contention that the popularity of Kuhn's concept of 'paradigmatic shift' owes most of its appeal to its ambiguous nature. It can be constructed as a key concept, which is both ambiguous as far as content is concerned (thus legitimizing continuous modifications in many directions) and remains psychologically attractive (thus gaining popularity in different groups and networks). This mix of ambiguity and attractiveness has also been traced by Feyerabend (1967) in his studies of the mechanisms of transformation of either artistic or scientific practice. A paradigm means something different to historians and philosophers of science and to natural scientists themselves, it means something different again to the historians of particular scientific disciplines, say biology or biochemistry and, last but not least, to the historians of social sciences and of the humanities, and to sociologists, psychologists, economists, historians of art and literary scholars. Its ambiguity, far from being its weakness, turned out to be its most important strength, and Popper's subsequent ventures into evolutionary epistemology as the cornerstone of 'objective knowledge' could not change it. Ironically, Galileo's tricks and the concept of a paradigm (evoked by Kuhn in *Structure of Scientific Revolutions*) won out against the concept of an evolutionary difference between an Einstein and an amoeba (which Popper evokes in *Objective Knowledge*). The uses of ambiguity (in itself a title claimed by literary scholars) in engineering a compromise without a consensus are best described by Boltanski and Thévenot (2006) (who propose a much more complex theoretical frame for analysis of 'economies of worth'):

> A compromise can be worked out more easily when it can be made to accommodate beings or qualities that are ambiguous in the sense that they may derive, depending on the way they are understood, from more than one world. This is the case, for example, with 'authority' and 'responsibility': each of these terms may qualify the relation between a father and his children in the domestic world or the relation between a supervisor and his subordinates in the industrial world ... Figures of the common good also lend themselves to compromises: thus one can refer to 'society' and maintain an ambiguous reference to polite society (domestic), civic society as a political body, or society as studied by social sciences (with its regularities and its laws, the latter has a strong industrial component).
>
> (Boltanski and Thévenot, 2006, pp. 279–80)

Boltanski and Thévenot offer an interesting interpretative clue, which might be worth pursuing in order to explain the astonishingly rapid spread of the Kuhnian concept of paradigms across the social sciences and the humanities (and even into the more popular genres of public discourse in the media). They describe six worlds – the world of fame, the domestic world, the market world, the industrial world, the civic and the inspired world. Their distinctions are based on a fairly unconventional ontology, which resembles an earlier ontological concept of the 'prefabrication of sensory information' introduced by Jacques Ranciere (2004). The idea that artists create their works of art under social and historical constraints is not very new. New, however, is the intuition that prefabrication of sensory data about the world creates the cards with which artists can play in designing new meanings. This idea had been expressed by Ranciere in philosophy, primarily in aesthetics, but it travelled to sociology, political sciences and economics. Boltanski, himself active as an art and media critic may have sensed it 'in the air'. This is not an elective affinity, since there is no reference to Ranciere in the book *On Justification*. However, Boltanski and Thévenot go further than Ranciere, because they generalize the process of 'creating value' in order to account for all values, not only the sensory 'inputs' to the process of creating aesthetic values. Describing the world of fame, they display an affinity to Feyerabend, although once again this is not an elective affinity, because they do not refer to the idea that a concept must be logically empty and psychologically attractive in order to merit attention and an 'aura' of value. Unwittingly treading in Feyerabend's footsteps, the authors declare that:

> In the world of fame there are few things that can consolidate and stabilize the relation between worth, which comes exclusively from the opinion of the others, and the bearer of worth, an entity (a person or a thing) that is not qualified by properties inscribed in its being in a lasting way. This nonessentialist and purely relational character of the worth of fame may be precisely what has encouraged its adoption as a universal standard of measure by the schools of thought in social sciences that like to highlight the structural and relativist properties of the social world.
>
> (Boltanski and Thévenot, 2006, p. 178)

The outsourcing of meanings is both accelerated and facilitated by practical professional ideologies, whose ambiguities (logically empty, thus continually modified, psychologically attractive, thus continually defended) identify and empower individuals and groups.[13] Individuals and groups then start broadening the fields of democratic negotiation of meaning and increasing the repertory of flexible responses to organizational crises. Such ambiguities are often exploited, for instance in an ongoing negotiation of past meanings. We do, for instance continually renegotiate our reconstructions of historical events. We ask the following questions. How was Columbus's 'discovery' of America perceived by the native populations? How is it interpreted today by those who identify with the conquered, not the conquerors? What exactly did those processes of interaction between Columbus and the Indians mean to these actors then and what do we think about their consequences now?

Both diligent reconstruction and creative rewriting of history are important parts of the re-engineering of meanings attached to contemporary agents, agencies and events. Those who re-engineer meanings do not always have to be aware of the fact. They sometimes think they introduce slight modifications because of newly found 'evidence'. They are sometimes shocked that their views can fuel a revolutionary movement. Erasmus of Rotterdam was no more amused by the popularity of his writings among the Protestant reformers than was Darwin with Marx's dedication.[14]

2
The Past Tense of Meaning (Lost and Gained in Historical Translations)

We have managed to arrive at the question of the past of meaning without having given a definition of 'the meaning of meaning'.[1] However, the introduction to the cultural and historical background of contemporary management of meaning (as outlined in the previous chapter) had to precede a more analytical approach. Otherwise two important points would have been compromised. Cold War influences would have been reduced to third-rate stage props in a drama populated by rational knowledge producers and those producers themselves would have become ghosts in an organizational machine defined piecemeal. Management of meaning would have been defined at the outset. Its definition would have been tacitly chosen as a preferred mode of creating/inventing or discovering/detecting a meaning. Following an introduction which places our discussion in a historical context, we can proceed forewarned that the meaning of meaning is itself a hotly debated issue. How do we go about it? First, we have to keep in mind that social locations or contexts – which provide the 'scaffolding' for meaning under construction – can move and change:

> Part of what gives cultural practice its potency is the ability of actors to play upon the multiple meanings of symbols – thereby redefining situations in ways that they believe will favor their purposes. Creative cultural action commonly entails the purposeful or spontaneous importation of meanings from one social location or context to another.
>
> (Sewell, 2005, p. 168)

Second, we have to be aware of our habits of mind, trained and reinforced by our professional routines. Defining 'management of meaning'[2] (past, present or future) usually begins with a definition of 'management' and a definition of 'meaning'. This is followed by the explanation of the two terms and the added value of linking them with an 'of'. Our understanding of what management is, thus becomes outsourced to the authors of a dictionary, which we accept as authoritative in a given domain of knowledge. A dictionary includes the descriptions and definitions of meanings of words. Since there are many definitions of most words, and ambiguities are the rule rather than exceptions, it is usual to look for common denominators in those definitions. An attempt must be made to sum these up in a brief and possibly abstract text, disseminated preferably in a printed form. In the process of, for instance, defining management, we are usually inclined to neglect any incoherence of terms (which would limit validity) or mutability of an object (which would limit applicability) of definitions encountered so far. We try to explain these difficulties away with the complexity and diversity of data sources. We tend to stress the need to hone and polish definitions, upgrading them incrementally all the time. Nor are we quick to change the very concept of *management*, which has the solidity of a separate, autonomous noun, leading a proud, distinct, easily identifiable existence. We cannot so easily change it into the flexible and less rigid concept of 'managing', which reflects, as a gerund, a more fluid, verb-active, situation-dependent and contingent nature of managerial actions. That this remains something of a hurdle to be overcome is astonishing insofar as around the same time that Ogden and Richards published their famous study of *The Meaning of Meaning* (subtitled, *A Study of the Influence of Language upon Thought and the Science of Symbolism*) in 1923, another philosopher of science, Alfred N. Whitehead, had been busy with *Science in the Modern World*, published two years later in 1925, in which the author, influenced by Einstein's theory of relativity, proposed a new ontology, which he labelled 'event-ism' and which included events in four spatiotemporal dimensions as its basic building blocks. What was new? Events replaced material objects filling three-dimensional space. Time did not have to be added separately in the course of the philosophical analysis of these objects. Whitehead's ideas failed to influence the mainstream philosophy of science (at least at the time), but kept recurring in many guises.[3] Even in Ogden and Richard's *The Meaning of Meaning* from 1923, we can find a supplementary essay by Bronislaw Malinowski on 'The problem of meaning in primitive languages', where Malinowski explicitly states that language should: 'in its primitive function ... be regarded as a mode of action, rather than as a countersign of thought' (Malinowski, 1969, p. 296).

A growing number of contemporary theoreticians of organization and change management (for example, Weick, Tsoukas, Chia) do not share this reluctance to switch to gerunds. Charging the theoreticians of organizations with the accusation that they overlook multiple ways in which actions generate their own meanings, Weick pleads for the use of gerunds rather than nouns in describing organizational realities:

> In turbulent periods, orderliness is limited to short-lived transactions, intelligence is reduced to local expertise, and determinacy covers only those events close together in time and space. While no one questions that it would be desirable to have grand and stable designs in times of turbulence, the organization is not sufficiently homogeneous to support concerted action, nor is the environment sufficiently determinant to encourage accurate, long term prediction. Instead, the way out of turbulence may lie in continuous improvisation in response to continuous change in local details. Designing replaces design.
>
> (Weick, 2001, p. 88)

This is what happens, according to Weick, in organizations. But this cannot easily be described, particularly if we want definitions to 'control' our meanings and authors of dictionaries to manage these meanings for us. Grand structural designs are easier to define with nouns than are single cases of piecemeal social engineering (interacts) with gerunds. Company codes of conduct disseminated by top managers are more visible than discrete acts of designing and fine-tuning performed in real interactions. Thus if we become hostages to the authors of dictionaries, we are bound to repeat that the very word '*manager*' comes from the Italian *maneggiare*, which in turn sends us back to the Latin *manus* and was used in order to name the actions of an equestrian riding a horse and controlling its movement with reins held in the hands. Management is therefore linked to a visible 'hand' leading dumb 'horsepower' on behalf of the 'brains' situated in the body that also owns the hand. Ontological hierarchy is tacitly re-affirmed. *From a brain down to a hand and further down to a horse.* Definition of management imposes on us a heavy ontological duty of hierarchic evaluation of social worlds according to their proximity to mental or manual work. And after this initial explanation, a list of actions usually follows. The list includes activities linked by theoreticians of organization to a manager's job. These activities are usually explicitly named in formal job descriptions designed by professional bureaucracies. What do managers do when they manage? They supposedly plan, organize, lead, coordinate and control. This is what management and managing mean. Let us examine the word 'meaning' within the context of managing.

With *meaning* we are entering a more sophisticated game, because we cannot continue pretending that it is, as was the case with management, an objective reality. An objective reality is supposed to wait 'out there' until a researcher comes and provides its best, most accurate and economic, abstract definition. However, *meaning* did not wait to be discovered and defined. It is the underlying concept, traditionally studied in rhetoric, grammar and logic, which made the creation of dictionaries possible. It had to be invented when linguistic communication became not only widespread but also sophisticated (for instance, when different natural languages had to be translated one into another). Once invented, the concept of meaning had to be 'translated' into instructions for coining new words in order to facilitate the construction of meanings. We construct and reconstruct meanings of many phenomena, relations, actions and events. But we also have to find out what games people play, because we all play with meanings. Dictionaries would not be needed if we did not believe that we can detect and remember the meaning of words we speak or hear. According to our dictionary-based view of meaning, meaning is a relation between a word and an entry in a dictionary constructed precisely in order to answer the question 'what do you mean by (this word)?'

However, as historical dictionaries amply illustrate, the meanings of words in natural languages are not determined once and for all. We learn how to do things with words, but we have to keep re-learning and un-learning as we go along. Meanings migrate and change over time and space, both geographical and social. Some meanings have emerged from the past, some have been dropped, some maintained, some modified, some trumped by context-determined ones. Moreover, not only have the meanings changed, so have our ways of establishing and maintaining meanings. This means, in other words, that the meaning of meaning also changes, that one should probably speak about the meanings of meanings.

In order to understand the meaning of a word 'naming' anything – an interaction, an event, an object, a relation or an aspect – we can use three approaches. The first one has already been presented – it is called *defining*. We can define a manager as somebody who plans, organizes, leads, co-ordinates and controls in formal organizations that tend to evolve towards professional bureaucracies. But we can also examine the activities of individuals in an organization and start *interpreting* their behaviour. In this case, we may interpret some of the activities – for instance planning, organizing, leading, coordinating and designing – as differentiating managers from the managed. The same applies for situations in which we interpret a sudden application of brakes as a driver's proper interpretation of a change of traffic lights from green to red. He or she interprets the red lights as a sign saying 'stop'. His or her interpretation might have been different if Mao had had his way and 'red' had become a 'go' sign to extend the honour of the red flag of the communists to traffic regulation. Then the driver would have braked upon seeing green. Likewise, when I nod my head, my partner tacitly understands that I approve or confirm, and when I turn it from side to side – that I disapprove or deny. However, in India exactly the reverse applies for a correct understanding of nodding or shaking one's head.

When we interpret the words 'I do' pronounced by a man and a woman in front of the priest at the altar, we understand their meaning as an expression of consent. Each of them says 'I do' and they mean to marry one another. We interpret their actions as an expression of their will to meet the requirements associated with this status. They are getting married and they mean it. Likewise, the obscene words used by city rappers can be interpreted as a protest against hypocritical pretences to politeness, good manners and decorum upheld by the more affluent citizenry. 'Why are you so goddam polite?' asks an irritated jury member of his colleague in *Twelve Angry Men*. 'For the same reason you are so impolite' answers the other. 'This is the way I was brought up.' We interpret 'dirty' words as a protest against assumed middle-class hypocrisy. In spite of the fact that the wealthy understand very well the unnecessary suffering of the poorest they decide to ignore it. This fuels rage expressed in some rap (almost immediately taken up by the media in order to spice the cultural content of TV and boost programme popularity). Analysing rap lyrics, or managerial decrees, or organizational announcements, we are busy with a systematic reflection on our communications. We communicate, therefore we interpret. Our communications, as was discovered long ago, involve us in a continuous communicative/interpretative process, which is at present highly mobile and individualized and becomes increasingly distributed in time and space. Let us note that in interpreting we do not rush immediately to the dictionary; rather we interpret in a given situation, 'on the spot'. We produce interpretations by improvising. It means that we, as receivers of communication, are much more 'in charge' of the results of interpretation than we would have been in the case of the definition imposed by the sender and immortalized, solidified, frozen and locked (for instance in a printed object or in an immutable PDF file). Interpretations strengthen the consumer's, not the producer's market of meanings.[4] We can decide to follow the interpretative rather than the defining approach to the management of meaning and thus preserve for ourselves a certain liberty to overlook, ignore, change, manipulate and modify the meanings we attach to the object of our interpretation. In doing so, we follow our intuition that interpretations empower (the reader, listener or a viewer of a communicated message) and definitions – in a sense – disenfranchise or at least constrain (the interpreting receivers). Interpretations open up, definitions lock out. Definitions are imposed and repeated, interpretations are invented and fed back to the sender of organizational communications by interactive receivers. Nor is this all.

When definitions are proposed and interpretations expressed, negotiations begin. Thus we reach the third approach to the management of meaning – *negotiating*. In our daily management of meaning we negotiate and renegotiate meanings almost incessantly – although from the point of view of most organizational routines, we do not consider ourselves to be active negotiators. More often than not, we see ourselves as slightly bending or stretching the constraints and rules and either getting away with it or not. We do not normally see ourselves as communicating, outspoken citizens, as empowered individuals participating in a process of negotiation in all locations, including families, schools, churches, companies, institutions, streets, shopping malls, chatrooms and the like. Perhaps we are not encouraged to do so by the hierarchical structure of the religious (for example, churches) and scientific-rational (for example, universities) institutions, both of which are modelled after the professional bureaucracy of the Catholic Church. Let us – for instance – imagine we decide that 60 per cent of correct answers during the multiple choice test means that a student gets a 'pass' instead of a 'fail'. Let us assume that students are anxious that this would put too many of them under the threshold of the lowest passing grade and urge us to lower the barrier. If we hope to avoid too much work with a re-sit exam in a few months, we may grudgingly make use of our lecturer's discretion and agree that 55 per cent is enough. Students are relieved, we grade accordingly and we save ourselves some work. By doing so, however, we have just renegotiated the meaning of the multiple choice exam. We have changed it. We have participated in the interactive, negotiated, social construction of reality, which requires an ongoing negotiation of meanings. The most important party in these negotiations is not the students, who have to wait until the threshold is announced, nor academic teachers, as the authors of multiple choice questions, but mediating gate-keepers, the academic power holders (for instance deans or heads of educational commissions). Negotiations strengthen the mediators', not the producers' or consumers' market of meanings. The influence of negotiations upon the market of meanings has been less frequently researched than it deserves to be. For instance, discussions around Kuhn's study *The Structure of Scientific Revolutions* in the 1970s avoided mentioning James Bryant Conant, who shaped agendas for generations of researchers and launched Kuhn on his Harvard career (Fuller's study of Kuhnian doctrine within the framework of Cold War academic politics came out in 2000). The share of interpretations and negotiations in shaping meanings and the meanings of meanings in organizations had been undervalued, while the share of definitions had been overpriced. This state of affairs is beginning to change as new studies in the complexities of organizational knowledge pave the way for 'organizational epistemology', which allows us to access the organizationally situated 'web of meanings':

> As Berger (1963, 70) noted some time ago, 'memory itself is a reiterated act of interpretation. As we remember the past, we reconstruct it in accordance with our present ideas of what is important and what is not.' Actor's re-weaving may be minimal, such as, for example, in instances of single loop learning or Weick's 'embellishments' (1998). Alternatively, it may be maximal, such as when entirely new ways of doing things emerge, through metaphorical redescription (Lakoff, 1987, Rorty, 1989; 3–22). In either case, change there is, the web is reconfigured and change is brought about.
>
> (Tsoukas, 2005, p. 195)

Of the authors quoted by Tsoukas, Weick as a social psychologist studying organizations comes closest to the issues of organized management of meaning. Once again we recall that Weick was among the first of the social psychologists specializing in organizational sensemaking to notice that negotiating is essential for a management of meaning. He had also observed that it turned every manager into a historian, interpreting the history of his or her organization and trying to present current decisions as the necessary outcomes of past choices, events and developments:

> When one feels compelled to declare that a decision has been made, the gist of that feeling is that there is some outcome at hand that must have been occasioned by some earlier choice. Decision making consists of locating, articulating, and ratifying that earlier choice, bringing it forward to the present, and claiming it as a decision that has just been made.
>
> (Weick, 1995, p. 185)

Weick called the subsection of his book from which the above quote is taken, 'Manager as a Historian'. Management of meaning requires access to the lost and found of past organizational changes. Sensemaking activities rely upon defining, interpreting and negotiating – and this covers also historical defining (and changes of definitions), interpreting (and changes of interpretation) and negotiating (and renegotiating). Moreover, the expansion of telecommunications and the multiplication of the multimedia have resulted in an accelerated 'public review' of those negotiations that are considered significant for individuals and groups. Let us therefore examine the historically and socially differentiated patterns, the most general patterns of sensemaking, which impose constraints on most of our communications by shaping their channels and codes.

What are the most general patterns of sensemaking – the most abstract and universal ones? Which are usually classified by historians as the dominant modes of management of meaning in subsequent periods of past development in systematically studied societies? If we assume the western, Eurocentric point of view, the following three – partly overlapping – are mentioned most frequently in the western academic tradition:

- The religious pattern of sensemaking, embodied in the evolution of Christian doctrine and in the history of religious institutions.
- The rational-scientific pattern of sensemaking, embodied in the philosophy of the Enlightenment and in the rise of science and industry.
- The 'postmodern'[5] pattern of sensemaking, acquiring shape in the new networks of communities of practice and new clusters of knowledge producers.

The emergence of the rational-scientific pattern of sensemaking did not eliminate the religious one, nor did the arrival of the postmodern pattern of sensemaking replace the rational-scientific. All three are present in contemporary societies. The religious and the rational-scientific have gradually developed social mechanisms for demarcation (and divided their social domains) and do not clash as powerfully as they used to. However, there is a potential for competition and conflict between all these patterns of sensemaking, as demonstrated, for instance, by the recent debate on 'intelligent design'. In this debate, the most recent episode of which took place in a court in Pennsylvania in 2005, the defenders of the religious pattern of sensemaking demanded an equal share in designing the curriculum of biology classes in a high school. They wanted their approach, which favoured a religious sensemaking pattern, to be put on a par with a rational-scientific approach in the social construction of the high-school curriculum. This is the meaning of the so-called 'intelligent design' debate and subsequent trial. This meaning had been negotiated – in this particular case in courts, since the parties could not agree 'on the spot', that is, in meetings between parents and the local board of education. This case will be discussed later; now let us briefly review the differences between these three historically identified patterns of sensemaking.

The Christian pattern of sensemaking evolved out of the belief that in making sense of the world a man is guided by divine revelation. The meaning of the world is divinely revealed and men and women can gain access to this meaning if they accept certain rules derived (through interpretations and their negotiations among relevant communities and experts) from this revelation. In particular, believers should follow the instructions, which are called the commandments, and by following them construct a desirable, 'just' society. Such a society should facilitate each individual's pursuit of personal salvation. Systematic production of knowledge has a distinct place in this society, and in contemporary society this place is the university. Since divine revelation is the 'guide' for men and women, theological faculty must form its core. Theologians and their fellow-researchers in other, more practical disciplines (law, medicine, geography, astronomy) conduct a systematic study of the most fundamental and also less fundamental meanings of the world and of ourselves (the less fundamental meanings must be derived from the most fundamental – the meanings imposed by God on all creation). What is essential for this pattern of sensemaking? It is the position of God as the ultimate guarantor of all other meanings discovered and invented by men and women in all walks of life and in all domains of systematic study. There is a hidden order in everything that exists and this order was created before we started deciphering it. This pattern of sensemaking, which emerged in the history of Middle-Eastern and European societies, has been studied by historians of religion who have pointed out a certain continuity of themes in patterns of religious sensemaking, linking the ancient Egyptians (with their belief in the immortality of an individual soul), the Persians (with their Zoroastrian belief in the world as a stage for the struggle of Good against Evil), the Greeks (with their Platonic idea that reality perceived by the senses reflects only dimly a higher, more 'essential' world), the Romans (with their political division of the roles of a church and a state) and contemporary Europeans (with their gradual separation of church and state). They have pointed out as well the influence of the institutional history of the Roman popes and the

Byzantine pope-emperors. Historians of religion have also shown that attempts to explicitly articulate and codify the basic principles of this pattern of sensemaking reached their peak in the thirteenth century with the studies of St Thomas Aquinas who tried to develop a systematic logic of religion.[6]

For St Thomas the Bible was more valuable than any sensory data or any empirical discovery. However, beginning in the Renaissance, the changing structure of the university started to reflect a gradual shift in the practical hierarchy of university faculties, with sciences and the humanities gaining ground at the expense of the formerly dominant theology. The Bible was still considered vital for guiding human conduct, but not necessarily for studying perceptible nature and actually achievable society. While Galileo expressed it most succinctly in his polemic against cardinal Bellarmine, preferring empirical experiment in Pisa ('reading in the book of nature') to Bible study, the emergence of a new pattern of sensemaking started much earlier and took more time to acquire a generalized and articulate form. The emergence of the new pattern of sensemaking started during the late medieval and early Renaissance period. It lasted until the end of the nineteenth century. Between the 'Latin Renaissance' of the fourteenth century and the publication of Diderot and d'Alembert's *Encylopédie* in the late eighteenth, a new, scientific-rational pattern of sensemaking matured. If the religious one had been codified by St Thomas, the scientific-rational acquired its most complete articulation with the emergence of the Enlightenment. The Enlightenment promoted a pattern of sensemaking developed by scientists, scholars and philosophers, whose collective work, embodied in the new encyclopedia, guided and accompanied the social, political and industrial revolutions. According to the thinkers of the Enlightenment, men and women did not need to cling to a hypothesis that God exists in order to discover the nature of the world and to shape their collective and individual destinies. Human 'Reason',[7] embodied in science, art and politics, could guide individuals as well as societies towards inventions and discoveries, towards welfare and progress. Liberty, Equality and Fraternity were viewed as rational principles invented and implemented in order to secure the greatest happiness for the largest possible number of individuals, each of them busy with the full-time pursuit of happiness. Personal happiness (not the salvation of one's soul) and fulfilment of human possibilities in earthly life (not in an afterlife) became socially desirable aims. The creative development (self-regulated evolution) of individuals replaced salvation (a result of following a pre-designed plan) as the ultimate ideal.

The scientific-rational pattern of sensemaking became dominant over the course of the nineteenth and twentieth centuries. However, its clear domination did not mean that it went unchallenged and it was subject to growing critiques, especially in the twentieth century. Critics pointed out that scientific rationality had not prevented industrialized societies from the upheavals of two totalitarian revolutions (which ended in Soviet and Nazi genocide and concentration camps), from waging two world wars (the second of which ended in the Cold War) and from excluding most of the people of the world from the benefits enjoyed by the citizens of affluent democratic societies (in spite of the formal dismantling of the colonial system). The most salient points were made by those who pointed out that any attempt to implement abstract, utopian, revolutionary ideals usually ended in terror. These critics claimed that the bloodshed caused by revolutionaries tended to far outstrip the horrors that their revolutions were meant to prevent. The Jacobin terror during the French revolution of 1789 and the Bolshevik terror after the Russian revolution of 1917 are quoted as cases in point. In each case the ideals were rationally grounded and they were considered legitimate. Monarchy was obsolete, capitalism was unjust. In each case the revolutionaries gained popular support (the French Jacobins much more clearly so than the Russian Bolsheviks, who hijacked anti-tsarist and anti-war sentiments and managed to use terror for much longer – thus effectively silencing those who would have tried to delegitimize them). In each case scientific rationality had been evoked when legitimizing political actions. The Jacobins claimed that they had to use terror because they wanted to pre-empt the monarchist plots of aristocrats. Bolsheviks claimed that their terror could prevent the eruption of counter-revolutionary plots by capitalists and their allies. In each case the machinery of terror eventually turned against the revolutionaries themselves.

Writing *The Open Society and its Enemies* in exile in New Zealand during the Second World War, Karl Popper (who became Sir Karl Popper after a distinguished career at the London School of Economics) opposed piecemeal social engineering in a democratic ('open') society to the implementation of a single utopian order in a totalitarian ('closed') society. Popper was a moralist; he argued that modest piecemeal social engineering (protected by market democracies) is better for citizens and for mankind at large. But Popper was not only a moralist and a political scientist. He had also been a philosopher of science, who had been influenced by the Viennese neopositivists in his youth. As a philosopher of science, Popper defended the scientific-rational pattern of sensemaking. He defended it not only against Marx's 'historical materialism' (which replaced divine design with class cunning). He also defended it against a narrowly neopositivist interpretation (which had replaced revelation with purely empirical, sensory examination). The neopositivist doctrine had already run into difficulties trying to explain developments in theoretical physics and faced serious problems with the emergence of biology as the 'queen of sciences'. Popper's criticism of historical materialism (with its Hegelian and Platonic roots) and of the concept of a single immutable 'logic of scientific discovery' had thus been an attempt to strengthen this scientific pattern of sensemaking from within. However, pointing out the political, social and human consequences of applying 'closed' utopian doctrines to the real world meant that Popper – and many other authors, from Hayek and Orwell to Miłosz and Solzhenitsyn – were trying to criticize dangerous utopias by confronting their theoretical claims with realities. By pointing out some consequences of implementing utopias (concentration camps for those who opposed the new order) they embedded criticism in a broader public sphere, further from the institutional embeddings of academic discussions, closer to 'the really existing masses' and to the 'informed' sectors of laic, non-academic citizenry. Criticism of the scientific-rational sensemaking pattern came thus both from within and from without the scientific-rational establishment. This criticism was grounded in comparing 'scientific reason' both to earlier religious reason (hence the disenchantment of the world thesis) and to possible future patterns of sensemaking (hence the re-enchantment of the world thesis).

The new pattern of the management of meaning – the *postmodern* pattern of sensemaking – is still emerging from significant modifications to the sensemaking processes in contemporary, increasingly transparent and networked societies of mobile and hypercommunicative individuals. The point is that the religious pattern of sensemaking strongly privileged 'the sender, the ruler, the author'. *The message counted.* The scientific-rational pattern of sensemaking privileged 'the expert community, the responsive audience, the professional organization'. *The media counted.* These were, in a sense, exposed by McLuhan as the message. The postmodern pattern of sensemaking (the very name of which is improvised and contingent and will probably change in the twenty-first century) privileges individualized masses accessible through open networks, imagined communities and social change programmes directed towards the inclusion of those who were formerly systematically excluded (from citizenship and political participation, from access to education, jobs, food, respect, identity, self-expression and so on). *The mobilization of masses for a movement counts. The social negotiation of mediated messages counts*. Message – media – movements. The postmodern pattern of sensemaking is being articulated as a post-Enlightenment project that privileges neither churches nor states nor markets, but instead invents new social spaces for mobile networked communities, so that they do not have to 'choose between freedom and privacy':[8]

> We are no longer in an age of expert juridical constructions designed to inscribe the irreducible 'power of the people' in oligarchic constitutions. This figure of the political and of political science is behind us. State power and the power of wealth tendentially unite in a sole expert management of monetary and population flows. Together they combine their efforts to reduce the space of politics.
>
> (Ranciere, 2006, p. 95)[9]

The postmodern pattern of sensemaking, like the religious and the rational-scientific patterns before it, has its own ideal: that of a transparent flow of social communications in an open, *multicultural* and democratic society, built around constant negotiation and renegotiation of meanings within complex and diverse social flows and transformations. Individuals are not expected to strive only for personal fulfilment or for individual salvation. For individuals, an ideal state of affairs is a creative, participative and open-ended socialization, which enables them to enjoy the diversity of 'others' and to contribute to a sustainable development (development that is manageable from the point of view of preventing an explosive clash of inequalities). For societies and groups, the ideal is a managed increase of inclusion and access to goods, services and relationships, and the gradual reduction and elimination of the systematic discrimination and exclusion of individuals and groups from real and virtual communities. Communication, interaction, feedback and self-reflection combine and recombine in fluid, networked, evolving social worlds. Individual, organizational and social actors perform rituals, play roles, break out of routines, invent themselves and construct social worlds. The postmodern pattern of sensemaking makes us focus not on an abstract society (as did the scientific-rational one) or on an individual soul (as did the religious one), but on intermediate, interactive and organizational realities. Organizational realities, that is, organizing and organized realities, are viewed and processed as social without becoming a distant abstraction in an individual experience. In other words, whether we like the 'postmodernism' label or not (most researchers are reluctant to accept it and some reject it virulently as irresponsible chatter) the focus of research slowly shifts towards organizations and organizing. This is a conscious choice by theoreticians of organizational knowledge and epistemology:

> Our problem is not only that we do not know enough but, more fundamentally, that we do not know what we need to know. This kind of 'radical uncertainty' (Piore, 1995, 120) or a second-order ignorance, adds additional force to Hayek's insight that in a social system knowledge is essentially dispersed. It is dispersed not only in the sense that knowledge is not, and cannot be, concentrated in a single mind but also that no single mind can specify in advance what kind of practical knowledge is going to be *relevant,* when and where ... Normative expectations and dispositions are activated within particular interactive situations, and how such activation occurs is always a *local* matter.
>
> (Tsoukas, 2005, pp. 105–7; emphasis in the original)

It can be claimed that postmodernists drew on Marx and Freud. Marx claimed to have detected the hidden plot of human history. He believed that in listening to the spirit of the ages one hears a symphony of progress played by the struggling lower classes. Freud claimed to have discovered the hidden plot of individual socialization and the rise of personal identity. He believed that this plot could be revealed as the history of individuals trying to liberate themselves from internalized repression. But postmodernists learned not only from theoretical doctrines. Postmodernist critics also drew conclusions from the failures of organizations, institutions and ideologies managed on behalf of Marx's and Freud's followers. The communist organizers who managed the working-class movements legitimized their actions with reference to Marxian doctrine but did not encourage a transparent analysis of their own organizational practices. The Gulag and an omnipotent secret police waging a war of terror against its own society were the inventions of communism in action. The practising psychoanalysts who applied Freud's ideas legitimized their actions with reference to Freud, but did not encourage transparency in the bitter organizational struggles for his legacy. Sectarianism, fractionalism and breaking with academic communities were neo-psychoanalytical inventions. Did postmodernism offer a way out?

Postmodernist critics focus on an intermediate level of managed and organized realities. Societies and individuals meet in organizations. Individuals try to make sense – to manage meanings. Gathering, analysing and interpreting concrete and local stories, postmodernists (Boje, 2007; Czarniawska, 1997; Gabriel, 2004; Tsoukas, 2005) claim to redress the wrongs and compensate the imbalances of theoretical (knowledge-producing) practices in contemporary societies. These wrongs and imbalances are the result of the dominance of a single organizational form, namely the large professional bureaucracy, which had been given a new lease of life with the advent of virtual networks and telecommunications multimedia. In attempting to subject the media and the virtual networks to their corporate mega-narratives (for example, those of Nike, McDonald's, Wal-Mart, Microsoft), corporations tend to suppress or isolate local narratives and microstorias. (Microstorias are individual 'stories', personal interpretations of experience by employees, which are often suppressed by the dominant 'macrostorias', those controlled by top management and disseminated by public relations organizations.)

The roots of the postmodern critique of the scientific-rational pattern of sensemaking are complex and are to be found entangled in the fringes of the scientific-rational academic establishment itself. Here, among the marginalized and discriminated-against critics of the 'core' scientific-rational doctrines we may detect echoes of dogmatic struggles between Christian communities (schisms, heresies, conflicts between eastern Orthodox and western Catholic churches and so on). The roots lie in phenomenology, psychoanalysis and critical theory (in its original Frankfurt School form), within the academic community and on its margins. They also draw upon non-academic sources, mainly social and political movements (which are not deprived of academic representatives): anticolonialism (with its postcolonialist reflection), environmentalism (with the antiglobalist or alterglobalist philosophies), feminism (which studies both 'glass ceilings' in professional bureaucracies and the iconic manipulation of the female body) and anti-consumerism (in the guise of both 'slow food' in Italy and George Ritzer's *The McDonaldization of Society* in the USA). Let us take a closer look at the roots of the postmodernist pattern of sensemaking, beginning with the three academic and epistemological influences cited above: phenomenology, critical theory and psychoanalysis.

Phenomenology

The phenomenological critique of 'Universal Reason' dates back to Husserl's 'transcendental phenomenology'. Husserl distrusted the Kantian construction of the categories of mind. These categories were supposed to form a stage on which dramatic ideas had to perform the dance of thinking. Husserl assumed that intuitive experience of phenomena always preceded any logical operations and that these experiences, continually turned around and taken into 'brackets' in our minds, were

more significant than any stage designs, including logical and philosophical categories. The latter came along with the acts of thinking
and behaving, which were intentionally performed by human agents.
Husserl considered philosophers to be the 'functionaries of mankind',
professionally testing the most widely-held universal principles of dealing with sensory experiences in a systematic way. However, his influence
on European thought came mainly through his followers, none of
whom had been loyal to the master. First, his two closest protégés,
Martin Heidegger and Roman Ingarden, turned his 'transcendental phenomenology', respectively, into 'existentialist' and 'realist' ontology.
Husserl also inspired two brilliant female students, Hannah Arendt and
Edith Stein, of whom the former turned to political sciences and the
theory of totalitarianism (and to the psychological explanation of 'the
banality of evil'), while the latter converted to Christianity and became
a Catholic nun.[10] However, his main influence has been upon French
philosophers – Emmanuel Levinas, Jean-Paul Sartre, Paul Ricoeur and
Maurice Merleau-Ponty. All of them questioned the abstract 'essence'
of revelation and reason, and wanted to root knowledge in a critical
analysis of individual existence. One of the unexpected results of this
shift in philosophical attention, mediated by Alfred Schutz in social
sciences, was a development of studies of everyday life and daily experiences of individuals undertaken in the areas of sociology, ethnography
and social psychology (including the social psychology of organizing),
of which Peter Berger and Thomas Luckmann are the best known cases
in point (see Berger and Luckmann, 1966) Discussing the contribution
of phenomenology to contemporary sociological research, one of the
sociologists continuing the phenomenological tradition wrote that:

> The City of God was replaced by the City of Man; the familiar other
> gave way to the unfamiliar self ... Phenomenology is the most radical
> development of humanism: an attempt to assimilate the unfamiliar
> to the self-transparency of *experience*. In defining humanity in terms
> of its own experience, rather than enigmatically in terms of putative
> 'nature' or self-generated 'divine' that cannot be thought without pre-
> suming its reality outside humanity itself, it seemed that the project
> of modernity would indeed come to an end; by reaching its goal. But
> experience, in becoming the focus of attention, also became opaque;
> rendered impenetrable by the act of looking. It is just the reflection of
> this look, the glassy stare of experience objectified, which instigated
> and resisted phenomenological analysis.
>
> (Ferguson, 2006, p. 212; emphasis in the original)

One might then say that the contribution of phenomenology to the postmodern pattern of sensemaking was a new focus on the shared experiences of interacting, communicating, collaborating human individuals 'thrown' into the world of 'others' encountered in real-life experiences. Will the ideal of a City for Mobile Civil Society, the 'Cosmopolis',[11] replace the ideals of the City of God and the City of Man expressed in the earlier patterns of sensemaking?

Critical theory

The second source of the theoretical critique of the scientific-rational pattern of sensemaking was the critical theory of society developed on the fringes of the academic world, in a privately financed institute for social research started under Max Horkheimer and Theodor Adorno in Frankfurt am Main in 1930. The group of researchers clustered around Horkheimer and Adorno had been doubly marginalized from the mainstream of German academic life. First, they tended to be influenced by Marxian social theory without necessarily being enthusiastic about either the communist party or a social-democratic party as the political guardian of Marxist doctrine. Thus their exclusion from accepted academic environments was not compensated by the broader popular support of organized political parties (which would have offered them a chance to reach the masses in spite of the academic boycott). Second, they were mostly Jewish and thus tended to be discriminated against in academic policies no matter what their paradigmatic and political loyalties were. The influence of this group grew as the result of the enforced migrations between 1933 and 1940. When the Nazis came to power, the group had to leave for Paris, and when the Germans invaded France, they had to escape to the United States. Thus the fundamental study of ethnocentric attitudes (which were believed to generate right-wing and totalitarian political sympathies) – 'The Authoritarian Personality' – were conducted and published in the United States. Horkheimer and Adorno's major criticism of the scientific-rational pattern of sensemaking was delivered in their *Dialectic of Enlightenment* (1944), where they diagnosed the status of 'the Enlightenment project'.

At the peak of the Enlightenment project's popularity, Jean Jacques Rousseau complained that man had been born free, but – due to obsolete social arrangements – 'was everywhere in chains'. Paraphrasing Rousseau, Horkheimer and Adorno announced in the preface to *Dialectic of Enlightenment* that they wanted to explain why humanity had not only failed to break the chains (as promised by the authors of the Enlightenment project) and to achieve freedom between 1789 and 1944, but had indeed fared even worse, sinking into a state of barbarism symbolized by the concentration camps of the totalitarian systems. Concentration camps and the industrialization of genocide were – according to them – manifestations of the same profoundly European development. They were the symptoms of the gradual growth of 'instrumental reason' (represented by the scientific rationalization of all walks of life that results in a 'disenchantment of the world' as Max Weber had put it) at the expense of 'substantial reason', or a value-guided pattern of sensemaking. The latter had been increasingly neglected and largely rejected – classified as religious or mythological, and therefore obsolete and superfluous. Mankind decided that it did not need the hypothesis that God existed. Mythologies were fables invented in mankind's childhood. This created a dangerous imbalance. The rise of the west to power and world domination is underpinned by both the mythical Odyssey towards the values (expressed in mythologies and revealed in religions) that granted meaning to human life, and the rational quest for the control of Nature, which delivered instruments for 'conquering' nature and solving social problems. The latter gave science a privileged position among knowledge producers, because knowledge provided by sciences contributed to the explosive growth of wealth (however, it also contributed to the growth of destructive power).

Critical theorists claimed that the totalitarian threat was not an external attack upon the European tradition. It was not an isolated and contingent deviation from the course of reason caused by barbarians from outside 'the west'. It emerged from the same fundamental crisis of western civilization as the attempts to save it. Soviets and Nazis tried to rationalize their social, economic and demographic policies and to impose universal, mythological ideologies on disenfranchised masses. They legitimized their terror with a mythological vision of an ideal – class or race – society.

Moreover, profoundly shocked by popular culture as promulgated by the American mass media, Horkheimer and Adorno concluded that there was no fundamental difference between the US and Nazi or Soviet 'audiences' – they were all kept in check and controlled by 'cultural industries' producing cultural content calculated to keep the masses docile and disenfranchised. As Walter Benjamin (1969) – who hovered on the fringes of the Frankfurt School (and who had thus been on a fringe of a fringe of the respectable academic world in Germany) – had put it, the introduction of the mass media (radio, film, press) meant that two types of celebrities dominated the attention of their audiences – film stars and dictators. None of them had a stake in contributing to the authentic liberation and emancipation of the masses.

Horkheimer and Adorno initiated their diagnosis of the human condition of their times as independent and uncompromised critics, but both were eventually embraced by the academic community (both returned to Germany after the Second World War), and their later contributions to critical theory – 'negative dialectics' and 'the logic of disintegration' – were proposed from within the establishment, not from without. The main influence of critical theory has been on the work of their fringe collaborators – Herbert Marcuse, Erich Fromm and Wilhelm Reich are all cases in point. All three attempted a critical synthesis of Marxism and psychoanalysis. Marcuse did so in *Eros and Civilization* and *Reason and Revolution* and finally in *One-Dimensional Man*. This last attempt to demonstrate that the apparent freedom of the western consumer disguised the 'repressive tolerance' of the market system turned Marcuse into an intellectual authority admired by the rebellious students of 1968 fighting police on the barricades of Paris and Warsaw, Berkeley and Prague, Mexico City and Frankfurt am Main. Fromm's synthesis appeared in *Escape from Freedom* and Reich's in *The Functions of Orgasm*. Adorno was surprised by the popularity of Marcuse and did not share his hopes for either the revolutionary potential of students in the western world or for that of peasants in the third world. When a female student blocked his way to the speaker's podium in 1968 in Frankfurt and bared her breasts in revolutionary challenge to break with the conventions of an academic lecture, he closed his eyes, turned around, left the hall and retired from active university life.

His assistant, Jurgen Habermas, has transformed the tradition of critical theory into a theory of emancipatory and communicative action in the evolving public sphere. This communicative action is conceived of as a liberating, interactive communication between networked free subjects fighting for the preservation and enlargement of their modern agora – or 'public sphere' – where a dialogue (free of domination, open and egalitarian) can be maintained between partners in a democratic civil society. This public sphere has to be defended against two imperial domains, that of a market rationalizing all actions according to the profit principle and of a state legitimizing all actions according to the hierarchies of power. But it is also a theory that fits the needs of specialized, organizationally partitioned experts, each of them sentenced to his or her expert domain within the social division of intellectual labour, because it helps them uphold the illusion of a universal common liberal ground:

> Much of the reception of Habermas's work in general takes place in the university, and for professors in the humanities there is undoubtedly a utopian element to his analysis. Habermas, like Adorno, attributes the impoverishment of culture to the inner dynamics of capitalist society. A cause of such impoverishment is the depolitization of the public sphere that accompanies the welfare state's involvement in a capitalist economy: society is now administered by bureaucracies and agencies rather than negotiated by political factions. Negotiations of the public sphere give way to client-consumer relations … An ever increasing overload of information led to the fragmenting of the public sphere through the development of specializations and expert cultures. Less and less can there be any common language or knowledge base for cultural elites to talk with one another. The various expert cultures housed in the university are largely split off both from society as a whole and from one another.
>
> (Beebee, 2002, p. 199)[12]

The impulse of critical theory has not been limited to Habermas and his followers (for example, Axel Honneth). Many other researchers in the social sciences also express their belief in the Enlightenment as the 'unfinished project', pointing out that radical large-scale re-engineering of social institutions and organizations had barely begun and that a longer time-scale is needed to pronounce the project either 'dead' or 'successful':

> What is Enlightenment? To have the courage to make use of one's cosmopolitan vision and to acknowledge one's multiple identities – to combine forms of life founded on language, skin, color, nationality or religion with the awareness that, in a radically insecure world, all are equal and everyone is different.[13]

Psychoanalysis

Psychoanalysis is the third main source of the postmodernist critique of the scientific-rational pattern of sensemaking. In broad terms, the historical long march of psychoanalysis through the institutions can be described as the reverse of that completed by critical theory. While critical theory started on the fringes of the academic world and gradually found its way into the established mainstream of research communities and producers of cultural content for the media and institutions, psychoanalysis started as an academic school of thought in psychiatry, a branch of psychology with strong medical (neurological) and therapeutic (medical clinics for mental disorders) links and has devolved to a collection of psychotherapeutic techniques, which remain controversial for most academic researchers in medicine, psychology and mainstream psychiatry. It has gradually been removed from academic establishments and marginalized where its representatives have managed to survive. In these instances psychoanalysis is currently known as a family of psychological theories (developed mainly by the American representatives of neo-psychoanalysis – Horney, Sullivan and others) with a troubled record of empirical verification. It has also been a powerful source of poetic inspiration in many different domains of social sciences (for instance, social psychology, the psychology of childhood, developmental psychology) and the humanities (literary, historical, philosophical, feminist, political – Lacan, Ricoeur, Kristeva, Irigaray, Žižek). Psychoanalysis has also inspired artists, even entire artistic movements. Surrealism would have been impossible without the Freudian theory of the unconscious.

Psychoanalysis was developed by Freud in his role as a medical doctor treating neurotic and hysterical patients in Vienna at the end of the nineteenth and the beginning of the twentieth centuries. His therapeutic experiences made him suspect that his patients' problems arose from their inability to cope with their true desires – primarily those of a sexual nature – as a result of social constraints on their behaviour and on their capacity to express themselves in explicit language. These constraints were particularly damaging in the sexual sphere, because individuals found themselves torn between their authentic desire (the 'id') and the equally authentic repression of these desires by the symbolic internalized 'controller' of one's behaviour (the 'super-ego'). Individual personality developed between those two powerful masters fighting for their share in determining behaviour; unconscious desires propel the individual towards sexual fulfilment, internalized norms repress these desires in order to channel behaviour into patterns acceptable to society. 'Ego' deals with both, giving us a feeling of becoming ourselves, of acquiring a unique identity, but also sowing the seeds of neurosis. The conflict is as tragic as the conflict between Platonic white and black horses, driving our souls towards the lower pleasures or higher values, each pulling at the same time and in opposite directions. Both are necessary if an individual is to function in society. Without satisfying our desires we cannot mobilize energies and lead a normal life. Without trying to realize higher values we cannot lead a meaningful life. Without internalized repression collaboration with others would be difficult. Without unconscious drives, there would be no emotional flavour and creativity in social life. But individuals may pay a high price for preserving both, and it is the role of the therapist to trace the history of repression in the patient's life through specially structured conversations (with the patient lying comfortably on a couch and a psychoanalyst sitting behind him or her and asking questions in order to free a patient's repressed memories), which are basically attempts to facilitate the patient's understanding of past behaviour. Unconscious conflicts and repressed wishes can then be brought out into the open and discussed. Their destructive potential as the sources of neuroses can be defused and the influence of repression upon a patient's personality neutralized (if a patient is honest and a therapist is skilled and devoted).

Freud's insights into the origin of neuroses as well as his interpretation of the meaning of dreams (when repressed feelings make use of relaxed self-censorship and 'float' towards consciousness) and linguistic 'slips' (when a person says something different to what was consciously intended, but which gives a clue to what they would have wanted to say, had there been no repression) became extremely popular. This enthusiasm began among the educated elites of European societies and subsequently – especially after his ideas became popular in the United States – spread to the middle classes. Freud's ideas (aided by the development of reliable contraceptives – the 'pill') paved the way for the so-called 'sexual revolution', anticipated from the 1930s to the 1950s but completed in the 1960s. The educated elites, especially their artistic avant-gardes, did much to advertise Freud's ideas and to link them to the postulates of the liberation of an individual from artificial constraints imposed by so-called 'Victorian' sexual morality. Margaret Mead's *Coming of Age in Samoa* is nowadays considered not so much as a piece of research as an ideological manifesto inspired by psychoanalysis. Mead wanted to demonstrate that a normal society with happier individuals was possible – if only the sexual life of the young were not as heavily policed and constrained as was the case in the western world. Alfred Kinsey's empirical reports on human sexual behaviour (male in 1948 and female in 1953; Kinsey et al., 1975) functioned as far more than scientific studies of spheres of behaviour that had previously been protected by social taboos from the research communities. Kinsey, trained as a zoologist, had overcome the difficulties posed by the taboo, but ultimately he found that his studies had more impact outside academia than within it. His reports provided fuel for public debates on the limits of repression (sexual morality, birth control, the emancipation of women) and the possibilities of increasing areas of tolerance in contemporary societies. No wonder it was picked up by the feminists (for example, in the Hite report; Hite, 2004).

Meanwhile, academic intellectuals – philosophers of science (Popper, Bunge), philosophers (Wittgenstein, Grünbaum, Nagel), psychologists (Eysenck, Crews), sociologists (Gellner) and others – had subjected psychoanalysis to a thorough critique. Popper excluded Freudian theory from the realm of science, claiming that it was not falsifiable – and only those theories which can be subjected to an attempted falsification (and survive it) merit a tentative label of 'scientificity'. Moreover, the average length of a course of psychotherapy in the United States grew to just under six years in the last decades of the twentieth century (with prices varying from US$10 to US$250 for a one-hour session with a trained 'shrink') while the success rate of individual therapies declined. As one of the critics put it:

> Freud and his followers established psychoanalysis outside the university system by creating their own training institutes. For the goal of these institutes was less research and intellectual activity than the protection and transmission of doctrine from generation to generation. It was politics and religiosity rather than ideas that gave birth to institutional psychoanalysis in the 1920s.
>
> (Dufresne, 2003, p. 150)

In order to have a more balanced view of the contribution of psychoanalysis to the postmodern pattern of sensemaking, one should look at the interface between psychoanalysis as an academic discipline and a more general humanist cultural critique. Even the most negative critics agree that Freud has had a profound impact on our culture. For instance, Philip Rieff, an American sociologist and cultural critic has analysed the impact of Freud's theory upon western humanities and social mores.[14] Rieff was particularly interested in the possibility of maintaining and rejuvenating a culture in which the central place (sacred values) has been evacuated, authorities have been undermined and ideals have lost their power to hold. Rieff called this postmodern pattern of sensemaking an *anti-culture* – quoting an ironic poem 'Annus Mirabilis' by Philip Larkin, who had described the sexual revolution as a social process that had profoundly influenced all professions, including the academic one.

Rieff thought that following the culture dominated by religion and the culture dominated by science we are now living in a 'third culture', which he called 'postmodern' and associated with facilitated, managed care for smooth functioning without 'the sacred' core values of the 'first culture' and without the 'secularized and rationalized' core values of the 'second culture'. He described this third culture as: 'a condition of human imaginations in which self-erasure and fusion with the other become dominant ... But this is an abstraction of sameness that does not exist' (Rieff, 2006, pp. 130–1).[15]

Rieff concluded that Freud had become more easily accepted as a creative artist than as a scientist. Indeed, considering the impact of Freud's writings, we may consider him as a dramatist writing a dramatic fiction (on the manifestations of the Oedipus complex), as a novelist reconstructing the soul of another artist (for instance, of Leonardo da Vinci) and as a visual performing artist staging a therapeutic performance as a quasi-artistic happening (the drama of therapeutic sessions on a couch, the partly fictitious twists and turns of individual therapies). But even more important was the contribution of Freud to the dismantling of the concept of an individual personality, which replaced the concept of a personal soul when the religious pattern of sensemaking gave way to the scientific-rational one. Perhaps the most succinct description of the contribution made by psychoanalysis to the postmodernist pattern of sensemaking with respect to this dismantling has been provided by Slavoj Žižek, who commented on the ideological message sent by Freud through the medium of psychoanalysis (again, in this particular sense the medium had, indeed, been a message, although this had not immediately been obvious and had to be gradually understood and interpreted as such):

> The ideal addressee of our speech, the ideal listener, is the psychoanalyst, the very opposite of the Master-figure that guarantees meaning; what happens at the end of the analysis, with the distribution of transference – that is to say, the fall of the 'subject supposed to know' – is that the patient accepts the absence of such guarantee ... there is no face-to-face encounter between patient and analyst, since the patient lies on the couch and the analyst sits behind him – analysis penetrates the deepest mysteries of the subject by bypassing the face. This avoiding of face-to-face encounter enables the patient to 'lose face' and blurt out the most embarrassing details. In this precise sense, the face is a fetish: while it appears to be a manifestation of the imperfect vulnerable abyss of the person behind the object-body, it conceals the obscene real core of the subject.
>
> (Žižek, 2003, p. 170)

In contemporary management sciences the psychoanalytical inspiration can be traced in many authors, primarily in the writings of Kets de Vries (for example, Kets de Vries and Miller, 1984; Kets de Vries, 2001) and Yiannis Gabriel (1999). They have profited from the gradual recognition that the validity of any psychoanalytical contribution to contemporary knowledge-production cannot be easily established within the traditional academic philosophies of science:

> Instead of the empirical basis in the body, or the hermeneutic basis in the mind, psychoanalysis goes back to the psychophysical basis of the person, as the source from which all thinking must arise. From this nascent philosophical foundation, psychoanalysis appears neither as inadequate science nor as overblown hermeneutics. It is revealed, instead, as a form of enquiry, which potentially challenges the empirical-hermeneutic divide, by pointing to the unity beneath the scientific ground of matter and the interpretational sphere of mind.
>
> (Gomez, 2005, p. 15)

* * *

Having presented three major sources of the postmodern turn in socially accepted patterns of sensemaking let us now consider three cases lost and found in historical translations. These are the case of the controversy between supporters of the theory of 'intelligent design' and the 'Darwinians', the case of the Brent Spar oil rig controversy between Shell and Greenpeace, and the case of the 'glass ceiling' and discrimination against female researchers in academic bureaucracies. In the first case there is a clash between two different patterns of sensemaking: the religious and the scientific-rational one. In the second case, there is a clash between the instrumental and the environmentalist pattern of sensemaking, both of which claim to be the superior variants of a scientific-rational one. In the third case, there is a clash between a social construction of the meaning of gender differences in professional bureaucracies and a feminist pattern of sensemaking. The feminists point out the limitations of the scientific-rationalist pattern of sensemaking and its embeddedness in male-dominated professional bureaucracies, thus proposing a postmodern pattern as a vehicle of their critical thought and as the ideology of their emancipating movement. All three cases are symptomatic for complex, open, increasingly networked societies and all three allow us to brace ourselves for the management of meaning in the present tense.

3
Cases in Point

(a) The return of religious sensemaking: the case of intelligent design

The return of the religious pattern of sensemaking into mainstream public debate in western societies has been widely noted by philosophers of culture and acknowledged by the media. All major institutional religions have seen increases in membership, and the prognoses of secularization as the inevitable aftermath of modernization and the growth of material welfare have been quietly shelved. This may be the result of the promise of stepping 'outside' material life, which religion – as opposed to science, scholarship, philosophy and ideology – offers, while humanist scholars deem it impossible: 'Perhaps it is impossible to generalize intelligently about human life, because in order to do so we would have to step outside it' (Eagleton, 2007, p. 138).

The most spectacular events (the rise of fundamentalisms) have led to speculation about a forthcoming 'clash of civilizations' along the borderline separating religious communities. But even the most sensational moments (for example, the Danish cartoon 'war', the riots after the pope's quote from a Byzantine emperor) failed to trigger major international conflict. Most of these alleged 'clashes' were in fact successful compromises that had been blown up by the media in the course of their regular dramatization and 'theatricalization' of daily life online and on screen. Sometimes the differences expressed in these cases had been hijacked by extremist parties in attempts to accelerate the political mobilization of their own support. For instance, the French courts ruled against the Muslim female head cover in public places (including schools and courts of law), but at the same time religious tolerance allowed radical imams to get footholds in fast-growing mosques in the city suburbs inhabited by the Muslim immigrants. Nor is this 'clashing' limited to the conflicts between a secular western state and a religious Muslim community. Public debates about a formal acknowledgment of the role of Christian roots in the development of European civilization accompanied the attempt to introduce the Constitution of the European Union. As a result of differences of opinion among potential future members of the EU, the preamble mentioning the Christian tradition was dropped, while the Constitution itself was rejected in national referenda in France and in the Netherlands. Attempts to reinsert religion into the legal institutions of the United States were manifested in the placing of the ten commandments carved in stone in prominent positions in and around public buildings, specifically courts of law. In some cases, the strict observance of the separation of the political and the religious sphere has led to the removal of these stone tablets by the federal authorities in the face of objections from the local (state) constituency's protests. In the case of the theory of 'intelligent design', court action was also necessary to decide the issue.

On 19 October 2004, Dover Area School District in Pennsylvania came up with a press release informing the general public that high school biology teachers would henceforth be obliged to read the following statement to their students commencing the ninth grade biology class:

> The Pennsylvania Academic Standards require students to learn about Darwin's Theory of Evolution and eventually to take a standardized test of which evolution is a part.

> Because Darwin's Theory is a theory, it continues to be tested as new evidence is being discovered. The theory is not a fact. Gaps in theory exist for which there is no evidence. A theory is defined as a well-tested explanation that unifies a broad range of observations.

> Intelligent Design is an explanation of the origin of life that differs from Darwin's views. The reference book, *Of Pandas and People*, is available for students who might be interested in gaining an understanding of what Intelligent Design really involves.

> With respect to any theory, students are encouraged to keep an open mind. The school leaves the discussion of the Origins of Life to individual students and their families. As standards-driven district, class instruction focuses upon preparing students to achieve proficiency on standard-based assessments.

> (The United States District Court, 2005, pp. 1–2)

The statement was issued as a response to lobbying pressure exercised by those parents of high school students who thought that the school curriculum reflected partiality to the opinions of its devisers and as a consequence devoted too much attention to a single theory concerning the origins of life, at the expense of all other theories. Democracy involves answerability and the school board promptly responded to the claims of taxpaying parents with the above statement. However, at this point parents who agreed that the Darwinian theory of evolution should be privileged in biology classes protested in their turn. They went to court in the role of taxpayers who disagreed with the way in which the school authorities spent their money. Clearly, the democratic constituency had been divided. There were those who wanted to maintain the status quo in which the academic community imposed a monopoly view of the scientific-rational pattern of sensemaking on the school curriculum. And there were those who questioned this monopoly and wanted to weaken it. Parents who wanted to preserve the scientific-rational monopoly mobilized convincing expertise in their cause and ultimately convinced the court and won their case. On 20 December 2005, Judge John E. Jones III of Harrisburg, Pennsylvania, ruled in the case of *Kitzmiller et al. v. Dover Area School District in Pennsylvania*. Eleven parents whose children attended schools in which the theory of 'intelligent design' was taught on a par with the Darwinian theory of biological evolution had questioned the school authorities' decision and the judge ruled in their favour. The verdict left Dover Area School District with a debt of $1 million (in estimated legal costs) and forced them to discontinue teaching the theory of intelligent design in biology classes as a counterbalance to Darwin's theory of evolution. The judge's conclusion was that the theory of intelligent design (ID) was not science and was not therefore entitled to equal treatment with the theory of biological evolution. He decided that ID in fact constituted a form of creationism, which meant that it was religion in disguise, promoted by individuals who clearly had religious motivations, and that by undermining secular science teaching it violated a constitutional separation of church and state. More specifically, in Judge Jones's 139-page opinion one can find the following argument:

> After a searching review of the record and applicable case laws, we find that while ID arguments may be true, a proposition on which the court takes no position, ID is not a science. We find that ID fails on three different levels, any one of which is sufficient to preclude a determination that ID is science. They are: (1) ID violates the centuries old ground rules of science by invoking and permitting

supernatural causation; (2) the argument of irreducible complexity, central to ID, employs the same flawed and illogical contrived dualism that doomed creation science in the 1980s; and (3) ID's negative attacks on evolution have been refuted by the scientific community.

(Ibid., p. 64)

The defence lawyers for the Dover Area School District managers of the board of education tried to utilize arguments drawn from contemporary philosophers of science, all of whom are profoundly critical of methodological research procedures and sceptical about the theoretical coherence of large-scale theories, including Darwinian theory. Their experts, including a contemporary philosopher of science, Steven Fuller, felt that the justification of the verdict was based on the attribution of 'wrong motives' and not 'wrong methods'. According to Fuller, who appeared on the witness stand and subsequently commented on the entire case, the judge assumed that there was no difference in motivation between those who promoted religion-based inquiry (for instance, a study of intelligent design) and those who conducted scientific inquiry (for instance, studying the evolution of species as reconstructed by palaeontologists and biologists). In each case, in the context of discovery there is a place for a thousand motives and multiple serendipities (heuristics are to a large extent contingent and discretionary). What makes them different is that in science, as opposed to religion, all products of scientific inquiry have to be submitted to an impartial scrutiny of the researchers' peers and only some of them can be approved within the context of justification (as opposed to the context of discovery). Genuine distinction, according to Fuller, can only be truly explained and guide our future decisions with respect to educational issues (such as, among others, inclusion in or exclusion from school curricula) if we focus on the context of justification. We should not be asking where theories come from but what they have to go through. We have to pay attention to the scientific method and its reiterative working (which makes the opinions of scientific experts vulnerable to later criticism and potential rejection, no matter what motives might have underlain their research in the 'discovery' context).

Interestingly enough, Fuller follows Popper rather than Kuhn at this point. Popper was the last major philosopher of science regularly to criticize biological research reports and to chastise biologists for flawed research and methodological failures in theory-building (somehow demonstrating in personal conduct that the context of justification is too important to be left to routines and bureaucratic peer control).

Judge Jones's ruling will probably cause as much public discussion as did the Scopes trial in the nineteenth century, or the 'equal time' school trials of 1982 in Little Rock, Arkansas (when the state tried to mandate teaching creationism alongside evolution) and of 1987 in Louisiana (where creationists' claim to an equal share in school curricula was also rejected). However, the issue has not been closed definitely once and forever. What is at stake is a clash of two principles, both of which are central to our social and political organization (laws, governments) and to our management of meaning – in this case our management of the inequalities between two bodies of thought, two patterns of sensemaking, the religious and the rational-scientific.

In open, democratic societies, the right of the individual to express opinions and to attract the attention of politicians and public servants is taken for granted. It is also taken for granted that science offers the most impartial, unbiased, knowledge about the world. Scientific knowledge is considered 'valuable' because of potential applications. It is also considered 'open' to potential modifications, improvements and regular critical scans. Thus democratic societies are both democratic (in politics) and aristocratic (in granting privileges to scientists as knowledge producers). We vote as democrats, listening to the people, but we explain most processes in the natural and social world as logocrats, listening to the aristocracy of knowledge producers. As court trials have demonstrated, none of these attributes (unbiased, open, valuable) applies to the explanations offered by the followers of 'creationist' or 'intelligent design' theories. What is at issue, however, are priorities: does the principle of democracy, which subjects school curricula to parental approval (they have the right as taxpaying citizens to determine what their children will be taught) or the principle of rationality, which subjects curricula to the expert approval of academic communities (they have the right to determine what is good for the intellectual development of a child) come first? The answer is found in the court rulings, but it is not final. Rather, it reflects the present consensus, which allows the academic authorities to exercise their right to decide what will be taught in schools even against the explicit will of constituencies. What matters is the consensus among members of a scientific community about the superiority of Darwin's theory of evolution. If this consensus crumbles, different curricula may be proposed by splinter groups within the academic community, and, over time, court rulings in similar situations might start reflecting a different balance of social forces. Would this, however, mean a second chance for the religious pattern of sensemaking? This is hard to predict. A lack of consensus in the rational-scientific area (consilience, as one of the sociobiologists dreaming about the unity of science put it) does not necessitate a return to the previous, religious pattern of sensemaking (though it may very well be indicative of a general return to religion, as recent reversals of secularization suggests). It could also mean that the issue will not be decided between individual parties, which could be identified and served by a court of law as the neutral third party, but by emergent movements and clusters of different organizational entities (for example, the media, political parties, NGOs and the like) initiated and managed by a network of voluntary, semi-voluntary and professional actors competing for public attention in the media and for policy change in parliamentary democracies.

This is what happened in the case of the Brent Spar oil platform. This issue was never brought to a court of law. It was played out in the media and orchestrated as a dramatic struggle between a heroic NGO and a huge, bureaucratic and malevolent corporation. Had an attempt been made to bring it to the courts, the case would have been likely to have been massively unwieldy and to have required an international court, given that both protagonists – multinational company Shell and Greenpeace – operate worldwide.

(b) Experts, ideologies and the media: the case of the Brent Spar oil rig

The Brent Spar oil rig has become infamous in the contemporary history of the environmental movement because of the conflict that surrounded its decommissioning in 1995. The controversy fuelled continuous media attention and provided extremely vivid images that fired the imagination of the masses and ensured that Brent Spar became a household word. The two main protagonists, the two principal organizational actors playing the leading roles in this widely-televised drama, were one of the world's largest multinational oil corporations, Royal Dutch Shell, and a large global, non-governmental organization devoted to the preservation of biodiversity and protection of threatened environments, Greenpeace International. The two clashed over the potential risks involved in sinking the oil rig Brent Spar (Shell's preferred solution, with some inevitable oil spillage conceded) in the Atlantic. Their difference, supported by scientific expertise, was prompted by different 'universalisms': 'The multiple temporalities in which we live may cause us some analytic confusion, but they are far easier to think about and to handle than multiple universalisms' (Wallerstein, 2004, p. 83).

Having closed the rig in 1991, Shell solicited the permission of the British government to sink the rig in the Atlantic. The authorities were persuaded by expert reports delivered by scientists from Aberdeen University in Scotland. Their opinion was that sinking the rig at a depth of 2.5 km would inflict only limited damage on underwater life. First, there were only negligible remnants of oil in the underwater storage tanks that would come to rest at the sea bottom. Second, while the spilling of oil remnants was possible (sinking the rig would involve blowing it up), it was also possible that this could be avoided and that the construction would hold in spite of sinking. This deep-sea solution was considerably cheaper than the alternative decommissioning technique of on-shore dismantling. Greenpeace responded to these expert opinions by promptly commissioning a 'second scientific opinion'. Convinced that Shell was basically interested in cutting costs without due diligence in ecological matters, the Greenpeace activists pointed out that very little is known about deep-sea ecosystems and that any damage predictions are thus inevitably imprecise, because so little is known about the organisms that might be exposed to danger. Greenpeace quoted research for Shell by the Fisheries Research Services, which described the variety of underwater life in three locations among which a final dumping site had to be chosen, and in which the environmentalists noted – although the research was very limited – that the researchers had found much richer deep-sea life than they had anticipated. Second, the Greenpeace experts observed that most of the estimates of the extent of damage to the environment from underwater leaks of oil remnants were based on questionable extrapolations of quite different and small-scale events. Third, Greenpeace experts (aided by new samples taken by the activists who occupied the platform) calculated the volume of possible oil remnants and came up with a much higher estimate than that provided by Shell. According to the Greenpeace experts, the volume of these hazardous wastes remaining in underwater storage tanks could have been a hundred times higher than Shell's estimates, not 50 tons but more than 5000 tons. In conclusion, Greenpeace asked Shell and the British government to reconsider their decision and not to dump the oil rig in the deep ocean.

This difference of expert opinions, clear as it was, would in normal circumstances have remained a relatively minor issue buried in organizational dossiers, among other expert reports and attachments. However, a dramatic action undertaken by Greenpeace activists who managed to occupy the abandoned platform, preventing its final towing away and disposal, had been filmed and the cassette delivered to the media, which televised the event all over the world.

The smuggling of the video recording of the 'battle for Brent Spar' to TV stations and their prompt transmission of the event to the viewing public changed the political dimensions of the conflict. Further, the symbolic occupation of the abandoned rig by Greenpeace activists (April–May 1995) and the attempts by Shell – using ships and helicopters – to remove them coincided with the emergence of a new Shell marketing campaign in Germany with a heavy stress on environmental protection, clean energy and ecological concerns. The former led to dramatic media images of a multinational Goliath brutally removing brave small David in order shamelessly to pollute the environment, without regard to international treaties and public sensitivities. Once the activists had been removed, the towing of the platform to its final location had been started (11 June 1995). The latter led to a widespread boycott of Shell gas stations in Germany (including a boycott by German government ministers) and to occasional attacks (cutting the hoses, smashing the shops, setting stations on fire). German chancellor, Helmut Kohl, protested the issue to British prime minister, John Major, during the G7 conference, which took place in Halifax, Nova Scotia, while eleven European states proposed a moratorium on deep-sea disposal of oil rigs (only Great Britain and Norway were against the proposal). European public opinion, aware of the ambiguities of Shell's position, gave Greenpeace the benefit of the doubt. Shell conceded in a public announcement issued on 20 June 1995:

> Shell's position as a major European enterprise has become untenable. The Spar had gained a symbolic significance out of all proportion to its environmental impact. In consequence, Shell companies were faced with increasingly intense public criticism, mostly in continental northern Europe. Many politicians and ministers were openly hostile and several called for consumer boycotts. There was violence against Shell service stations, accompanied by threats to Shell staff.[1]

Meanwhile, Shell commissioned an independent auditor, a Norwegian company Det Norske Veritas, to check the expert reports. The auditors confirmed the accuracy of Shell's expertise and Greenpeace promptly apologized in public for gross exaggeration of the estimates concerning the volume of remaining oil. Prompt apology saved the NGO from any public backlash. Shell apologized for having tried to criminalize the environmentalists and suggested forming a joint Shell/Greenpeace discussion group for reviewing potential environmental risks in future. Both organizations were willing to let the public know that they were learning – Greenpeace from imprecise expertise with an ideological flavour, Shell from insensitivity to the consequences of adverse media coverage for their corporate reputation. However, falling sales and the growing crisis in Germany forced Shell to stop the towing and to look for another option.

Ultimately, the rig was towed to a Norwegian fjord and elements of the structure were re-used in order to develop harbour facilities near the port of Stavanger in south Norway. The battle for scientific expertise was won by Shell, but the war for the disposal of Brent Spar was won by Greenpeace, which had suggested on-shore disposal all along. Greenpeace had won on two fronts: in the media (that is in the virtual public agora) and in politics (where civil society's mobilization influenced politicians). Public opinion had been mobilized much more effectively by Greenpeace than by Shell. They contrived to manage the meaning of oil rig disposal and to convince broad segments of the public and key politicians in the European Union that sinking Brent Spar meant more dangerous waste and potentially unknown risks to the environment than Shell led them to believe. Both parties have also learned how to recognize the limits of their influence. Greenpeace learned that ideological zeal can blind them to hard facts and superior expertise. Shell learned that focus on hard facts can blind them to the consequences of flexing their multinational muscle and disregarding organizational actors, who might be smaller but are still capable of representing the interests of civil society as a principal stakeholder. By establishing a joint commission for discussing sensitive issues linked to environmental protection both organizations had learned how to manage their differences. The greatest winners are the growing number of commercial PR consultancies that teach corporate clients how to translate expert reports into dramatized media messages. Media messages have to be dramatized and launched in order to extend the protective umbrella of a scientific-rational pattern of sensemaking over managerial decision-making, but at the same time they also aim to smuggle in an organization's ideological message and to impose it on mass audiences – enhanced with a 'halo' of 'objectivity' and 'rational backing'.

However, what happens if the learning process cannot be as swift as in the Shell/Greenpeace case? In other words, what happens if the issues are much more complex and the expertise itself is being continuously negotiated by the most competent but divided research communities? What happens if it is not simply the question of one piece of expertise against another, or of one rational academic community against another? What happens, for instance, if a male academic official announces in public that female students are less intelligent than male students? How can we negotiate the meaning of IQ and of gender comparisons, which are notoriously burdened with clashes between the followers of scientific-rational ('modernist') and postmodern patterns of sensemaking?

(c) Acceptable inequalities? The case of female IQ (gendered soul inside the academic brain)

On Tuesday 8 November 2005, Rector Magnificus of the Erasmus University in Rotterdam, Steven Lamberts, spoke during the ceremony of awarding doctorate *honoris causa* to the American economist, Richard Thaler. His speech 'The Gender paradox in student population of the Erasmus University in Rotterdam' (Lamberts, 2005), opened with a list of managerial worries about the increasing numbers of students, the decreasing level of educational services and a remark on the differences between male and female applicants and students. He observed, quoting the official state statistics, that generally speaking, more girls than boys start studying at universities and college-level schools offering bachelors diplomas (20,000 versus 18,000 and 46,000 versus 41,000 respectively). Moreover, differences become even more evident when their academic careers are checked after eight years – by that time only 54 per cent of boys would have graduated, as opposed to 67 per cent of girls. Trying to explain this difference, the rector asked if this proved that women were more intelligent than men, but he rejected this hypothesis. He quoted a report published in the *British Journal of Psychology* by researchers from the University of Manchester (Irwin and Lynn, 2005), based on IQ tests administered to 80,000 individuals. According to these researchers, men had a higher IQ than women (with an average difference of 5 points) and this difference grew in the uppermost segments of the tested population (twice as many men have an IQ score of 125, a score of 130 is reached by three times more men than women, and scores of 155 increase the difference in favour of men by a ratio of 1:5).

Thus having suggested that men are more intelligent than women, the rector went on to complain that the percentage of women among first-year students of medicine at the Erasmus University had risen to 68 per cent. First-year students are selected on the basis of grades received in high schools and colleges – the better the grades, the higher their chances of getting selected. At seventeen or eighteen girls usually have better grades than boys and therefore 'appear' to be more intelligent. According to the rector, this might be just a misleading appearance, or the consequence of a blind trust in school grading, as the Manchester psychologists' research clearly suggested. Conclusion: the selection of candidates on the basis of grades obtained during their final school exams should be abolished since it creates an unnecessary – and unfair – barrier for boys that does not represent their actual intelligence.

Steven Lamberts turned to the university's statistics and observed that two-thirds of students in law, sociology, psychology, medicine, history, art and the management of health-care were female, while in the faculties of economics and business management 70 per cent of students were male. How to explain this difference in the gender composition of the student body?

> Could it be that the choice predominantly made by male students to study business, management and/or economics at our university, is related to the unconscious wish to enter a world of money, power and the involved risks? And could this choice be related to the stormy testosterone-driven growth of the young male into adulthood? ... My conclusion at this time, however, is that the Rotterdam School of Management and the Faculty of Economics are consistently successful in attracting on a yearly basis high numbers of male students. I want to emphasize that this is of crucial importance for our country as a knowledge society.
>
> (Lamberts, 2005)

Speaking after the rector, the dean of the Rotterdam School of Management, Han van Dissel, calmly observed that the rector should be thanked for providing a hormonal excuse for the existence of a glass ceiling limiting the professional careers of women within the academic bureaucracy. Then the media stepped in. On Saturday 12 November many major daily newspapers carried critical accounts of the speech on their front pages. *De Volkskrant*'s headline was 'Rector of Erasmus finds boys smarter than girls', while *AD* spoke of 'Sexism in rector's annual address'. When interviewed by *De Volkskrant* on 15 November and asked if he had had any negative responses, the rector dismissively answered that he had only had some angry emails from women within the university. Meanwhile, the speech triggered a petition by researchers participating in the ceremony, which was subsequently signed by 300 employees of the university, including a few full professors, and a letter from the department of 'business and society management' to the president of the board of directors of the university. The petition's authors demanded an appropriate political and academic apology instead of a dismissive remark about a few angry emails. They pointed out that Steven

Lamberts had failed to mention that Irwin and Lynn's study had been subjected to a very damning and equally widely publicized critique in *Nature*. The letter to the president of the board of directors, who happened to be a woman, suggested that more public dialogue on gender balance in education was needed and that a task force should be formed 'to examine the role and position of women and men in each faculty and student body'.

The interest of the media in further developments quickly waned, but the response from within the university was more robust. Employees signing the petition expressed disbelief that in spite of similar incidents in the past, including the much publicized events at Harvard University (whose president was forced to step down soon after he had made disparaging remarks about women), attempts were still being made to legitimize gender inequalities. Signing the petition had been widely seen as a signal of concern and dissent. The following fragment of one of the comments attached to signatures, from a junior academic researcher (a woman), stands for many other expressions of similar sentiments:

> The naive trust of the rector in the authority of top ranked journals is amazing and embarrassing. Next to this, the factual correctness of the – indeed highly controversial – article is not the issue here. A person in the position of the rector has the social and moral obligation to handle matters that might encourage discrimination in a responsible way.[2]

There were others who refused to sign the petition but offered explanations for their refusal. One reason quoted by a senior professor (male) was that he did not believe in the 'ill-will' of the speaker and did not consider a political and academic apology to be 'politically correct'(since the peer status of the quoted journal made the rector's mistake understandable and therefore excusable), another was that sending a petition to be signed as a general email contributed to the circulation of spam among colleagues (junior academic researcher, male) and thus should have been limited to some discussion forum, in order not to 'become number 1 irritation-vehicle'. This latter comment provoked a response: one of the senior professors (male) replied that he did not find the petition disruptive of corporate communications and suggested that the label 'spam' might be replaced with 'responsible participation in the making up of a collective mind'. Clearly, academic professionals differed with respect to their definitions of the legitimate will to know: 'Democracy requires that citizens be willing to make some effort to find out how the world around them works ... When democracy becomes modeled on consumption, becomes user-friendly, the will to know fades' (Sennett, 2006, p. 171).

The response on the part of both the president and the rector was indirect: they did not address the petition at all and they left the letter about forming the task force unanswered. However, they undertook some damage control: a month after the controversial speech the university's board of directors announced that a special office was to be established at the university with a female researcher and female manager in order to participate in a nationwide study of the situation of female employees within universities. In effect, the university simply linked up to an existing nationwide research programme that had so far failed to produce any significant results as far as the position of women in hierarchical research organizations was concerned. Nevertheless, funds were allocated, presumably meeting policy guidelines for the president, the rector and the dean. At the same time the establishment of a new position – 'ambassador of diversity' – was announced and the dean of the Rotterdam School of Management became one of them. All this was announced during a meeting organized by the rector and the president in the Senate Hall of the university, to which some of those who signed the petition had been invited. The assembled employees were not satisfied with the proposed measures, which were presented in a patronizing way and illustrated with a video film on discrimination against female researchers in biochemical labs at MIT twenty years before. Female researchers present at the meeting complained about the inadequacy of these measures, the primitive level of didacticism in the presented film, and a failure to commit the board of directors to the creation of a 'gender watchdog', which might have provided a real chance for women to voice their complaints and would potentially have made a difference. However, no action plan was formed and although the measures proposed by the president and the rector were generally deemed inadequate, no alternative action was initiated. The rector and the president made vague promises to raise these issues in public discussion with the employees and a further promise was made to organize an open forum on gender issues on 8 March, International Women's Day. In an ironic twist of bureaucratic fate, the female president of the university was subsequently forced to resign by an all-male alliance of the rector and deans.

From the point of view of an opportunity to reduce a democratic deficit, the dissent started after the rector's speech did not result in any palpable improvement of women's chances of professional upward mobility within the university. The problem of gender inequality was re-branded as a managerial problem of acquiring more reliable knowledge (on the hurdles preventing women from reaching men's levels of academic success) and then translated into prompt but arguably superficial administrative action. This action amounted to the reduced response of the 'window dressing' type – the establishment of a single office with one part-time researcher (for the duration of the project) and the assignment of a junior female employee to run it on a daily basis. At the end of the project the report on the situation of women would be produced and the future of the office was further unclear. The timing of the managerial response was effective: the rector and the president waited until signatures on the petition stabilized at around 300 and the lack of further growth signalled a failure to mobilize more than one-tenth of the university's employees, then suggested their remedy for a translated, re-branded version of the problem, took note of the voices of dissent during the public discussion about their proposal and asked the most active participants to take part in a public panel discussion on International Women's Day two months later. The most important issue, that of a gender watchdog (a kind of gender ombudsman), was stonewalled by the top managers of the university, then patiently sidetracked in ensuing discussions and quietly removed from future agendas. This left the glass ceiling off the agenda, especially the disturbing fact that although more women than men start as PhD students, their advantage disappears as the first tenured track positions of assistant professors are filled and becomes a clear disadvantage when full professorships are allocated (there are seventeen male professors for each female professor, and the business school currently employs only one woman as a full-time professor).

The 'academic brain' is still supposed to be male, definable in terms of IQ and measured primarily in terms of papers published in selected journals. The difficulties experienced by women while anchoring their identities in academic communities and the difficulties that they experience in trying to enrich the social capital of universities by involving both men and women in 'socializing' these increasingly streamlined bureaucracies (making them better places to work in) testify to a more general discrepancy between an official ideology of the 'diverse workplace' (in terms of age, race, gender and so on) and the reality of managed inequalities. These difficulties also clearly indicate that women do not stand any chance of improving their chances of successfully pursuing an academic career if they wait for more gender-friendly expert reports. The scientific-rational pattern of sensemaking makes us almost entirely blind to gender inequalities, since we tend to assume that 'human being' is by definition either a male or a female and thus the same applies to both genders – disregarding empirical evidence that realities do not confirm this gender equality. The roots of inequality and discrimination cannot be rooted in biology forever. After all, almost everybody (now) agrees that women are not genetically inferior as far as brain development goes, while social child care can be expanded and household tasks traditionally perceived as 'female' roles can be divided more equally between male and female partners. Thus relevant research in this context would be articulated by a feminist movement attempting to overhaul – step by step – the *hidden* injuries of gender inequalities that have been built into family socialization, school interactions, professional careers, media stereotypes and numerous other processes, which continue to rehearse male advantages in institutional settings and legitimize them with subsequent tacit ideologies. Successful challenging of male superiority requires a critical (for instance, but not exclusively, postmodern) pattern of sensemaking.[3]

An ironic reflection of these gender discrimination problems had been happening, almost simultaneously, in the lower ranks of the university's hierarchy. One of the women who cleaned the Erasmus University offices in Rotterdam approached one of the PhD students in business management (with whom she shared Afghan roots) and asked her for help. Cleaning staff (mostly non-European and predominantly Moroccan women) had been allowed less than one minute to clean each office and felt that this meant they could not perform their duties well. They were pressed by their supervisors to complete their jobs precisely in the allotted time and problems were aggravated by flawed communications. The cleaning company employed exclusively foreign women, only some of whom spoke either Dutch or English. The university administrator of office building could not force the cleaning company's manager to change the rules. One can detect the gender issue emerging in the resistance of low-paid female cleaners against their male foremen. Women resisted being forced to do a poor job, opposing both their supervisors' targets and their gender superiority. What they were fighting for was recognition as responsible, concerned and rational employees, rather than merely existing as anonymous cogs in a service machine. They did not want to lose the opportunity to be recognized as reliable service-providers. Having experienced the double stigmatization as immigrant labourers and as women (their supervisors were all men) they protested against lowering their already low status even further by being forced to deliver a mediocre, low-quality performance. In this particular case compromise was possible, since the university agreed to increase the cleaning organization's fee, which enabled foremen to allocate more time per office. However, this compromise only became possible after the cleaning staff reached out to the client company's personnel and their complaint became 'visible' in inter-organizational communications.

The rector's speech on gendered student brains had been prompted by a highly positivist vision of human intelligence. Intelligence, according to this vision, can be precisely determined as an intellectual skill that can be isolated and measured during and after psychological testing of individuals. This vision is underlain by a biological explanation of gender differences neatly reduced to the level of hormones influencing behaviour in early youth. Finally, the rector's speech had demonstrated an unshakeable faith in the indisputable rationality of academic bureaucracies. Professional bureaucracies have trouble noticing that thinking bodies are gendered (especially if they are to be promoted to higher academic positions) and so are the cleaning bodies (mostly foreign and female, outsourced and temporary or part-time employees). Managing to glimpse hidden affinities between gender inequalities linked to the glass ceilings in academic competition and gender inequalities between immigrant women working for facility maintenance companies and their male competitors (who tend to be employed as supervisors of female teams) on lower-end job markets, might offer a clue to alternative, more gender-balanced ways of managing inequalities. However, most of the representatives of the academic research community would consider the problems of outsourced labour on their premises as marginal at best, preferring them to remain invisible most of the time. The stability of 'nickel and dimed' labour, like the stability of gender gaps depends crucially on our ability to sweep under the carpet many inequalities, including the gender flavour of distinction between paid (for example, academic researcher), underpaid (for example, outsourced cleaning services) and unpaid (for example, domestic chores, particularly child rearing) labour.[4]

* * *

All three cases – the case of the concept of 'intelligent design' picked up by concerned citizens, the case of the concept of the 'second expert opinion' on environmental impact used by an NGO, and the case of gender inequalities picked up by a privileged member of the academic bureaucracy – hark back to inequalities inherited from the sensemaking patterns and practices of the past.

First, we have inherited the Enlightenment's concept of universal rationality, which paved the way for the monopoly of scientific rationality, with a tacit assumption that academic communities are preferred suppliers of expertise for public decision-making. Democracy stops at the academic expert's door. Peer approved merit prevails over democratic process, no matter how narrowly and technically defined.

Second, we have inherited the market economy and its accompanying liberal, open society illusion of a free 'marketplace' of ideas in which different paradigms and different expert communities compete. But competition does not always prevent the emergence of monopolies and oligopolies and victory in competition may be reached at the expense of methodological and ethical reliability. The mobilization of social and political support does influence the construction of rational expertise (the experts of Greenpeace versus the experts of Shell).

Third, we are slowly creating an increasingly omnipresent and virtual, multimedia-driven and individually accessed world of instant communications. With the individualization of mobile communications we have created new virtual agoras, spaces for individual reflection on social issues outside political institutions. Mobile, instant, individualized communications turn even relatively trivial issues and events in the daily lives of local communities into potential stepping stones towards a general mobilization of concerned citizens for a meaningful political action. Although these virtual agoras have been used only sporadically (Seattle anti-WTO protests remain the most significant cases of rapid political mobilization of ecologists and alternative globalists), there is probably more to come. In any case, universities learn quickly. In spring 2008 the Erasmus University in Rotterdam published a well-designed hard-cover brochure on 'A career in science? Female professors on their profession and their lives' and disseminated it among the employees (2500 copies had been conceived and composed by a professional PR company, Lansu + Paulis Communicatiepartners from Leiden) in a cleverly designed attempt to improve the gender image of the institution. The rector's foreword, dated March 2008, begins with 'congratulations, Madame, on earning your Master's degree or doctor of medicine diploma' and continues:

> You have reached a significant moment and are ready to take the next step along your career track. Although becoming a professor may not be the first thing that comes to mind, why not consider it? A career in science is fascinating, multifaceted and challenging.

> We are keen on giving you a glimpse of what it involves. A number of female professors working at Erasmus University Rotterdam and Erasmus Medical Center will have their say in this publication. They will discuss their careers, when they knew they wanted to be a

Illustration 3.1 'Gender', Navid Nuur. A billboard by a contemporary artist making a creative comment on dead-end streets in attempts to increase gender equality in professional bureaucracies (courtesy of the artist)

professor, and what they are working on. They make suggestions and talk about the world of science.

Erasmus University Rotterdam offers talented women opportunities to work at its research institutes and faculties. Promising young female Master's or doctoral degree course graduates who are curious, inquisitive and flexible will find a place at one of the many academic disciplines offered at EUR. As time passes, a job as a professor may be within your grasp!

(EUR, 2008, p. 79)

Happy ending?

4

The Present Tense of Meaning (Underground Passages between Hierarchies, the Cunning of Calculating Reason and the Return of Utopian Virtues)

We have considered three cases – the debate over intelligent design, arguments over the disposal of an oil rig platform and the existence of gender insensitivity among academic professionals – as exemplars of the recent history of the management of meaning. In the case of intelligent design we discussed an attempt to 'legalize' the return of religion into mainstream socialization (educational curricula). In the case of the Brent Spar oil platform we saw a premonition of things to come in a changing multimedia landscape, in which the power of images and mobilizing messages far exceeds the power of rational and balanced analysis. Last not least, we saw in the case of gender insensitivity within professional bureaucracies the manifestation of systematic inequality managed by discreet exclusion. We concluded that our intellectual inheritance (the past tense of meaning) includes:

- the universalist concept of manageable rationality (embodied in professional bureaucracies)
- the liberal concept of a marketplace as the matrix for shaping organizations and interactions (of exchanges, of interactions, of ideas and influences)

and that these components of our inheritance should be seen against the background of our

- growing awareness of the need for a new concept of increasingly complex multimedia communications (which allows for a much more rapid recycling and dissemination of meanings). These increasingly complex media communications often require a less systematic and more creative approach:

One management consultant claimed marketing was about to cure its Don Giovanni complex of seducing as many buyers as possible; her partner saw the advent of new firms basing their success on an inner ethos attracting an audience much as Kandinsky wanted spiritual art to do. A trendy marketer insisted that what he was doing was best called 'curating' and that Krishnamurti had more to say to marketing managers than Philip Kotler did. Henrik Schrat, a German concept artist, introduced a 'manager-in-residence' to his English art school.

(Guillet de Monthoux, 2004, pp. 348–9)

The religious zeal of the proponents of intelligent design, the ideological zeal of the proponents of 'green' solutions to all problems and the 'paternalistic/patriarchal' zeal of professional academic communities – all these mixes of passions and interests demonstrate links to the past patterns of the management of meaning. The quotation from Pierre Guillet de Monthoux demonstrates some of the new links between present patterns of management of meaning designed with the future tense in mind. Architects and managers need to acquire the 'aura' of a work of art or of an artistic process in order to endow management with a less instrumental and more 'substantial', 'symbolic' meaning.[1] (We noted this in Chapter 1, when considering Larson's studies of postmodern architects.) Guillet de Monthoux makes a similar case for consultants and academics in management education in the quotation above. The past does not disappear, rather religion is often replaced by art as a more 'impartial' custodian of symbolic values for professional communities (because the institutional infrastructure of contemporary artistic production and consumption appears less centralized and dogmatized than institutional churches). Going to an exhibition of art in a city museum on a Sunday does not only symbolically replace a visit to a local church, but also, equally symbolically, emphasizes our intuitive search for a 'living experience' of values, which we expect to encounter in an artist's work as earlier ages might have expected to find sustenance for the soul in a priest.

The case of intelligent design showed us a successful attempt by the representatives of the scientific-rational pattern of sensemaking to defeat the representatives of religious sensemaking. They won in the educational domain by claiming a monopoly on the production of valid knowledge, by evoking the law in order to influence a political decision and by deliberately challenging an attempt to open the debate and enable

the conflict to take on the role of a valuable resource for local deliberative democracy. The legacy of universalist rationality (managed by
research communities) and the quasi-monopoly of the preferred supplier of acceptable knowledge (academically trained teachers) prevailed.
Academic professionals successfully defended children and themselves
against the return of the religious pattern of sensemaking. 'Democracy'
(represented by the court of law) decided to hold to the scientific rather
than revealed or religiously 'usable' truth.

In the second case we observed the outcome of a clash between different expert reports coloured by ideological and political preferences –
the case was decided outside the academic world, in the virtual agora
of the mass media and in the streets and in their Shell gas stations
(interestingly, Greenpeace did not offer a similarly media-rich on-screen
counter-presence to Shell – no luxurious corporate offices, no logo on
omnipresent gas stations, just youngish citizens angry and mobilized for
action against a multinational). The media won a temporary victory for
the ideologically green party and it was in the media that the case was
decided (in the end, the oil platform was towed away and recycled rather
than buried in the deep ocean). It was ironic that Greenpeace's expert
reports impelled the company to check the actual amount of potentially
harmful residues in the rig and thus to confirm which of the expert
communities was right. The result (that Greenpeace's reports of potential spillage were exaggerated) came too late to influence the actual oil rig
disposal, but not too late to flag up the need to defuse similarly explosive
potential ideological clashes in the future (hence there was a much more
careful policy later in dealing with oil deposits in Nigeria). Shell and
Greenpeace decided to establish a joint commission on ecological issues
and to discuss potential conflict areas. Both academic communities managed to remain in business (and did not suffer visible damage to their
reputations), while the reputations of their sponsors (Shell, depicted
as a heartless and greedy corporation and Greenpeace, revealed as a
Machiavellian media manipulator) suffered. The media decided to stay
with the most dramatic show in town. The occupation of the oil platform captured public attention and spoke to the imagination of millions
of viewers, listeners and readers, while the empirical testing of expert
claims by actual investigation of the contents of the rig's tanks had no
such publicity value.

The third case introduced one of the contemporary forms of the 'class'
('race', 'religion', 'gender' or 'age') type of social conflicts and struggles. There is an increasing pressure exerted by emergent social actors
(in this case, women systematically encountering 'glass ceilings' when

following career paths in professional bureaucracies) on the representatives of the scientific-rational pattern of sensemaking. This pressure has been duly noted and described as the struggle for recognition or 'a moral grammar of social conflicts' (Honneth, 1994)[2] or as the desire to 'include' the excluded (for whom the illegal, often racially and religiously 'strange' immigrants surviving in western metropolises are a favourite media image).

Pro-feminist protesters against the rector's speech in Rotterdam pointed out the ambiguities of the academic status of the expert report in question (IQ tests on gendered samples of adolescents) and profited from the attention of the mass media (mobilizing individualized communications for political action). However, they also realized that their case would not be won on expert panels, via emails or on TV screens. It should be noted that only print media and only quality newspapers reported the incident, while TV programme makers and local community interactive radio broadcasters ignored it. Pro-feminist political organizers '*in spe*' realized that successful social action would have to be conducted on the organizational (and to a certain extent the political) level. They would have to neutralize the managerial (the rector, deans and president of the university can be viewed as a top management team) 'diversity management' initiative and to expose it as ideological 'window-dressing'.[3] They would have to replace it with a bottom-up initiative of concerned 'corporate citizens'. On the other hand members of the managerial power elite also realized that they could not simply wait the crisis out. In a modernist setting (before the late 1960s), they would have suppressed the protest; in the 1970s they would have formed a joint commission of feminists and managers; in the postmodern period they followed the advice of their PR consultants. They established 'diversity ambassadors' and swept all 'minorities' (women, foreign exchange students, racial and religious minorities, social classes, generations) under one carpet. The women who triggered the protest recognized that they had been neutralized as a protest movement. They had lost the chance of turning a single incident into a political issue and of turning this issue into a process generating a political subject (putting 'women' as candidates for new political representation alongside the other categories of underdogs – immigrants, asylum seekers, refugees, Asians, Africans, students). Last but not least, participants in the protest action realized that the contemporary theoretical landscape of organizational and managerial sciences had changed. Contemporary managers have an armoury of sophisticated instruments at their disposal as far as ideological persuasion or bureaucratic controls go. They can, for instance launch a 'diversity management' campaign instead of making a genuine effort towards participative, deliberative democracy within a professional bureaucracy and instead of designing testable, palpable, 'real' egalitarian measures. Political mobilization of deprived, excluded and discontented groups have failed – so far – to produce a new political 'subject' capable of threatening the status quo. This anticlimactic ending to the incident in question also suggests that neither PhD students nor female researchers had much hope that their values – gender equality in this case – 'will be executable and impactful at work or in society in general' (Giacalone et al., 2008, p. 488) and thus were discouraged from forming a political agency working against 'glass ceilings'.

This lack of a 'viable' political subject, deplored by left-wing academic intellectuals (Bourdieu and Žižek, Foucault and Burawoy, Bauman and Rorty, Spivak and Said, Laclau and Mouffe, Hardt and Negri, Ranciere and Anderson, Wallerstein and Arrighi, and many others), is not the result of any scarcity of critical theories in the ideological marketplace. From Marcuse's embracing of rebellious students and from Fanon's appeals to the 'wretched' peasants of the third world to Said's theory of critical 'orientalism' and to Hardt's and Negri's analyses of 'multitudes' there has been no scarcity of radical theories and ideas. But the contemporary theoretical landscape of organizational and managerial sciences has emerged not only from the intellectual traditions of postmodernism and critical self-reflection that were noted in the previous chapter. It has also been constructed and maintained by current institutional environments. They have shaped the processes of organizing and institutionalizing knowledge production and dissemination not only in academic communities, but also in other institutional settings, including politics and mass-mediated communications. From the point of academic establishments, the 'postmodern' climate for patterning the present sensemaking processes emerged from powerful 'tectonic' movements (I call them 'tectonic' because they shaped the academic archipelago through which we have to navigate). Each of these tectonic movements that shaped the continents of organizational sciences and the sciences of management may be broken down into a bundle of volcanic eruptions, or processes, which we may consider as 'clusters'. Let us have a look at three clusters of processes in turn.

First, there is the astonishing persistence and perseverance of the *hierarchic cluster* in all walks of life and areas of organization. The hierarchic organization emerged together with the rise of professionalism and remains the dominant mode of controlling recurrent patterns of interactions, that is, of 'organizing and managing'. Not many people question the persistence and flexibility of this organizational super-matrix and yet its perseverance offers one of the most challenging problems for social sciences, especially for the sociology of organizations and theories of management. If we start an organization or establish a company, we begin with the construction of a hierarchical pyramid. It does not help to call some patterns of interaction 'ritual chains' and to explain them from the point of view of individuals clustering around face-to-face events. The implicit shadow of a pyramid as the 'proper' matrix for organizing looms very large. This also holds true for the management of meaning. Max Weber (iron cages) and Adam Smith (division of labour) are the sociological and economic patron saints of researchers working on this cluster of problems, but we should not forget, in the second half of the twentieth century, Nicos Mouzelis and Michel Foucault. We simply cannot imagine a viable and robust alternative to a formal bureaucracy as the most practical form of organizing, in spite of having designed many social movements, in spite of having generated many alternative networks and in spite of recurrent dreams of liberty, equality and the brotherhood/sisterhood of participative democracy. The formal rationality of professional bureaucracy prevails, regardless of our increasingly frequently voiced concerns about the necessity to listen to the 'polyphony' of voices from various levels of organizational hierarchies. Professional bureaucracy survives all attempts to rely on bottom-up decision-making procedures and to 'empower' the powerless members of formal hierarchies. In order to question this formal rationality of professional bureaucracies, a more 'populist' approach would have to be seen to be respectable. This is what Laclau seems to suggest in his study of 'the populist reason', where he blames the failure of thinkers on the left to come up with the new proletariat on their mistaken search for an 'already existing and shaped' privileged candidate for the title of revolutionary underclass of the decade. What they should be looking for – according to Laclau – is not any specific social group but a socio-political demand that would be capable of mobilizing, shaping and institutionalizing a new sociopolitical actor, emerging out of aggregated social demands: 'This aggregation presupposes an essential asymmetry between the community as a whole (the *populus*) and the underdog (the *plebs*) ... the latter is always a partiality that identifies itself with the community at large' (Laclau, 2005, p. 224).

This demand, in turn, cannot be theoretically reduced to a continuous sequence of socio-political evolution leading towards some preconceived aim (eternal salvation, victorious revolution, classless society, affluent consumer paradise), because: 'History is rather a discontinuous succession of hegemonic formations that cannot be ordered by a script transcending their contingent historicity' (ibid., p. 226).

Second, we are dealing with the real global domination of market exchange as the privileged and increasingly spectacular (which means 'made theatrical', 'dramatized' and media-communicated) form of social interaction. This domination of the *market exchange cluster* extends far beyond the economic sphere. The persistence and expansion of market exchange also means that calculated and contracted trade-offs become the dominant mechanism of managing the emergence and negotiation of all values, not only economic ones, continuously accelerating and conquering an increasing number of domains of social life. Georg Simmel (in his *Philosophy of Money*), Thorstein Veblen (*The Theory of the Leisure Class*) and Guy Debord (*Society of the Spectacle*) are the patron saints of researchers focusing on this cluster of problems, but among the economists Amartya Sen (1999, 2005) is often mentioned as the author of the concepts of rationality and development as fundamentally dependent on free exchange, of which markets are a necessary if insufficient precondition.[4] We simply cannot imagine a viable alternative to the regulated and negotiable market in a democratic institutional framework as far as negotiations about the use of available resources go.[5] Rituals of conspicuous consumption have shaped the space of our cities and prompted the invention of the virtual media worlds that are currently fighting for individual attention. But all these consumption rituals are intimately linked to the systematic, ubiquitous, regulated exchanges measured in common currency, to commodified exchanges and reified values. Instrumental rationality prevails. Some of these consequences have been reconstructed by Charles Taylor in his interpretation of the prevailing 'social imaginaries':

> The original importance of people working steadily in a profession came from the fact that they thereby placed themselves in 'settled courses' to use Puritanical expression. If ordered life became a demand, not just for a military or a spiritual/intellectual elite but for the mass of ordinary people, then everyone had to become ordered and serious about what they were doing, and of necessity had to be doing, in life, namely working in some productive occupation. A truly ordered society requires that one take these economic occupations seriously and prescribe discipline for them ... The affirmation of ordinary life is part of the background to the central place given to the economic in our lives, as also for the tremendous importance we put on family life, or relationships.
>
> (Taylor, 2004, pp. 73, 74)

Taylor's suggestions are not isolated; quite a number of sociologists point out the empirically testable 'spillover' of economic, instrumental rationality into personal, intimate relationships (see, for instance, Swidler, 2003; Zelizer, 2005) and the emergence of an 'emotional culture' around economic relations and interactions (for example, Nussbaum, 2001; Agger, 2004; Illouz, 2007). Economic rationality has spilled over into all interactions and patterned relationships, but the reverse spillover has also taken place. Participation in economic activities and relationships built in the economic sphere have been intensely 'flavoured' with cultural and emotional 'additives':

> capitalism has made us Rousseauian with a vengeance, not only in the sense that emotional fields of action have made identity exposed and publicly narrated, not only in the sense that emotions have become instruments of social classification, but also in the sense that there are now new hierarchies of emotional well-being, understood as the capacity to achieve socially and historically situated forms of happiness and well-being.
>
> (Illouz, 2007, p. 73)

Our third cluster is the alternative and countercultural *cluster of social movements and telemediated mobilizations*. This signals the persistence of the concept of a social movement matrix as a privileged mode of political change. The concept of a social, political and cultural movement harks back to a simplified 'Renaissance' model of creative reconfiguration and transfer of cultural and technological resources and to the working class movements that followed the industrial revolution. They have been glued together (the concept of a cultural renaissance and the concept of the social movement of an underclass) to form the matrix of a revolutionary project epitomized by the working class movements of the late nineteenth and early twentieth centuries. The idea behind this 'fusion' of the concept of Renaissance ideas and the concept of a working class ushered onto the centre of the historical stage by the industrial revolution evokes a powerful vision. The working class paradise was designed as a dream of upward cultural mobility for the masses. Leftist thinkers of the first half of the twentieth century imagined the 'gardens of art' as gated treasures, which had to be opened to a broad public as if they were 'imaginary musea' (Malraux). If in the past they were gardens for the sophisticated comfort of the elite, in future they should become accessible to the masses, enhancing the quality of life and 'gentrifying' the inner experiences of those formerly excluded from sharing cultural achievements. Malraux's 'imaginary museum' in which mankind's best works of art become accessible to the global masses through the possibilities offered by photographic reproduction is a case in point.

In reality, of course, the Italian Renaissance, which gives its name to the entire movement (*rinascimento*), was a process of slow maturation and the outcome of the confluence of numerous broadly distributed components. It is traceable to the long transfer of knowledge from the ancient learning centres of India and China to Persia and subsequently to the Arab-Byzantine-Latin-Italian nexus, finally resulting in the familiar revolution in the arts and crafts in Italy in the late fifteenth and sixteenth centuries. A contemporary variant of this utopian dream – of a 'second renaissance'[6] – takes us to California, especially to Silicon Valley and its imitations in the late twentieth and early twenty-first centuries (arguably, Manuel Castells, Antonio Melucci, Paul Feyerabend and Bruno Latour could be chosen as candidates to the positions of patron saints of this cluster).[7] Utopian ideas of (counter)rationality, (counter)culture and (counter)polis prevail and analogies to the industrial revolution and the subsequent inclusion of working-class parties in parliaments are obvious:

> With the convergence between internet and mobile communications and the gradual diffusion of broadband capacity, the communicating power of the internet is being distributed in all realms of social life, as the electric grid and the electrical engine distributed energy in the industrial society.
>
> (Castells, 2007, p. 246)[8]

It is interesting that not only sociologists, such as Castells, but also electronic engineers turning their minds towards management, economics and organization theory, such as the late Claudio Ciborra, tried to make use of the Renaissance as a matrix, an ideal type, a metaphor for sociocultural revolutionary change. Ciborra duly noted that the breakthrough of the Renaissance painters was mostly formal – they reached new levels of realism, but remained embedded in 'idealized' contents of mythological and biblical figures. It took the Dutch Golden Age and the painters of the Italian Baroque to introduce daily life as a theme worthy of an artistic work and real moods and the emotions displayed by actual individuals rather than ideal types as a content proper to artistic processing and the audience's expectations. At the end of the introduction to his book on labyrinths of information, Ciborra, evoking Raphael, Vermeer,

Caravaggio and Monteverdi, writes that one should critically reflect on scientific rationality and on a 'narrow model of rational, ideal actors':

> by focusing on the mundane and the existential, I want to contribute to a transition of the field towards the Age of the Baroque in the deployment and management of technology in organizations and society. Passion and improvisation, moods and bricolage, emotions and workaday chores, existence and procedures will become integral to systems design and use, casting new shadows and lights on the unfolding world of technology.
>
> (Ciborra, 2002, p. 9)

Do we not hear the echo of Guillet de Monthoux in the quotation above? Ciborra's introduction is interesting not only because it contributes to the growing criticism of the narrow concept of a rational agent, which still dominates paradigmatic ideological schisms and institutional power struggles as part and parcel of an even narrower concept of scientifically supported rationalism. It is also interesting in that the author tries to demonstrate that the emergent (and often powerful) whirlwinds of cultural, social and political processes of change, later labelled, for example, 'Renaissance', are often late responses to much earlier and subsequently hidden, neglected influences. The suppressed organizational memory of the elite medieval Catholic clergy (about their Arab predecessors) is a case in point. In pre-Renaissance Italy most educated monks embarking on a course of lifelong study and most young Venetians preparing for a career in commerce and diplomacy had to learn Arabic as well as Latin. The almost complete forgetting of the Arab part of the cultural legacy once considered indispensable for a well-educated, competent politician, merchant, artist or intellectual in pre-Renaissance Europe is itself a fascinating historical consequence of the erasure of cultures and societies that were subjected to re-ranking in the course of subsequent European colonial expansion and within the framework of 'orientalization'. Pre-Renaissance monks still had to read in Latin and Arabic, but in the Renaissance Shakespeare's key to the heritage of ancient Greece and Rome had already been reduced to a little Latin and less Greek. This erasing of Arab influences was accompanied by changing historical representations and revisions of social memories, which are also subject to whirlwinds of change. Renaissance art was exposed to the inventions and reinterpretations of the Baroque (which, as we have seen, introduced quotidian themes and emotions to art), but nowadays, we tend to lump these movements together, seeing the contributions of the Renaissance and the Baroque as more or less simultaneous on the historical stage, as primarily contributions to a 'world cultural heritage' and as if their representatives (the artists – painters, sculptors, architects, philosophers, poets, thinkers) were able to understand their respective contributions in a fair and objective manner. No wonder that we often end up inflating the value of the Renaissance and depreciating the value of the Baroque. While the latter lends itself less easily to ideological applications of the propaganda of universal rationality in history, the Renaissance has long served as the prime argument in defence of western, European, cultural supremacy.

Let us examine these three clusters of sensemaking processes which shape the present tense of meaning in our societies. Exploring underground passages between the political control of contemporary societies, academic production and the dissemination of knowledge and the neutralization of oppositional alternatives could help us understand the following processes:

- The 'eternal' return of professional bureaucracies in an age of networking organizations and individualized, mobile communications (with networks 'floating' on hierarchies that re-establish themselves as the dominant organizational form, re-emerging in knowledge-intensive organizations).
- The victorious commercialization of rationalized interactions and the theoretical justifications of value creation and emotional bookkeeping, reflected in the language of academic professionals legitimizing their rationality but also looking for alternative valuation procedures.
- The successful growth of mediascapes and their professional clusters of 'symbolic analysts' turning multimedia into the 'fourth estate' exercising its influence by tacit monopolies on providing navigational tools for individuals immersed in tele-multimediated communications.

Following these underground passages could – perhaps – help us explain the ways in which we make sense of our sensemaking at present. We could then hope to understand why so many potentially 'progressive' and 'robust' programmes, schools, movements or paradigms exert their influence not in the area for which they had originally been designed, but in different, sometimes strikingly unanticipated 'locations'. Social Darwinism comes to mind (mechanisms of biological evolution were 'read' into social processes), as does the 'therapeutic culture' initiated by Freud and intended for psychoanalytical practice, but broadly accepted outside of psychiatry[9] (for instance in quality of working life

Illustration 4.1 Pawel Althamer, apartment building in Warsaw on New Year's Eve, 1999/2000 (courtesy of the artist)

and professional coaching programmes), and many other cases of 'inventions' spilling over to varied cultural domains, from literary theory and criticism to urban planning, from the re-engineering of the architecture of networked communities of knowledge and open databases to the stimulation of diversity by subcultural artists (see Illustration 4.1).

(a) Patterning the sensemaking processes 1: the professional bureaucracy cluster and attempts to leave the pyramid behind

One of the most commonly reiterated themes in the documented history of organized societies is a protest against soulless red tape, of which Kafka's short novel *The Trial* is the most succinct literary manifestation. All societies are bureaucratically organized, but we tend to use the term 'bureaucracy' to refer only to those in which formally distinguished patterns of organizing and managing have been recorded and incorporated in the legitimizing narratives of contemporary academic communities. These narratives routinely leave aside the Indian, Chinese, Persian or Arab civilizations, influences and interdependencies, reserving praise for the fine tuning of the rational mode of thinking and acting of the 'west'.[10] The same narratives also neglect the underdogs' version of events and the 'microstorias' of the representatives of the lower classes, focusing instead on the dominant narratives of 'hegemons'. The objective nature of the iron cages of social divisions of labour are often evoked in place of a class analysis. Rebellion against bureaucratization may mask different class backgrounds and schemes and is thus more safely aimed against a universal and multiform monster of 'red tape' than against a more precisely pinpointed upper class. The universal complaint against the increasing bureaucratization of all walks of life (that which is supposed to lock individuals in the 'iron cages' of social division of labour and to subject increasing number of their activities to professional control[11]) does not usually address a single culprit, although the elite's desire to exercise authoritarian control is mentioned among the potential causes of bureaucracy's reiteration, as is the attempt of the masses to escape the 'dictatorship of the cousins' (or the informal and arbitrary controls of traditional societies as Malinowski so aptly summed it up) for more objective rules and more impartial rulers. Curiously enough, apart from some early sociologists observing the emergent trade unions at the end of the nineteenth and in the early years of the twentieth centuries (Michels's 'iron law of oligarchy', Pareto's 'circulation of elites') not many sociologists of bureaucracy have looked into professional bureaucracies as supporters of their own cause. No matter who wins in political, cultural or economic struggles, the victor usually either imposes a new form of bureaucratic control (creates new ministries or agencies, designs new provinces or counties, funds new schools for public servants and so on) or takes the previous bureaucracy over, working through its hierarchically organized professionals. A bureaucratic specialist can apparently survive even the most violent political revolution. 'Good specialist, although not a party member' sounded like a label for a second-category citizen of the Soviet society, but it also expressed reluctant respect for a purely formal, professional expertise, which deserved recognition in spite of the lack of enthusiastically declared loyalty to the new regime. Talleyrand served professionally as head of the French state police, surviving the revolutionaries, Napoleon and the restoration of the monarchy. Yugoslavian, Hungarian and Polish intellectuals observing the late-communist intelligentsia concluded that members of professional bureaucracies tend to dominate in state-controlled societies no matter what ideological colours are being flown. They spoke of the pathology of organizational structures (Staniszkis, 1984, 1992), of a class struggle in a classless society (Djilas, 1957; Starski, 1981) or of providing cadres for all involved parties. Konrad and Szelenyi (1979) called their study of the elites of professional bureaucracies *The Intellectuals on the Road to Class Power*; Derber et al.'s (1990) study was subtitled *Professionals and the Rise of a New Mandarin Order*. The growth of formal, professional organizations, constructed as hierarchies, is perceived as an underlying mechanism of 'normal' social development, which emerges in all complex societies and withstands attempts to curb or counter it, in spite of 'abnormal', revolutionary attempts to break the continuity of the bureaucratic control of social processes.

One might say, paraphrasing Kuhn and transferring him from the scientific to the political realm, that long periods of 'normal politics' (parliamentary elections, competition between party programmes) are punctuated by brief periods of turbulence – 'political revolutions' (the overthrow of the system, the radical change of political parties, the inclusion of the previously marginalized and criminalized segments of society) – after which bureaucracies learn to live with new ideologies and restore their institutionalized power by maintaining the successful exclusion of 'the masses' from political decision-making. Neither is this a phenomenon observed only in past communist and present post-communist societies. In western European societies the 'class domination' of professional bureaucracies, that is of party cadres and political marketing firms also excludes most of the voters and citizens from political decision-making. Masses are not always passive, resigned and cynical, as witnessed by successive populist waves of protest at the end of the twentieth and the beginning of the twenty-first centuries. The extreme right of Heider in Austria and Le Pen in France, or the extreme anti-establishmentism of Fortuyn in the Netherlands and Lepper's 'self-defence' in Poland may easily be quoted as cases in point. None of them were successful: Heider was gradually marginalized and slowly tucked away in the political institutions and removed from the sight of the media; Le Pen's critique was taken over by mainstream politicians (Sarkozy) and his own party, the national front, ceased to count; Fortuyn was murdered by an animal-rights activist on the eve of potential electoral victory (which might have made him prime minister of the Netherlands);[12] and Lepper, in spite of making it briefly to the government, clearly played a junior role and was swiftly removed from the political stage after he became entangled in legal cases.

Bureaucracies not only survive, they also trigger processes that protect them from systematic 'outside' influences and stimulate their growth – no matter how many checks and balances are invented to limit their expansion and to subject them to either autocratic or democratic controls. As Foucault noted, one of the strategies which bureaucracies use to prolong their domination is to supervise and implement the individualization and internalization of power relations.[13] The first removes critical focus from organizations and institutions, the second involves every individual in self-control, which reduces the costs of managing him or her.

Fear of being locked into the 'iron cages' of the social division of labour (manifested in the post-1968 generations' desire to achieve recognition as creative individuals, preferably in art-like projects) can be replaced by a fear of being manipulated by 'hidden persuaders' guiding individuals towards the 'velvet cages' of high-tech, knowledge-intensive organizations (where creativity is unleashed only in order to tap new resources in the market economy's never-ending drive for profit). These professional organizations may appear to cater to individual needs, but the aim is always to train an individual to internalize the impulse to continually improve performance. Contemporary surveillance techniques can make the employees of many companies feel that they are under the omnipresent watchful eye of the 'Big Brother' of electronic control, turning their workplace into a cell in a Benthamite 'panopticon'. In view of contemporary psychological techniques, they may feel the not quite invisible hand of an HR specialist describing employees as 'high potentials', designing their career 'pathing' and 'nudging' most of them towards the internalization of self-disciplinary measures (which ease the burden of managerial control and implant control mechanisms in an individual's personality).

Thus the fear of being 'locked' into a rigid structure – of becoming a personal cog in an impersonal, bureaucratic pyramidal machine – does not disappear in any contemporary formal organization, no matter how much its managers may claim that theirs is a relaxed community of professionals, where no formal constraints are present, and where the creative self-realization of corporate citizens is strongly supported. Not many sociologists of organizations have managed to continue tracing this 'eternal return' of the hierarchic organizations consistently and persistently, but those who deal with bureaucracies have done so most often – Mouzelis's warning being a case in point: 'No amount of theorizing or rather philosophizing about the ontology of the subject and the nature of interaction can help bridge the micro-macro gap as long as human interaction continues to be conceptualized in a hierarchical vacuum' (Mouzelis, 1995, p. 26). In other words, most of the theoretical studies of formal organizations, which focus on micro-level analysis, do not sufficiently account for the mezzo-level (organizations, institutions, hierarchies, power pyramids, formal and informal pecking orders) and macro-level (class, rank, stratum, cultural capital, educational tracks) constraints and influences, which leads to a number of distortions in the descriptions and analyses of organizational realities.

The most important distortion is the astonishing absence of analyses of the power asymmetries and inequalities that so sharply differentiate 'corporate citizens' or employees of a professional bureaucracy into, on the one hand, 'the best and the brightest' lured with tenure and, on the other, 'temps' kept in line through threats of redundancy. There are very few studies of the hidden injuries caused by these legitimized differences and enforced inequalities imposed by the bureaucratic class on professionals, and even fewer on the hidden injuries caused by academic bureaucracies and manifested in the packaging of knowledge for general 'consumption'.[14]

This is what Mouzelis (1995) means, according to my interpretation, when he speaks of a 'hierarchical vacuum' in which all our theoretical and practical conceptualizations of organizing processes take place. The hierarchy and the inequality implied by it are taken for granted and not accounted for as the basic cause of distortions and boundaries of rationality. Even less visible is the dangerous power of top representatives of professional bureaucracies to orchestrate peer control, perform gate-keeping selection and interpret the criteria of professional evaluation (all the time appealing to the ideals of institutional democracy with checks and balances and to the history of professional autonomy with peer control rather than societal stakeholders). Institutional power plus ideological domination equals the stability of a bureaucratic mode of organizing and secures a quiet growth of hegemonic managerialism, which most academic professionals are unable (or unwilling) to recognize, let alone to deal with.

Let us drive this general point home. Hypothesizing in a theoretical vacuum, we are unable to account for the inbuilt inequality of the academic hierarchies. A paper presented by a brilliant PhD student as one of the five squeezed into a single session running parallel to five other sessions does not have the same impact nor does it attract the same attention as the long presentation by a keynote speaker, which can be attended by everyone and is mentioned in most reports of the event. The same holds true in the peer reviewed journals: while all reviewers follow certain guidelines, some bias and prejudice on their part is inevitable. An unknown PhD will have to wait longer to be reviewed than a more familiar name, and when reviewed, will face a much higher chance of being rejected or criticized in a possibly very discouraging, sometimes even hostile way. Somebody from outside the close network of researchers pursuing the same academic specialization, promoting the same methodological agenda or simply exploiting some thematic focus for institutional advancement will always be sacrificed in the long queues for publication. And all this unequal treatment is sheltered by the umbrella alibi of a scientific rationality managed by an autonomous academic community with peer reviews, gate-keepers and high standards of criticism and falsification.

Nobody asks why, for instance, the subversive collection of critical essays *Manifestos for the Business School of Tomorrow* failed to attract attention or to make waves in the larger academic meetings, in more prestigious professional associations or among the more influential segments of the educated public at large. Nobody wanted to credit the editors, Campbell Jones and Damian O'Doherty, with publishing – let us say – Steffen Böhm's interpretation of Margaret Thatcher's famous statement 'there is no such thing as society', where we could read that:

> Neo-liberal management is today's hegemony of organisation. The discourses of neo-liberal management attempt to naturalise themselves and thus render invisible the multitude of different organisational worlds possible. One of the most basic and most urgent political actions is to disentangle the forced hegemonic bond between management and organisation. That is, management needs to be exposed as the hegemony of organisation. It is precisely this act of exposition which makes possible the imagination of different worlds and societies.
>
> (Böhm, 2005, p. 211)[15]

It is as if we had all tacitly assumed that this manifesto, issued outside the commercial distribution channels under the 'creative commons' umbrella, somehow does not fit into the mainstream discourse, that a discussion of a 'degree zero' of society risks shedding too extreme a light on our professional status as editors, teachers, experts, researchers, managers – in short, as members of an ever-expanding academic branch of wider educational and research bureaucracies. We fail to acknowledge or to treat seriously the challenges that this self-bureaucratization poses because we will not risk deviating too far from the ordinary course of routine academic action, that is from 'being rational'. Why are we afraid of appearing irrational? If deviations from 'true rationality' are detected, they are usually blamed on the original sin of human researchers whose presumed 'bounded rationality' makes it harder for them to see the light of reason at all times. Let us subject the concept of 'bounded rationality' to a closer inspection.

'Bounded rationality' is a euphemism reflecting an attempt to ground a concept in individual efficiencies measured on a scale from 'absolute rationality' (attainable probably only by perfect minds cleansed of their bodily and relational human stains) to absolute irrationality (measured according to the educational progress of an individual through formal schooling – the shorter it is and the less successful, the more irrational an individual is supposed to be). One's inability to be fully rational is thus conceptualized as something theoretically solid, as an outcome of exact measurement and benchmarking (to an ideal). In practice we employ the concept of a necessarily imperfect, limited rationality, differing from a universalist ideal, but somehow approximating it in the longer run and in spite of interparadigmatic revolutions (which change our measuring criteria). Thus it is easy to overlook the utopian assumption that the rationality in question is a limited, 'bound' case of an unlimited, unbounded rationality at large (and a tacit suggestion that the latter actually exists as a Platonic essence and the mother of all rationalities). Consequently there is no need to bother with the increasing dangers of incommensurability (see Essers, 2007) as paradigms change and clash and values conflict.

Needless to say, this choice is itself an outcome of highly biased and power-sensitive influences. It could have been different. What would have happened if we had looked for the binding factors of bounded rationality not inside an imperfect, sinful individual, but outside him, in our at least partly corrupt, pathological, dysfunctional professional community? Shouldn't the concept of 'bounded rationality' be grounded in the bureaucratic limitations imposed on an individual's range of options? These limitations are at work even before the individual begins to solve problems and generate projects for available courses of action. Tacit belief in a formally defined professional bureaucracy (as a privileged mode of organizing any inquiry and of managing any activity) is in itself a distortion of a rational inquiry. All inquiry subsequently is tainted (by tacitly accepted hierarchizations of institutional settings and by the equally implicit assumption of a hierarchic vacuum), no matter what it is directed towards. Inquiry into everything, most notably into organizing and managing, has already had its cards marked.

Distortions are not limited to the level of actual interactions, which occur in social spaces prefabricated by hierarchies (which resemble the slots allocated to tracks and papers during large scientific conferences). They also extend to the level of reflexive and critical practices. We copy – albeit not always wittingly – inequalities and pecking orders into the creation of our professional ideologies, philosophies and methodologies. Macro-differences in power limit the repertoires for organizational underdogs to draw on in response to perceived and experienced inequalities. The underdogs' opportunities for identifying, analysing and expressing their responses to these micro-effects of macro-differences in power are not totally eliminated in formal bureaucracies (as they would be if bureaucracies resembled Big Brother's society in *1984*), but they are severely curbed (as they are when bureaucracies resemble the military in *Catch-22* or the psychiatric ward in *One Flew Over the Cuckoo's Nest*).[16] This leads to a democratic deficit, which is further exacerbated when states and markets start to exploit so-called 'knowledge resources' by introducing 'chief knowledge officers', 'executive PhDs' and by treating academic communities:

> much as indigenous people sitting on rich mineral deposit. The interesting feature in this development is the extent to which businesses will allow their training, practices and expenditures to be structured by academic considerations, which are seen as helping to stabilize their dynamic environments. Of special note is the 'Fenix' initiative between the Stockholm Business School and Chalmers Institute of Technology, which is now supported by most of the Swedish multinational corporations.
>
> (Fuller, 2000, p. 422)

Contemporary democratic deficits are also reflected in the almost complete decay and fading away of the avatars of participative democracy within academic communities following the rebellions and reforms of 1968; for instance in the real and palpable decay of the university and faculty councils, in which students, administrative staff and academics are all duly represented, but which have no power to influence the dean's or rector's decisions. This gradual shrinking of the role of employee councils is the shadow of another process, namely that of the reinforcing of the principle of hierarchy in professional bureaucracies. The dean, a top manager of a faculty, originally selected by his peers, other university professors, is increasingly being nominated by the university's president and a board of directors; selection is no longer necessarily from the pool of professors, but increasingly often from a headhunter's consultancy database. He (it is usually a 'he') is less dependent on his constituency than he would have been had he been elected by the votes of his peers and collaborators. Thus he can consider other faculty members as a 'client base'. Clients are granted faculty and university-level councils as a safety valve through which they can voice complaints. They can play the roles of corporate citizens, but soon discover that the councils do not work as an instrument of actual, relevant and salient co-deciding about the university's policies. Sociologists of organization who had entered the academic profession around 1968 sense this dangerous ambiguity of subverted democratic safeguards. They resent the ease with which the academic liberties won by rebellious students in 1968 can be subverted by the upper crust of academic bureaucracies, but they tend to offer a mild rebuke instead of a stern warning:

> The challenge for future power theory ... is 'to manage with power' where you recognize, diagnose, and respect diversity of interests and seek to translate and enroll members within organizational courses of action, while at the same time listening to what the others are saying, modifying your position accordingly, and choosing the appropriate strategies and tactics to accomplish whatever is chosen. Sometimes, after taking all that into consideration, it still means making others do what they would not otherwise have done, against their resistance. Power can be like that. Yet, it does not have to be so. Coercive power should be the refuge of last resort for the diplomatically challenged and structurally secure, not the hallmark of management's right to manage.
>
> (Clegg et al., 2005, p. 185)

Historically, the best chances of evading the 'cages' imposed on the underdogs by the powers that be were provided either by escaping their territorial range (as in the moving western frontier of the USA) or by the skilful manipulation of overlapping bureaucracies (as in the feminist exploitation of the rivalry between religious and state authorities in contemporary Malaysia, where religious *ulams* counter female emancipation as state-educated professionals by claiming rights to regulate civil legal matters, while the state secures female access to education and jobs) (Ong, 2006, pp. 31–52). In the contemporary educational landscape there are also migrations of academic professionals, some of which are triggered by attempts to escape the bureaucratic control of their home institutions.

In this context, the development of MBA programmes and of schools of business in Europe has (broadly) been fiercely opposed by the academic elites of many traditional universities and enthusiastically supported by the younger and less privileged members of the academic profession. The MBA programme of the oldest Dutch university, in Leiden, was the last to emerge in the Dutch academic landscape and closed down in 2007 after unsuccessful attempts to integrate managerial courses linked to a commercial MBA programme within a traditional academic structure. To illustrate the degree of distrust with which the establishment of the business school had been approached in Leiden, let us recall that the dean of the business school (a Dutch PhD from Wharton) had previously been bureaucratically attached to the department of … biology (where his professorship had been 'parked') and had never been viewed as an equal partner or even a peer by the other Leiden professors. Prior to the dismantling of the entire MBA programme, the rector of the university frankly admitted that the recruitment of students for MBAs cannibalizes the social sciences' pool of potential students and that in his view it should thus be discontinued. I do not claim that escaping bureaucratic controls is the only factor triggering academic migrations, but a more thorough and systematic study of these institutional attachments might help us to understand the size, range and scale of itinerant experts' travels. For instance, two of the three authors of the above quote, Clegg and Kornberger, are listed on the cover of their *Managing and Organizations* as being attached not only to the school of management at Sidney's University of Technology, but also to Aston, Amsterdam and Maastricht (Clegg) and to the University of Innsbruck (Kornberger). These affiliations have a PR value: they demonstrate the importance of the expertise represented by an academic professional for different university centres. Affiliation to more than one institution also demonstrates the symbolic bond between academic centres in different locations but answering the same call for knowledge production according to the same rules and principles observed by their respective bureaucracies.

The historical spread of the bureaucratic form of organization in Europe (religious, political, social, scientific, medical, legal and so on) was primarily the result of imitation. Historical translations of the principles of organizing had been 'exchanged', imposed, stolen or copied, usually with some degree of conflict occurring between rival bureaucracies flexing their muscles and trying to extend the limits of their influence. For instance, for a long time European clergy were not under the jurisdiction of secular courts of law and if clergy members were brought to justice on any account they were tried in the canonical court. If two or more bureaucracies claimed rights over a given population, the conflict increased the chances of groups and individuals escaping their 'cages' (controls). The hierarchy of the church provided a model on which emerging state bureaucracies in medieval and early modern Europe were based, subsequently dividing areas of competence. This is why Carl Schmitt's studies of the relationship between Roman Catholicism and the political form of European societies labelled 'nation-states' attracted the attention of contemporary leftist thinkers (see Mouffe, 1999). If the church hierarchy had been copied more or less spontaneously by the emergent state administrations, then new professional categories, especially elites, such as merchants in Europe's most prosperous cities, could discover some space to navigate between the two. Class struggles are not a recent invention, nor are the political and legal instruments for fighting them out:

> In the Middle Ages, feudal lords routinely appropriated profits from merchants, arbitrarily slapping on 'taxes' or tolls. To shelter their earnings, merchants ultimately aligned with monarchs and the developing national state to establish a unified political and legal framework for protecting private property.
>
> (Derber et al., 1990, p. 17)

The fact that both church leaders and state officials needed large sums of money, which could be lent from the (un-ruined) top merchants, made it easier for the 'third estate' to navigate towards a civil society within the political and legal protection of the nation-state framework. Easier, but still not very easy. Chantal Mouffe's anthology of critical leftist essays about Carl Schmitt and Karl Marx includes a study by Jorge E. Dotti, who reminds us that the Soviet Union, according to Schmitt, implemented the principle of 'cuius religion eius oeconomia' ('Whose religion, his economy', a pastiche of the well-known principle, 'Whose rule, his religion', introduced into Europe after the Thirty Years War by the Treaty of Münster). Had the medieval feudal rulers employed the same principle, there would have been no 'social space' for a politically differentiated civil society, since feudal state managers would have reduced politics to their own, feudal, elite, state-run, corporate control of economic resources, eliminating, as Schmitt had put it 'the nucleus of the idea of politics, the inevitable moral decision' (in *Political Theology*; Schmitt, 1979). Luckily for the republicans and the third estate, the power holders, both religious and secular, had outsourced the financing of their wars to independent entrepreneurs. Dotti sums his critical review of Schmitt's reading of Marx by pointing out a certain Romantic remnant discovered by the author of *Political Theology*. Schmitt noticed that in Marx's historical materialism a single individual is reduced to a tool in the hands of the supreme historical necessity (a secularized God) and that avoiding this reduction is the precondition for successful social change:

> The search for the novel kind of linking between what belongs to the private sphere of each human being, what is proper to society, and what constitutes the responsibility of the state, brings with it a rethinking of the notion of sovereignty, with a view to its responsible revitalization and with the assumption of a metaphysics which

legitimizes the priority of the political over the economic in the republican anticorporatist sense.

(Dotti, 1999, p. 113)

The lack of a single, all-encompassing and all-controlling bureaucracy and conflicts between bureaucracies controlling some aspects of social processes spelled a relative growth of freedom of social manoeuvre for the more commercially active subjects of their control (citizens). Bureaucatic wars stimulated the growth of what we would call 'civil society' in the political jargon of contemporary liberalism. This copying of the bureaucratic technology of rule did not stop with the urbanization and secularization of western societies and with their gradual industrialization. Bureaucratization of war and tax collecting reinforced the state, which then became nation-state:

> Many aspects of bureaucracy in the armies developed during the military revolution in Europe in the late sixteenth and seventeenth centuries ... whereas tax administration did not bureaucratize in most of Europe until the late eighteenth and nineteenth centuries (English excise administration in the late seventeenth century is an outlier). In fact, bureaucratic military organization served as a model for bureaucratizing civil administration, in Prussia and elsewhere.
>
> (Kiser and Baer, 2005, p. 241)

We observe conscious 'copying translations' by alternative power elites looking for practical toolkits for control all through the twentieth century (especially in the decolonizing countries, which had to invent their political form after gaining independence from their colonial occupiers).

This copying includes the application of the organizational model of industrial bureaucracy to most contemporary activities. In organizational terms, more often than not we observe a pyramid, with top management, and their reliable high priests (ministers and top officials), mandarins or experts (academic and technocratic communities) ruling over stratified levels of employees and outsourced networks. Writing shortly before the breakdown of state socialism, Derber et al. concluded that:

> In both East and West, we have pictures of new societies dominated, or coming to be dominated, by experts. If the spirits of witch doctors and the God of the Middle Ages are dying, their ghosts are reappearing – in white coats. The specter of logocracy now haunts capitalism and socialism alike.
>
> (Derber et al., 1990, p. 24)[17]

Their observation still holds true after the breakdown of state socialism in Russia and the selective transformation into state capitalism in
China. From the very beginning of the state socialist experiment, practical imitation of what were perceived as being successful governance
methods was accompanied by ideological condemnation of capitalism as
a whole. For instance, the principles of Taylorism/Fordism were quickly
copied by the Bolsheviks in order to accelerate the coercive industrialization of Russia after 1917 in spite of the fact that they had been created
in a different institutional and political setting. Clearly, not only the
New Economic Policy reflected the flexibility of the new Soviet ruling
elite – so did their ability to copy the most advanced managerial techniques from the United States, a world leader in industrialization and
in the development of mass consumption. A communist worker might
remain under the ideological spell of the ideal of a classless society, but
on the job he was controlled by the rules of 'Stakhanovite competition'
(a competition between workers to perform above the imposed norm),
which resembled Taylor's pay incentives implemented in Ford's car factories. True, the direct pay increase had been abandoned in order to
exploit the ideological significance of more productive work for the same
pay (propaganda presented the over-performing workers as individuals
motivated solely by their dedication to the working-class cause and their
Bolshevik leaders). However, additional remuneration assumed the form
of social recognition, significant bonuses and special privileges, all of
them important in a country suffering famine and with large-scale state
terror problems. Analogies between the 'capitalist' and 'communist' (or
'state socialist') managerial controls and workers' strategies to oppose
them were the subject of Michael Burawoy in his comparative study of
US and Hungarian industrial workers in the 1970s (see Burawoy, 1985).

Today, after the fall of communism, what is astonishing is the almost
total absence of any historical reconstructions of ideological sensemaking procedures in state socialist societies – a fertile empirical field of
research into technologies of domination and persuasion, which have
become more accessible to researchers than their western counterparts.
If these are not entirely neglected, then it is due to the current interest
of Polish or Hungarian, Czech or Romanian intellectuals in the shadows
that they cast upon the present political scene, not as a result of the fascinating analogies between the tacit ideological mix of competition and
cooperation across the Iron Curtain and its continuation through other
means after the fall of the Soviet Union and of the Warsaw Pact. Very
few scholars point out the significance of, let us say, the post-communist
legacy of 'politicized technologies of power holding' in contemporary

Russia (and to a lesser extent in the Ukraine) as the determining factor in 'faking democracy' or 'Darwinizing history' (Wilson, 2005; Lynch, 2005; Pomper, 2002), especially in view of the evolution of the neopatrimonial, 'superpresidentialist' political system in Russia:

> The rise to power and genuine popularity of Putin reflects a deep-seated reaction throughout Russia to the failure of a perceived liberal experiment. Putin has exploited a charismatic legitimacy, reinforced by the instrumentalities of elections, to consolidate the superpresidential system bequeathed to him by Boris Yeltsin ... The temptations of 'rent seeking' – to exploit privileged institutional access to 'extractive' export revenue – gravely weaken incentives to build rule-governed institutional regime.
>
> (Lynch, 2005, pp. 242–3)

The best-known example of the global imitation of a pattern of organizing and managing remains the nation-state, which emerged in Europe between the late medieval and early industrial periods. The nation-state as the privileged organizational form, a matrix, a dominant pattern of macro-organization, spread through colonization until the nineteenth century and through decolonization in the twentieth. The idea of the nation-state further spread as a result of postcolonial imitation by indigenous political elites who completed the process of decolonization (having obtained their education at Oxford or the Sorbonne, as did, for instance, Pol Pot, thus having incorporated their tacit preference for the bureaucracy of the nation-state with their educational milk). By the late twentieth century, nation-states as represented in the United Nations covered most of the world (the stateless Kurdish or Palestinian nations being among the exceptions). When the nation-state first emerged in Europe, it was something of a mix between the bureaucratic state whose lineage goes back to the Peace Treaty of Münster and the end of the religious wars in the seventeenth century and the somewhat romanticized ideology of own kin, folk or nation. Ideologies of national folklores, cultures and histories spread in the eighteenth and early nineteenth centuries with the development of mass printed media. There were also increasing numbers of professionals belonging to a middle class and working in expanding state and market bureaucracies. Today about 200 sovereign states hold United Nations membership and they are still the key elements of international governance, although their role has been limited by some 66,000 transnational corporations and by regional and global governance structures (including, for instance, the European Union, the North Atlantic Treaty Organization, the World Bank or the United Nations itself).[18] Paradoxically, although state bureaucracies in the United States and Rwanda, in Switzerland and Miramar, in China and in Canada have shown no tendency to wither away and atrophy, social scientists have started to write and speak on globalization and on the retreat of the state as if emergent and fragile attempts at global governance, limited to crisis situations and far from the systematic efficiency of state bureaucracies, have already replaced the nation-state centred world order.

A side effect of this shift in the attention of researchers and politicians has been a relative neglect of the problems of bureaucracy and an attempt to re-conceptualize global governance by trying to define new institutional or rapidly institutionalizing actors – most notably civil societies and communication networks – listing them along with states and markets (see, for instance, Tehranian, 2007) but devoting most attention to them at the expense of states (reduced to passive regulators) and markets (reduced to a stage for multinational corporations).

The gradual disappearance of the problems of bureaucratic organization below the radars of sociologists and researchers involved in the theory of organization and management is also due to the overpsychologizing, 'neo-institutionalizing' and under-socializing of organizational theory in general and organizational change theory in particular over the past two decades.[19]

This imbalance can be empirically verified by any visitor to a major academic bookshop in western Europe. The shrinking space allocated to books written by sociologists contrasts sharply with the expanding space allocated to books written by psychologists (and, surprisingly enough, philosophers and theologians). What does this shift reflect, apart from the lack of embedding of sociological research projects in the political initiatives of a civil society whose members observe markets and states fighting above their heads in the virtual spaces of an increasingly dense multimedia? It certainly reflects a relative neglect of organizational, social, institutional and structural influences upon our behaviour. For instance, in a standard contemporary work of social psychology on the authoritarian dynamic, the author looks for a hidden 'predisposition' towards being 'an authoritarian personality' and responding negatively towards 'the other':

It is about the kind of people who – by virtue of deep-seated predispositions neither they nor we have much capacity to alter – will always be imperfect democratic citizens, and only discouraged from infringing others' rights and liberties by responsible leadership, the force of law, fortuitous societal conditions, and near-constant reassurance ... Individuals possess fairly stable predispositions to intolerance of difference, that is, varying levels of willingness 'to put up with' people, ideas, and behaviors. Our attitudes toward minorities, immigrants and foreigners could not be predicted from our views on dissidents, deviants and criminals (and vice versa) if not for some relatively enduring predisposition to be intolerant of all manner of difference.

(Stenner, 2005, pp. 1–2)

This over-psychologized view of an individual member of society is certainly biased towards a psychological as opposed to a sociological explanation and in favour of an essentialist psychologist theoretical construct (similar to 'personality' or 'drive') at the expense of a sociological, relational and historical understanding (similar to 'class position' and 'cultural capital'). Stenner argues against seeing a tolerant or intolerant individual as a 'social animal'; her view is clearly under-socialized and under-sociologized. The organizational and managerial aspects of the individual's environment are reduced to secondary factors – 'force of law', 'fortuitous societal conditions', 'responsible leadership' – while the primary cause of authoritarian, intolerant behaviour is to be sought deep inside the individual soul/personality, not in the exposure to hierarchic power relations in families, schools and jobs, nor in the dominant position of the state bureaucracy in regulating individual life in contemporary societies.[20] This approach, typical for psychologists, social psychologists and organizational scientists, especially those who claim expertise in organizational behaviour and need psychological alibis to establish their credentials, certainly reflects a relative neglect of power struggles (including the class struggle and the struggle of genders or races, intertwined in complex braids). The reductionism of 'rational choice theory' manifested by social psychologists, economists and sociologists has often been deplored by critical social scientists, even those who are not hostile to rationalist and individualist assumptions. The reductionism of rational choice theory is usually described as reliance on two basic assumptions, which are, in Andreski's words, 'rules of thumb' allowing a researcher to:

pre-empt the unthinking or uncritical reification of collective phenomena:

- Sociological explanation should, in principle, be expressible in terms of the properties, beliefs, dispositions and actions of individual human beings;

- Human agents normally try to act in accordance with their own sense of what is rational and reasonable in the light of their knowledge and preferences. Their choice of action may take into account the likely actions of other actors.

(Beckford, 2000, p. 220)[21]

The imbalance between academically prospering psychologists and academically impoverished sociologists also reflects the relative professional power of psychologists (reflected in their ability to publish more books and command more status) and a relative lack of power on the part of sociologists (unable to command the attention of the reading public or to attract the best and the brightest students). Another indicator is that sociologists are relatively less frequently asked to consult for companies or governments, a fact which certainly does not attract enough research attention from either academic side (why aren't psychologists studying the sources of their success or sociologists researching their failure?) There are many complex reasons, many competing 'causes' triggering contextual constraints and many overlapping flows (of events, ideas, individuals, groups, generations, fashions, technologies, ideologies and the like) which should be studied if we are to understand how we arrived at our present predicament. One of them could be found in the spread of formal professional organizations (that is, bureaucracies) as the privileged mode of shaping social processes and the simultaneous atrophy of the methodological and political self-reflection of professional communities (which would have to start questioning their own bureaucratization).

This means that both managers (who practice managing) and researchers in management theory (who theorize about it) are themselves shaped and professionally formed and controlled by increasingly formalized professions, which, almost by definition and often tacitly, tend to favour professional bureaucracy with an *unquestioned* institutionalized hierarchy as the organizing instrument of choice.

My (and most academic professionals') educated guess is that we fail to pay proper attention to the spread of professional bureaucracy because we are profoundly divided and ambiguous about our own status in the ever-growing hyper-bureaucracies of academia (including all their educational and research levels and forms). To put it in a nutshell: two ideological desires fill our professional souls. First, we see ourselves as Platonian walking philosophers (elite thinkers in institutional gardens), but, second, we are also populists assisting citizens to become more knowledgeable and committed to civic action (leaders emancipating

masses). Let us tackle the Platonic temptation first. We would like to identify ourselves with the avant-garde elites of knowledge-intensive firms
and institutions (it is lonely and cold at the elitist top of the profession,
but it is the most prestigious game in a professional company town).
Hence the proliferation of all types and kinds of rankings that reaffirm
our superiority. If we do come up as top ranked individuals and institutions, we believe that some day our ideas will be the ruling ideas. They
may thus justify our claims to be the top members of a meritocracy (with
merit conveniently defined by ourselves and our peers).

The ideology of upward social mobility (in its professional expert form)
has prevented the majority of professionals in hierarchic organizations
from taking a more radically critical attitude (risking an abrupt end to
their ascendance towards the institutional peak of the profession). If we
identify with the 'top',[22] we are more motivated to ascend there than to
pull its members down. Rocking the boat, while not an absolute taboo,
is not exactly an encouraged and daily occurrence and remains a morally
ambiguous, exceptional exercise of professional discretion (for example,
the whistle-blowing in the Enron case). The most interesting part of this
ideology of professional upward mobility is that it has survived the erosion of its material basis (that is, stable professional bureaucracies with
life-long professional upward mobility). It has survived the erosion of
an 'organization man' (depicted as a white male professional in a grey
suit devoting his lifelong career to a slow progress up the corporate ladder). Most of the sons and daughters of the organization men of the
1960s became itinerant professionals with a patchy job record reflecting volatile economies, part-time employment, project-like involvement
and a switch from full-time corporate citizenship to temporary consulting and limited forms of employment. They had not abandoned their
parent's ideals – only this time progress was measured according to individual ability to touch the creative base, to introduce higher, aesthetic
and ethical values to one's work, and not according to easily measurable
progress in climbing the bureaucratic ladder:

> For the children, creativity came to lie at the heart of their highly
> psychologized version of individualism. That is why clarion calls
> to greater creativity find such an enthusiastic audience, regardless
> of what creativity may concretely mean. For the offspring, cre-
> ativity, as the agency of authentic self-expression, simultaneously
> creates and expresses the authentic self ... Thus, the works matter
> far less than one's abstract sense of one's creativity. Moreover, the
> ideal of total originality – of the never-before-seen, one-of-a-kind

creation – requires for its fulfillment in the public world the achievement of Nobel-quality scientific breakthroughs, Edison-like inventions, and genius-level works of art, things of which few people are
capable. The only thing within easy reach that can fill such a tall
order is the private self, easily the most complicated thing personally
known to most people.

(Leinberger and Tucker, 1991, p. 417)

The ability to improvise in a creative and imaginative way, to become
like jazz players has been evoked (and revoked, as in the Hatch[23]–
Weick debate on the value of comparing organizational improvising to
improvisations inserted by jazz musicians into their performances) in
a rough analogy to Larson's comparison between legitimizing architectural projects and aesthetic creativity. Improvisation becomes important
if organizations (or rather their elites and theoretical designers) dream of
becoming a platform, or:

a chameleon-like organization conceived as a laboratory for rapid
restructuring. The platform turns out to be an unrecognized source
of productivity in the high-tech industries, because of its intrinsic potential to generate efficiently new combinations of resources,
routines, and structures which are able to match turbulent market
circumstances.

(Ciborra, 2002, p. 121)

Now, let us turn towards the populist temptation. Loyalty to top management is not the only motivating force in a professional's soul. As professionals, we would also like to side with the underdogs and to increase
their chances for advancement and for a fair recognition of their claims to
be included in the world in which we are entitled to shape opinions. We
would like our ideas to be written on banners carried by victorious crowds
storming the corporate Bastille. We would like to respond spontaneously
and emotionally to the appeals for populist solidarity (it is warm and
nourishing among the underdogs struggling for legitimate recognition)
and spread sustainable wealth, sophisticated culture and democratic participation to those who were formerly excluded, locked out, 'nickel and
dimed' (see Ehrenreich, 2002; Terkel, 2003). But we have been warned:
in trying to lead the masses, we have to enter the organizing bureaucracies that coordinate most domains of social activities and we have to risk
decision-making at a political rather than a scientific speed:

The science establishment has for too long had an unhealthy
monopoly on scientific and technological judgment and on the way

questions that contain a technological element had been framed. The inappropriateness of this monopoly ought to be obvious even within the technical domain: the technical point is that, at best, scientific knowledge takes a long time to make and therefore scientists are often pressed to make authoritative decisions on technical matters before there is any consensual scientific knowledge on which to base them ... Ownership of the universal and eternal has to be given up if the defense of science is to have integrity. We have to understand how to use *fallible* science and technology, as *science and technology*, in the long and sometimes indefinite run-in to what comes to count as scientific fact. The problem is not one of epistemology. It is simply a matter of how to use science and technology before there is consensus in the technical community.

(Collins and Evans, 2007, p. 8; italics in original)

A self-critical aside. Having said that, I could not resist the self-critical observation that even though the ideology of upward mobility and the ideology of siding with an underdog are political ideologies of professionals (we might call them, for instance, 'elitism' and 'populism' respectively), I have still chosen to present them as two contradictory forces driving an individual (soul, personality, consciousness) apart. In so doing I resorted to a psychological metaphor (which resembles Plato's immortal metaphor of two horses pulling the human soul in opposite directions) and not to a sociologically analysed metaphor of 'false consciousness' of salaried professionals in late capitalist societies (which would be more in tune with my attempt to restore critical sociological analysis in organizational and managerial sciences). Do I furnish yet another example of an over-psychologized and under-socialized approach towards the problem of the hegemony of hierarchic bureaucracies in the world of organizing, even as I attempt to overcome and undo this shift? Am I co-designing a new brand of theoretical opium for self-reflecting academic professionals who dream of restoring public intellectuals to their past, pre-Wikipedia glory?

Intellectuals inspired by 'populist' desires or ideologies would perhaps have become fellow-travellers or members of socialist or communist parties in the 1930s or 1940s, moving on to Maoist or Trotskyist movements and splinter parties in the 1960s. If, that is, they happened to live in capitalist societies. If they lived in communist countries, they mourned the loss of the 'fake bourgeois liberties' hailed as a true victory in official propaganda. (Interestingly, the public propaganda slogans and messages were mostly created by the very same intellectuals who privately longed for the 'bourgeois' privileges). In the 1960s intellectuals had invested their hopes in student rebellion[24] and in the wars of decolonization in the third world. In the 1980s and 1990s populist ideologues had largely withdrawn from the public sphere which had become viewed as a territory to be conquered only by a long march through the institutions. Instead of coordinating their various longer and shorter marches they started to found critical and fringe, alternative and bohemian professional conferences, periodicals, websites and associations.

If we want to reconcile these two impulses of academic professionals – the elitist and the populist – we usually end up as members of the alternative research club: say, with Critical Management Studies (CMS, along with Willmott, Alvesson, Gabriel, Knight or Burrell), or the Standing Conference on Organizational Symbolism (SCOS, together with Linstead or Czarniawska, Case and ten Bos, Jones and O'Doherty) or with the Standing Conference on Management and Organization Inquiry (sc'MOI, with Dugal, Boje, Hopfl, Oswick, Matthews or, indeed, myself). These semi-alternative and independent platforms for academic discussions offer a shelter from the bureaucratically controlled universities and schools of business in which participants spend most of their professional lives. But are they enough to provide a counterbalance to the mainstream establishment platforms of academic networking?

The Standing Conference on Organizational Symbolism started during an informal discussion in a Glasgow bar during the EGOS (European Group for Organizational Studies) conference in 1981. Steven Linstead[25] remembers talking to – among others – Barry Turner, Per Olof Berg, Antonio Strati and Rein Nauta. Participants agreed to conduct a small workshop at Exeter University in 1982 and followed this up with a meeting in Groningen in 1983.

> The big take-off was in Lund in 1984 when over 300 people turned up, including some Americans – there was a parallel stream for consultants, who Per Olof managed to convince to pay far more than the academics. Even so, the conference could not afford a dessert at hotel prices at the conference dinner, so cakes were smuggled in by the PhD student helpers and distributed under the tables! 'Notework' was started after this conference I think. 1985 was the traveling conference 3 days in the Antibes, and 3 days in Trento. 1986 was Montreal hosted by Robert Poupart at UQUAM and Milano was 1987 . . . things

became much more formalized after Milano as a result of the inclusion of Americans.

(Linstead, 2008)

The Standing Conference on Management and Organization Inquiry (sc'MOI) also started as an attempt to break away from a much larger organization, the International Academy of Business Disciplines (which itself had originated in an attempt to break away from the Academy of Management, as too large and too establishment-friendly and mainstream). At the annual conference of the IABD in San Antonio in March 2004, a critical organizational researcher specializing in narrative analysis and a storytelling approach towards management, David Boje, was slated to replace the outgoing president of IABD. However, as an entertainment during the first conference dinner he and a group of friends presented an improvised comedy show ridiculing the corporate ideology of McDonald's. Considering that the IABD's top representatives had invited a Bush lobbyist to give a keynote address, the contrast between Republican political correctness (San Antonio is surrounded by military bases and the USA was at war, it is close to Mexico from which illegal immigrants arrive in the USA and Huntington had just published his anti-Latin American credo *Who Are We?*) and the countercultural, contesting politics of a vegetarian pacifist and alternative academic could not have been greater. Some members of the IABD came to the conclusion that they might be tainted by association with an un-American symbolic figurehead. Gossip was traded and an extraordinary meeting called at seven in the morning, before breakfast and before the day's proceedings. Boje was forced to withdraw from the presidential elections (in public discussions he was accused of sexist language and a patronizing attitude towards – male, by the way – Middle Eastern participants and of hurting the religious feelings of one of the black participants – never of being too critical of current official US policies). What became clear was that although the IABD measured its members only in hundreds (rather than thousands, as AoM does) it had started to form a not-too-alternative academic niche attracting large numbers of researchers with Middle Eastern or Muslim backgrounds, extremely sensitive to criticism and cautious about their political image under the Bush administration. Witnessing the morning 'purge' of Boje by his IABD colleagues, who had been ready to elect him only a day before, recalled not only McCarthyism (as depicted in *Good Night and Good Luck*), but also the futility of rational choice and transaction theories, which are blind to contexts and climates, ideologies and hegemonic pressures. From the point of view of Boje and a group of researchers (including the present author) who had used the IABD for their personal networking, the time had come to move away from a formalized, too bureaucratic and too 'conformist' organization and to start counting members in tens rather than hundreds. That's how sc'MOI was born, networking researchers, their PhD students and – increasingly – consultants eager to make use of narrative methods in organizational analysis.

When we return to mainstream academic research, the emergence of the network theory of an organization looms large as the ideology of managers and those theorizing on organization and management. What is surprising in definitions of networks as the preferred organizational form of the future is the lack of critical analysis of the blatantly ideological and frankly utopian praise lavished upon them:

> When hierarchical forms are confronted by sharp fluctuations in demand and unanticipated changes, their liabilities are exposed. Networks are 'lighter on their feet' than hierarchies. In network modes of resource allocation transactions occur neither through discrete exchanges nor by administrative fiat, but through networks of individuals engaged in reciprocal, preferential, mutually supportive actions ... In essence, the parties to a network agree to forgo the right to pursue their own interests at the expense of others.
>
> (Powell, 2003, p. 318)

The disappearance of bureaucracy from the focus of academic interest has much to do with the emergence of the ideology of the network as the privileged organizational form of the future. The emergence of this ideology can be dated to the appearance of Walter W. Powell's seminal paper on 'Neither Market nor Hierarchy: Network Forms of Organization' in 1990 (see Powell, 2003; see also DiMaggio and Powell, 1983). Powell claimed that networks were a compromise solution that allowed us to combine the flexibility of market organizations with the solidity of bureaucracies. Markets work with prices, bureaucracies with routines, while networks, according to Powell, rely on 'relations' (hence, among others, the career of the Chinese '*guanxi*' in the managerial literature of the 1990s). The theme was picked up by a number of authors, including, among others, Sumantra Ghoshal and Nitin Nohria, who referred to the 'differentiated network' of a post-bureaucratic organization (Ghoshal and Nohria, 1997; Beer and Nohria, 2000). Powell claimed that after the processes described by Chandler as the emergence of 'big business' or of contemporary large business corporations (Chandler, 1977), which were in fact large 'professional bureaucracies', and after the processes described by Williamson as a gradual pushing out of the 'markets' by 'bureaucracies' in order to reduce the randomness and uncertainty of pure market transactions, a third tendency had emerged: simultaneously to downsize the bureaucracy and to expand the network of relations. Companies are selecting those (negative) relations with other companies, suppliers, clients and so on, which can and should be broken, and focusing on those that should be maintained, because network partners have resources that cannot be internally reproduced (for instance, they are creative, they can bring new technologies and so on). Thus companies try to reduce the number of hierarchical levels within their organization in order to become more competitive and in order to improve the horizontal networking between those who remain and are expected to respond more quickly, more effectively and more creatively to challenges than the more numerous but more bureaucratically controlled cogs in the machine. At the same time this domestically simplified organization becomes externally much more interrelated and partnered with the most diverse and ambiguous partners.

Elements of this network type of organization are often described only vaguely and theoretical descriptions frequently read as an ideological wish-list of top management, wanting to downsize and to expand at the same time. Bennett Harrison, commenting upon the 'lean and mean' landscape of corporate power in the age of flexibility, notices that this change in corporate shape, this shift from hierarchies to networks, corresponds to the changing composition of society more widely. Harrison tries to link this shift in the sociological landscape in which corporations are embedded to a new distribution of income, although it is not clear whether he sees the social environment as the cause and organizational shape as an effect, or the other way round:

> The class and associated wage structures that characterized nineteenth century industrial capitalism could be depicted as a *pyramid* with narrow top and wide base. The rapid growth of a wage earning middle class during the twentieth century (and especially in the years following World War II) effectively transformed the distribution of income into one with the shape of a *diamond*, featuring a small number of very rich individuals at the top, a declining fraction of very poor people at the bottom, and a burgeoning middle group.
>
> But economists, sociologists and journalists now almost universally agree that since the 1970s the distribution of income has been changing its shape again, becoming an *hourglass* with an expanding upper end of well-paid professionals (including Reich's symbolic analysts),

a growing mass of low-paid workers at the bottom, and a shrinking middle class made up of downwardly mobile former factory workers and middle managers made redundant by the philosophy of lean production. Moreover, it appears that this unsettling trend towards a polarization of earnings is occurring worldwide, albeit at varying rates. The consequences differ, also since countries have very different 'safety nets' in place to prop up those who cannot make it in the labor market.

Finding ways to maintain civilized labor and living standards in a world economy increasingly populated by forms of industrial organization that exacerbate such polarization will be no small feat.

(Harrison, 2003, p. 342; emphases in the original)

This last paragraph, on maintaining 'civilized labor and living standards' in spite of increasing polarization, reads like a warning of the necessity of disciplining the underdogs deprived of any rational hope of matching the living standards enjoyed by those at the top of the hourglass. What makes the current predicament of the lower classes even more acutely present in their daily experience is their continuous contact with the spectacle of conspicuous consumption through the multimedia. The consumer paradise of free individual lifestyles liberated from commonplace constraint is advertised continuously by glamorous TV soap operas such as *Dynasty, The Bold and the Beautiful* and *As the World Turns* and a plethora of other media. The have-nots are constantly faced with images of the unattainable, which was not the case in past epochs. Moral scruples at the perceived excesses of some lifestyles are dismissed as conservative attempts to hamper the liberation of an individual consumer on his or her way towards a successful contemporary lifestyle.

Sociologists assume that evolving social and organizational forms (which facilitated the neocon backlash between 1970 and 2000) increase inequalities in societies at large (for instance measured in salary differences between individuals and GDP differences between nation-states) and in particular in professional bureaucracies, which are the dominant form of organizing. Are the increased inequalities manageable? Or are our fears that they may become unmanageable well founded?

There are academic intellectuals investigating the potential influence of this dual shift towards increasing inequalities and a growing complexity of networking who interpret the combination of the two processes as an opportunity to develop a new, emancipative, liberating political praxis. So many new underdogs require guidance and a re-engineering of their identities into a force for political change that there is a growing need for emancipative projects for migrant labour and gays, for underpaid women and laid-off blacks, for the too young and the too old, the married and the unmarried. However, coaching a new social agency capable of large-scale change would be impossible without many new professionals trained in media communications and in the management of historical memories and social identities. Thus, other academic intellectuals see these developments in a less optimistic light. Growth in the numbers and training of coaches, therapists, identity articulators, communication and PR specialists – professionals for networked and mass-media communicated interactions – is to them a repetition of the past, not a rehearsal for a new hope. We are witnessing yet another historical reincarnation of the bureaucratic pyramid with the ever-present danger of authoritarian control. The spin doctors of contemporary social communications – PR, advertising and propaganda professionals – recreate bureaucracies with new rankings of professions. Professional bureaucracies tend to reproduce inequalities, hence breeding successive oligarchies (as Michels observed in the early industrial trade unions) and circulating their elites (as Pareto famously pointed out).

The more efficient emergent forces for political change want to become, the more they have tacitly to accept the most undemocratic, non-egalitarian, 'corrupt' (from the point of view of fair representation) and totalitarian managerial practices. This facilitates further enlargement and empowerment of the established bureaucracies or results in the design and gradual development of an alternative bureaucracy. Optimists stress increased individual mobility and individualized communications as opportunities for a liberating practice that are about to emerge from the conscious efforts of communicatively empowered underdogs. Pessimists claim that the monotonous humming of multimediated communications is more likely to pacify consumers and keep them at home or in the velvet cage of their individual consumer lifestyle than to prompt them to start organizing street marches or engaging in more sophisticated political organizing. As far as optimists are concerned, Castells and Norris note that:

> Social movements escaped their confinement in the fragmented space of places and seized the global space of flows, while not virtualizing themselves to death, keeping their local experience and landing sites in their struggle as the material foundation of their ultimate goal: the restoration of meaning in the new space/time

of our existence, made of both flows, places and their interaction. That is building networks of meaning in opposition to networks of instrumentality.

(Castells, 2007, p. 250)

Rising levels of human capital and societal modernization mean that today a more educated citizenry in postindustrial societies have moved increasingly from agencies of loyalty to agencies of choice, and from electoral repertoires toward mixed-action repertoires combining electoral activities and protest politics ... more likely to express themselves through a variety of ad hoc, contextual, and specific activities of choice, increasingly via new social movements, internet activism and transnational policy networks.

(Norris, 2002, p. 222)

Pessimists point out the difficulties in overcoming the effects of social divisions of labour in professional bureaucracies by turning them into networks. Networks still depend on hierarchies. Moreover, there is nothing 'automatic' in the link between critical theorizing and political organizing. Before an attractive ideological-political agenda can emerge, this agenda has to be articulated and legitimized across – and in spite of – academic, communicative and political baronies, fiefs and monarchies. This may be done according to a modified Marxian historical philosophy, as Arrighi does in tracing the 'spatial and other fixes of historical capitalism' within the framework of Wallersteinian 'world system theory' (see Arrighi, 2006). Arrighi assesses the possibilities of a new economic and political network, which he calls the 'government-business complex' and which he claims to have reconstructed in successive Genoese, Dutch, British and US attempts to establish a global market economy. He concludes that: 'In the present transition, it is not yet clear whether and how a governmental-business complex more powerful than the US complex can emerge and eventually provide a solution to the ongoing overaccumulation crisis' (Arrighi, 2006, p. 211).

Some pessimists assess the possibility of an emergent alternative agency on the 'underdog' side and ask themselves if the 'excluded' and 'discriminated against' can come up with an attractive ideology that would mobilize them, guide them and help them attract supporters, without losing their identity; an identity, incidentally, which is being constructed, designed, articulated and maintained by the very social and political, cultural and economic group that successfully managed to articulate 'class demands' and saved them from co-option by the powers that be.[26] They ask, as Said did, whether:

> in identifying and working through anti-dominant critiques, subaltern groups – women, blacks and so on – can resolve the dilemma of autonomous fields of experience and knowledge that are created as a consequence. A double kind of possessive exclusivism could set in: the sense of being an excluding insider by virtue of experience (only women can write for and about women, and only literature that treats women or Orientals well is good literature), and second, being an excluding insider by virtue of method (only Marxist, anti-orientalists, feminists can write about economics, Orientalism, women's literature). This is where we are now, at the threshold of fragmentation and specialization, which impose their own parochial dominations and fuzzy defensiveness.
>
> (Said, 2000, p. 215)[27]

Finally, there are those who are neither optimists nor pessimists but try to define the possible ideological space for political mobilization, as Wallerstein did, when speaking at Hong Kong's University of Science and Technology on 20 September 2000:

> If we look at the long historical evolution of modern world system we see that the choices among temporalities, universalisms, and particularisms have been a central locus of our political struggles. One of the weapons the powerful have had, is to misdefine these debates and thus to obscure them, in an imagery that argues that time and space are simply contexts within which we live rather than constructs that shape our lives. And universalism and particularism are defined as critical antinomy which we can use to analyze all social action and between whose priority we all have to choose, and once and for all. This has been helpful to the winners and not at all to the losers, which is the most urgent reason why we must unthink this antinomy and make far more complex our appreciation of the options that are available to all of us ... In a socially constructed world, it is we who construct the world.
>
> (Wallerstein, 2004, pp. 91, 96)

True, it is we who construct the social world, but, to paraphrase Marx, we do not construct it at will nor without constraints imposed on us by history (traditions, memories, trajectories, sunk costs) and society (classes, power relations, economic cages, resource mobilization, redesigning of social policies), culture (repertory of symbols to build identities and mobilize agencies, status wars, campaigns for recognition). Making sense of ourselves in the social world, we are also inventing and discovering new senses in which we shall be making sense of ourselves in future, or in which others and other, later 'ourselves', will be making sense of them-(our)-selves as members of emergent agencies in social worlds. Optimists claim that new agencies of change are emerging everywhere, that new identities are being forged with increasing velocity, while internet activists facilitate the uncontrolled spread of subversive ideas. Pessimists counter with arguments that the underdogs may have nothing to lose except their chains but they are chained in so many distant and different ways that global and class solidarity is a dream. Dreams of liberation can be realized only exceptionally and briefly – anti-discrimination legislation in the US Congress under Lyndon B. Johnson quoting Martin Luther King,[28] or 'Solidarność' in August 1980 in Poland (sweeping the nation and washing 10 million citizens away from communist dominated organizational forms into a non-violent trade union network with a political agenda).

Finally, alongside the optimists and the pessimists are 'neutralists' who agnostically refrain from positive or negative evaluations, and claim that we are not passive receivers of pre-coded mediated messages (watched over by not always benevolent professional bureaucracies) and can talk back to the multimedia, thus opening a public debate in virtual spaces and creating an opportunity to overcome prefabricated ideological assumptions disseminated by tele-multimedia. They quote approvingly the case of five young Lebanese from Beirut, whose photographic portrait – in a convertible, among victims of an Israeli air raid – won the World Press Photo Award for 2006. The routine responses of western audiences tended to be unfavourable (what are these young, smart and sophisticated yuppies doing, driving in a convertible through the debris of the air raid, using their cell phones to photograph smouldering ruins and despairing victims?) The protagonists of this photographic report were able to counter the slick assumptions of the western media. They explained that they were on a humanitarian assignment from a relief agency, documenting the consequences of the Israeli air raid against the civilian population. Moreover, their words were printed in the same newspapers that had previously printed only the photograph. The motivation of the professional bureaucrats and bureaucracies behind commercial media empires may have been ethically ambivalent (they might have been much more interested in capitalizing on the visual impact of the picture than in the intellectual discussion around it). Media magnates may have been showing off – saying 'look how interactive and responsive to our audiences we are'. But whatever the motivations, they were giving some underdogs a more structural, balanced and prospective voice. Hence the overall effect is one of a globally accessible renegotiation of the meaning of images disseminated by the mass media and thus offers a small contribution to the undermining of bureaucratic hegemony in the world of organizing.

(b) Patterning the sensemaking processes 2: the commercialization of interactions and alternatives to the iron cage of ranking

What do we reconstruct when we reconstruct the social world around ourselves? Reconstructing local consumer choices and streamlining global producers' inputs we are still within the supermarket rather than an agora, we are still tacitly accepting market exchange as the underlying blueprint for all social relations. We are, to paraphrase d'Iribarne (1989), within the logic of contract and we are not critically probing into the 'secret history of primitive accumulation' or into non-contractual patterns of interactions, or into contexts in which explanations in terms of interactions of autonomous agents make less sense. We are taking the scaffolding of contracts, exchanges and transactions for granted, although we should still be surprised to hear the Chinese government declare that 'being rich is glorious', which does not differ very much from the barely fictionalized Wall Street broker Gordon Gecko preaching that 'greed is good' in the film, *Wall Street*. In fact, there are not many studies devoted to the social, economic, political and cultural changes that must have been necessary in order to build and maintain 'market exchanges'. There are not many studies tracing the installation of political economy as a 'scientific ideology' legitimizing the commercialization of interactions and authorizing coercive, sometimes even violent, measures (see Perelman, 2000).[29]

> The so-called material world of governments, corporations, consumers and objects of consumption was arranged, managed, formatted and run with the help of economic expertise. The readiness with which it seemed that this world could be manipulated and modeled by economics reflected not only that it was a naturally 'quantitative' world, as Schumpeter suggested. It reflected this imbrication of the concepts and calculations of economic science in the world it was studying.
>
> (Tim Mitchell, 2005, p. 139)

The social world of commercialized interactions, with a single isolated transaction between rational individuals as a matrix is (as are all alternatives to it) a historical construct. Replaying a single exchange between individuals makes it possible to shape individual interactions, but does not necessarily facilitate detecting and analysing tacit collective choices embedded either in contextual realities or socializing (and enculturating) routines. We can break down a single job interview into sequenced exchanges between an interviewer and an interviewee and can design training modules to teach people how to prepare for this type of situation. But we have to leave cultural background and organizational embedding aside, even though they determine the climate and flavour of individual interactions, even though they make the social world around us meaningful, even though being aware of them is indispensable for making judgements, evaluating and making choices according to criteria of 'substantial' (and not only instrumental) rationality. We have 'made' the social world in which we move, and we maintain it by going about our business. It is, thus, 'we' who construct and justify the world, but it is also 'we' who are responsible for dismantling parts of it (in order to repair or remove them), reconstructing them, legitimizing changes and looking for improvement. In a sense, we legitimize by linking Lego-like building blocks supplied by political ideologies. These building blocks are always present in our culturally transmitted repertoires of evaluations and actions and have to be accounted for (by sociologists and cultural anthropologists) if we are to start interpreting and understanding individual actions. But they are not frozen into thin slices of one-to-one exchange routines.

The commercializing matrix owes its dissemination to, among other things, rational choice theory as a legitimizing vehicle. 'Rational choice' models focus on the individual as the basic calculating unit of the social universe. The world suddenly becomes a collection of prisoner's dilemma episodes. Thou shalt scheme, plot and count. Instead of following a more substantial rationality of choosing between conflicting values and shifting preferences, we are led to believe that simplified and isolated individuals behave as if they were continuously reinventing winning strategies in a prisoner's dilemma situation. They try to make their own reconstructions (of the social world reduced to a single exchange) on the basis of their own experience and their own preferences. They are supposed to be perfect carriers of instrumental rationality subjected to the cruel uncertainties of an interrogated prisoner. What the rational choice theoreticians ignore is the fact that we are never reducible to perfect carriers of instrumental rationality nor are we perfectly isolated islands.

We also remain 'us, ourselves' by accepting or changing our preferences as a result of ongoing self-reflexive evaluations of our routines and of our deviations from collective identity. Symbolic entities with which we identify are increasingly often subjected to self-critical reflection and we cannot assume that they continue to 'generate' similar attitudes and behaviours. Even as a single isolated individual in a one-to-one situation, we debate within our own individual personality, participating in an ongoing struggle between hierarchies of values linked to 'instrumental' and 'substantial' preferences (not always siding with 'ourselves', and sometimes forcing ourselves to do something that instrumental logic would not allow us to do).[30]

It is thus 'we' who construct the social world according to the tacitly assumed primacy of professional bureaucracies in the institutional framing of our activities. Bureaucracy would not thrive without our tacit and explicit support. It is also 'we' who construct the social world according to the tacitly assumed advantages of market exchanges performed by isolated 'I's. It is 'we' who construct 'I' decisions calculated in monetary terms and structured as consumer choices. Market calculations would not prevail in the structuring and patterning of social interactions (a gift follows a different logic of circulation to a commodity, obligations of honour follow different logic to contractual ones) if we did not calculate and insert the tacit pattern of market exchanges everywhere. In studying US managers and MBA teachers in Shanghai, Aihwa Ong focused on their concept of psychologized re-engineering of the young Chinese managerial cadres and noticed that:

> In business speak, intelligence is the capacity to think, plan, and act in a 'rational' way, according to specific goals such as increasing and maintaining company profit margins. Here business managers are invoking a Weberian notion of rationality, a capacity for rational consensus, cost-benefit calculations, and other techniques of the modern enterprise ... Reengineering became a metaphor for converting Chinese employees from particularistic cultural beings into self-disciplining professionals who can remanage themselves according to corporate rules and practices.
>
> (Ong, 2006, p. 223)

What deserves attention here is the language of corporate culture and the application of cross-cultural competence (individuals raised in one culture are supposed to be trained for jobs created in another) to the process of the social production of managers. These new Chinese managers have to be able and willing to fill the slots in organizational hierarchies designed and implemented in the expanding Chinese economy, which shapes its organizational forms under the influence of professional bureaucracies as the dominant mode of organizing and managing, but which legitimizes itself as geared to the production of profit in a market economy ('to be rich is glorious'). We should not pass by the supreme historical irony of this slogan on the red banners of the Chinese Communist Party. It is an astonishing 'marriage of convenience' marking the end of the Cold War! And yet it went almost unnoticed, as if the commercialization of social interactions had always been a 'natural' tendency of communist ideologies, socialist states and centrally planned economies. The new Chinese mandarins – managers – should, as we have seen, serve an abstract matrix of commercial enterprises (albeit in the discreet shadow of the communist state, whose cadres, 'managers of managers' remain under-investigated, covered by the veil of state security and party secrecy). Let us turn now towards this matrix, this second fundamental pattern of sensemaking processes, the one which has spread the intuitive logic of rational choice theory throughout the dense fabric of interpersonal relationships.

As well as the tacit acceptance of professional bureaucracy as the dominant form of organizing (with another assumption tucked neatly inside, namely that this form is best controlled by top management) contemporary sensemaking processes have been patterned by an equally tacit acceptance of the market exchange of commodities as the most universal 'shaping' instrument of all contacts, contracts and exchanges (with another assumption tucked neatly inside this, namely that this exchange is performed by rational isolated individuals, since 'there is no such thing as society'). In brief, the economic transaction, a rational exchange of goods and services, has been tacitly taken for granted as the basic underlying 'matrix' of most interactions. If transactions are repeatedly 'enacted', they lead to the emergence of routines and to the stabilization of relations. What do we do when we relate to others? According to this tacitly 'economized' view of relating to one another, we initiate and maintain patterns of exchange that form the spinal cord of relationships. The career of the 'prisoner's dilemma' in academic discussions testified to the widespread popularity of this tacit (market transaction = rationalized interaction) assumption. According to this vision we stand alone as independent agents, calculating our risks, making our decisions and living with their consequences. Let us note: not all relationships resemble an exchange between a seller and a buyer, but all of them are tacitly analysed in terms of an exchange, in terms of a deal that has to be closed (of a commodity for a commodity, of a commodity for money, of money for a service and so on). Placing the exchange of commodities in a central position among available matrixes of our relation-building activities makes for a peculiar, arbitrary and tacit 'quasi-commercialization' of interactions. Individuals are supposed to shape their relations with others according to comparable criteria of desirable exchange. Can the domination of this matrix really be empirically confirmed? Can investment of emotional care in intimate relationships be calculated, compared, bought and sold, monetized, as is the case in contemporary sex markets, and should this be the 'deep structure' and measure of personal relationships? (See Bernstein, 2007.) At the very least, the construction of relationships by individuals should surely be subjected to more critical and more sophisticated examination than a simple reference to transaction costs.[31]

Forming relationships (bonds of friendship, companionship or love spring to mind as eagerly as much weaker and fleeting 'mini-bonds', for instance expressing interest in a stranger in an incidental encounter) is usually conceptualized as conscious creation of instrumentally rationalized exchanges between rational individuals, which (relationships, exchanges) have to be audited from time to time so that individuals can assess their 'profits' and 'losses', 'assets' and 'liabilities'. The growing influence of the rational choice matrix (of which transaction costs analysis is the best known case in point) means that we tend to see the transaction between a seller and a buyer in a market as a blueprint for structuring interpersonal relationships that can be generalized to all spheres of human activity, most significantly to the domain of personal emotions and social movements. A commodity dominates, a gift fades away into the margins of a responsible individual life and survives as a personal folly in the bohemian clubs of poor artists creating their works of art as 'gifts for society', or at least for the society to come, which perhaps will be able to reward them, even if posthumously (see Hyde, 1983).

However, in structuring, for example, a marital relationship as a series of exchanges between partners, which should maximize both husband's and wife's emotional well-being and streamline the running of a household together with the shared raising of children, one may decide to subject these exchanges to a regular 'audit'. Am I getting more from this relationship than I have been investing into it? Marriage counsellors stand ready with checklists, which should clarify the question of whether the relationship is 'maximizing' one or the other partner's personal development and which should enable the identification of other signals of well-being and happiness. Here again, we have an over-psychologized and under-socialized approach towards relationship assessment. Ann Swidler reports that even if husbands and wives explicitly ask counsellors (or priests, ministers and rabbis) to help them make sense of their marriage in more 'collective' terms of living together, most of the advice they get is aimed at them as single autonomous individuals in hot pursuit of their sovereign plans. The entity called 'a married couple' is not a priority for therapeutic intervention[32] because it involves a shadow of 'collectivism' (of common interests and moral duties going beyond individual 'gain') and limits a sovereign rational subject in his or her autonomous choices.

In accepting the market blueprint for streamlining relationships according to a 'contractual' and 'atomized' model, we assume that the market exchange within political and legal regulations ('status quo') is and should be taken for granted. Market exchange should thus neither be 'deconstructed' nor criticized from the point of view of replacing it with a more desirable alternative (already envisioned and pre-designed) for masterminding relations. Envisioning and pre-designing of an alternative to markets by a benevolent bureaucracy acting on behalf of the masses had been tried before. This was historically the case with the alternative communist blueprint for the construction of a competitive economy by a professional state bureaucracy. The party and the state were supposed to be devoted to an 'objective', that is, impartial (from the point of rival classes claiming monopolies) control of all relations, as if an entire society could become a Benthamite panopticon, with all individual interactions perfectly visible to the party, state and secret police officials. This return to the idea of a purely bureaucratic control, with commercial exchanges closely structured by the state and profits taxed in advance, provided rational choice theory and the matrix of commercial exchanges between free individuals with an additional ideological appeal during the Cold War. 'We' were negotiating deals between free citizens. 'They' had to enact deals their rulers forced them to close. For reasons of ideological symmetry it made sense to assume that free, autonomous individuals undertake actions, which may add up to a mass process, but which are fundamentally structured as their private, separate choices based on a rational calculus (as opposed to enslaved individuals who had to follow collective choices while 'frozen' by state bureaucracies into their social slots and deprived of their chance to exercise discretion either in production or in consumption). Subjecting commercial transactions to state bureaucratic control in state socialist societies overshadowed the subjection of commercial activities to the bureaucratic control of large corporations in market democracies ('hidden persuaders' were studied only with respect to commercial advertising, especially subliminal messages). In particular these individual actions were rarely conceptualized as conscious acts of participation in collective actions, especially in regard to protest movements or consumer boycotts. Margaret Archer formulated her charges against rational choice theory very succinctly in her polemic directed against Jon Elster and Gary Becker:

> Rational choice theory in general cannot cope with the phenomenon of social movements. In part this is due to the methodological individualism which can only see society changed through aggregate actions rather than by collective action. In part, too, it derives from that purging of the emotions which condemns them as sources of irrational 'wish-fulfillment', rather than allowing that they can foster the vision and commitment which rationally support social movements pursuing the fulfillment of wishes.
>
> (Archer, 2000, p. 41)

The influence of this tacit rationalization, understood as a 'quasi-commercialization' of interpersonal relationships, has been visible in all walks of life, including academic communities. In the last decade of the twentieth century and in the first decade of the twenty-first century universities have been the focus of a number of new policies, most of them designed to 'commercialize' (or at least 'streamline' according to the principles of rational management in business companies) research and teaching. A research budget as an annual allocation by the ministry of education might have been cut, while 'bonuses' were allotted on the basis of performance and business corporations were encouraged to form proactive alliances with researchers and research centres. Teaching budgets were allotted according to the numbers of students enrolled, which led to an increase in the average size of classes and to a general lowering of standards.[33] These campaigns to 'rationalize' educational policies were prompted by the 'privatization' drives of the last decades of the twentieth century and influenced patterns of behaviour of teachers, researchers and managers, all of whom were subjected to annual 'audits' performed by department heads and deans, and to rankings influencing their promotion and tenure. Let us trace some of these more specific policies in order to find out what actually happens when they are implemented, and to discover their consequences for interpersonal relationships, if the latter have to be patterned after commercial exchanges and monitored regularly during business-like company audits.

Erasmus University in Rotterdam is a middle-sized Dutch university (24,000 students, 2200 employees in 2007), which focuses on medicine, law, economics and business management (these are the largest faculties) and forms the academic core of education in the province of South Holland (from which a majority of students are recruited). Rotterdam forms the southwestern end of the Dutch 'urban belt' running from the north-east to the south-west along the coast of the North Sea and extending from Amsterdam through Leiden (with the oldest university in the Netherlands) and the Hague (seat of the government and parliament) to Rotterdam and Dordrecht. The city of Rotterdam has one of the world's largest ports (although it lost the top position first to Singapore and then to Shanghai around the turn of the millennium) and attracts an increasing number of foreign students (mostly German and Chinese). Empirical evidence for the present case rests on official documents issued by the Rotterdam School of Management, which is the current name of the faculty of business management at Erasmus University. The 'BSc & MSc Student Code of Conduct', published in Dutch and English, lists a number of 'core values and attitudes'.

'Core values' are supposed to turn every single individual – student, administrator or teacher – into a rational agent following transparent rules of exchange and subject to impartial assessment by the benevolent institutional powers. These are:

- Professionalism (which boils down to the exhortation: 'everyone should deliver high quality in teaching and when taking courses', although the 'high quality' itself remains under-defined, as if readers would have clear tacit expectations and could easily compensate for this lack of clarity in the core value's description).
- Teamwork (stressing teamwork in spite of encouraging individual competitive behaviour presumably facilitates the development of leadership qualities, and the delivering of 'high potentials', individuals who can become leaders in their organizations. Since leadership is the highest stage of management attainable – delivering more leaders than the competition is a cherished aim for every university administration).
- Fair play ('accuracy and precision in judgements and assessments', without specifying what levels of accuracy are desirable and realistically attainable and without any mention of the in-built tensions between the commercial criteria of success in a business school recruitment policy on the one hand and the necessity to demand intelligence and effort on top of a fee when issuing grades on the other).

Five 'attitudes' are expected from lecturers, support staff and students. These are formulated as concretizations of values meant to increase the effectiveness and efficiency of an individual agent's exchanges:

- Honesty (this essentially means 'no plagiarism', which would contaminate the rankings and undermine trust in the quality of education, although it should also mean resistance to pressures with respect to individuals trying to cash in on their '*guanxi*' within state and academic bureaucracies and business communities).
- Respectfulness (concretized mainly as arriving in lecture halls on time and in students using decent language in emails. This 'attitude' is certainly desirable, but it is valued in view of notorious late-coming for lectures and in view of difficulties in banning mobile phones from lecture halls).[34]
- Accuracy ('attentiveness, precision and meticulousness', which presumably follow from the commercially relevant virtues of 'calculability' and 'reliability').
- Passion ('students are expected to show intellectual passion', presumably in pursuit of knowledge. This attitude, while certainly praiseworthy, remains a slightly isolated feature of an ideal student or teacher, because if it means the individual ability to generate emotional support for calculated choices, then it cannot be related to substantial rationality and to higher values motivating the quest for truth rather than grading or ranking).[35]
- Openness ('An open attitude means a willingness to communicate transparently and plainly. It also entails giving and receiving feedback relating to this. This includes calling on others to account for not complying with the code of conduct and, possibly, reporting any abuses to the persons responsible for this.' I have quoted the description of this attitude in length, because it clearly indicates that ethical transparency is preferred to emotional solidarity. The cult of transparency is a relatively recent phenomenon and is based on an assumption that more transparent interactions facilitate the democratization of academic bureaucracies and on a hope that the brave new world of information and communication technologies makes a desirable level of transparency possible).

None of these attitudes are described in terms of solidarity with fellow students (who are reduced to the role of suppliers – they supply themselves as partners for teaming up and thus increase one's individual scores and grades) or in terms of solidarity with fellow teachers (who are reduced to the role of suppliers of calculable packages of knowledge and skills geared to a job project of a student and valued in points and grades). None of the core values or attitudes would help much in advising an individual who was in a dilemma of some kind. Which core value would help if a student's career path devolved to a race for the accumulation of points and grades (which replace both the passion for knowledge and a quest for truth)? Neither could they advise a young researcher what to do if his or her passion counts only if it helps improve their ranking. A ranking can only be improved by publication in journals chosen by an arbitrary decision of one of the many research clubs and networks and established as a basis of some professional rankings to the exclusion of other rankings and their associated networks, clubs, paradigms, schools and theories.

Rotterdam is presented as a 'gateway to Europe' in Erasmus University's PR statements; as a place where individual transactions are swift and smooth. And why are they swift and smooth? Because they are facilitated as skilfully as business transactions resulting in cargo being loaded onto and unloaded from the ships. Students may be thus be seen as containers processed swiftly in modern container terminals. Rotterdam School of Management presents itself as 'a global learning environment' (because the passports of students sharing the same classrooms have different stamps, that is, almost half of them are non-Dutch). Two highly visible 'business-like exchange' policies implemented in most European and US universities between, roughly, 1997 and 2007, have also been reflected in policies introduced at the RSM. First, the coordination of research policies in the Erasmus Research Institute in Management (ERIM) was centralized. ERIM is a joint venture with the faculty of economics, but it is largely controlled by the Rotterdam School of Management, as a result of the recent change of fortunes in a power struggle between the established faculty of economics and a relative newcomer on the Erasmus turf (since December1984) – the school of business, or RSM (in full, Rotterdam School of Management Erasmus University). ERIM issued successive guidelines for monitoring the professional development of researchers and for their career structures. Young researchers are considered an investment and planned returns on investment are expected to grow if these young researchers publish in a limited number of the world's most prestigious academic publications. The overall intention of these measures is to facilitate the EUR's rise among Dutch, European and global universities.

According to a report commissioned from the Leiden-based Center for Science and Technology Studies, Erasmus University's research output (but not the impact) makes it the number one academic centre in the Netherlands, one of the top three in the European Union (along with INSEAD and the London Business School) and thirty-first in the world rankings. According to this report: 'We can draw the conclusion that Erasmus University is doing well in the field when we look at output numbers, but has a somewhat more modest position when we consider impact scores' (Leeuven and Raan, 2007, p. 25).[36]

The authors conclude:

> The results show that the world-wide ranking list of institutes based on EJL journals is headed by the University of California, University of Texas, and the University of Pennsylvania. The first Dutch university is EUR, in position 31. Among European organizations, EUR tops the ranking in 1999–2003, followed at some distance by the London Business School of the University of London and the French INSEAD.
>
> (Leeuven and Raan, 2007, appendix, p. 3)

The second policy implemented within the framework of streamlining and reforming the university is the centralization of the coordination of educational activities in an Educational Office headed by one of the vice-deans. Special commissions have been convened to develop a new curriculum for 'bachelor' ('Boost the bachelor' commission) and streamlined 'master' programmes offered by the RSM. The educational office issues regular teaching evaluations (the forms are accessed by students electronically after the course, filled and submitted, also electronically, to the office) and offers increasingly quantified and 'monetized' reviews of educational performance. Department heads can thus calculate what their department members have earned during the past academic year and compare these 'earnings' to the 'expenditures' (that is, the costs of a given teacher's salary). They can also check whether teachers had a lower or higher average evaluation for the courses they had taught and are thus able to decide upon a just measure of remuneration.

The centralization of managerial control – in both research and teaching activities – is well tuned to the tacit domination of the hierarchic organization (professional bureaucracy) that implements the marketization of the university's activities (the commercialization of performance criteria). The instruments for measuring research or teaching progress have been borrowed from business and are based on a strategic positioning within the academic market segmentation. Both of them (bureaucratic control and the tacit market matrix, which prompts cost calculations in terms of student numbers and graduation rates) reinforce the tacit structuring of interpersonal relations according to the rational choice/transaction costs approach. Students are assumed to be 'shopping' for courses and specializations, for coaches and topics. Researchers and teachers are supposed to be scouting for young talent. Teachers are supposed to be 'selling' their lectures and workshops, supervision and control. Students are supposed to be 'buying' into courses, classes and specializations. From the point of the top management, represented by the board of directors (presided over by the chairperson) and by the college of deans (presided over by the rector), the initiatives implemented in the past few years have contributed to the increased 'quality' of research and teaching delivered by Erasmus University's academic staff and reflected in the relevant rankings.[37] Successful teachers receive bonuses with the following explanations:

> The good evaluation results of your course as well as EUR/RSM quality policy, in relation to large scale courses, induced us to grant you this incentive. Of all XYZ program courses, 8 got an overall score of 7,1 or higher. You got, together with one colleague, the fourth highest score of 7,4. The bonus, together with the annual course reimbursement, will be transferred to your department's account shortly. Thanks for making this course a success.
>
> (Fragments of a letter from the educational office to one of the senior teachers, spring 2008)

Both these centralizing/commercializing policies have encountered – at times – professional resistance. Young researchers resent the arbitrary and mechanistic imposition of controls on their work inherent in forcing them to compete for publication space in an arbitrarily selected pool of journals. Even if the pool of top journals had been selected with the utmost care and due diligence, it could never reflect more than a transitory consensus among peers, subject to change over time and in light of the proliferation of new research methods, domains and networks. Senior researchers complain about a relative neglect of published books in comparison to articles published in the 'star' journals. They observe that books still tend to have a much broader and more profound impact than journals, which are often limited in their readership to a very narrow group of specialists. In teaching, attempts to quantify controls at the faculty level have triggered attempts to shelter some aspects of interpersonal relations from being patterned according to models of commercial exchange. Monitoring a PhD student's progress requires a competence in the coach-supervisor that cannot be reduced to 'rationalizing' benchmarks and standardized controls. Academic and administrative staff members thus spontaneously create some zones of more friendly, intellectually and emotionally 'customized'[38] and less competitive, calculative behaviour, where more disinterested contacts and social exchanges become possible. These acts of resistance to growing administrative control and to commercializing campaigns represent an attempt to regain the feeling of community that had previously been maintained by careful re-enacting of traditional rituals, such as the opening of an academic year with 'Gaudeamus' (which attracts a diminishing number of gowned professors every year), by inaugural and farewell lectures given by tenured members of faculty (which are increasingly frequently moved from a large aula to a smaller senate hall) and by Christmas and Easter parties.[39]

Boxed into the system of 'managed educational services', academic professionals search for alternative institutional platforms where they can exercise their skills, but escape the standardizing and commercialized gaze of university bureaucracies. Traditionally, some of these escapes were made towards consulting companies and joint ventures with consulting companies. These joint ventures often resulted in establishing training centres, for which the academics supplied trainers and consulting companies – corporate clients. This was the case with the Dutch platform created in 1958 by eight universities stimulated by their work with consulting companies. Jointly they formed the Foundation for Interacademic Education in Organizational Sciences (Stichting Interacademiale Opleiding Organisatiekunde – SIOO). In the 1980s the foundation expanded because of growing demand for 'change masters' and in 1994 two tenured Erasmus University professors relabelled the platform as the 'Interuniversity Centre for Organization and Change Management',[40] but kept the original acronym SIOO intact. The new rectors, Roel In't Veld and Henk van Dongen, who came from the academic domains of public administration (In't Veld) and organizational and personnel sciences (van Dongen), focused on change as an ongoing process, which can be managed only by a relevant and appropriate mix of academic knowledge and consulting skills. Combining the practical experience of consultants with the research-based theoretical knowledge of academic researchers, they offered open programmes, in-company modules and tailor-made training and educational projects. Since these activities were perceived as directly competing with the commercial activities of Erasmus University's Rotterdam School of Management (MBA, open programmes, in-company projects and tailor-made modules), both academics were forced into early retirement and the current list of SIOO's teachers does not include any EUR faculty members.[41]

More recently resistance to commercialization has led to attempts to establish alternative educational platforms, which would be free of the pressures of industrialized 'factories of knowledge', but which would not directly compete with the established educational (BSc, MSc, PhD) and training (MBA) services run by universities. In the case of the Erasmus University, the attempt to escape the velvet cages of the educational industry recently (2006) crystallized in the establishment of 'Academia Vitae' in Deventer (a small city in the east of the country) by a professor in the economics of culture, Arjo Klamer, who had spent part of his academic career in the United States and decided that a revival of a liberal arts education might generate a switch in educational supply, which, in turn, might help stimulate civic virtues and substantial rationality much better than the established, institutionalized system of higher education. It is too early as yet to evaluate the academy, since it is still searching for a position on the educational map of the Netherlands. Legitimizing the academy, Klamer uses the same argument for an appropriate mix of research-based knowledge and practice-based skills, phrasing it as an attempt to generate 'academic conversations that matter to life' (Klamer, 2007, p. xxi). The difference between the institutional entrepreneurs of 1994 and 2006 is to be found in the latter's deliberate avoiding of competition with their alma mater. Although Klamer's Academia Vitae opened as a potential alternative to established academic higher education institutions, he nonetheless tried – by trial and error and negotiations with politicians, mayors and peers[42] – to find a niche in between the existing institutions. For instance, Academia Vitae has profiled itself as the provider of an additional 'freshman year' for students who have graduated from secondary school but want to build up their academic knowledge and skills before starting the bachelor programme at one of the universities. In Academia Vitae's brochure we read that:

> Academia Vitae is a new initiative and aims to become the university of the future. Professor of economics Arjo Klamer experienced academic education at its best while he was in the US. On his return to The Netherlands, he decided that the inspiring US approach should also be possible in Europe. With liberal arts and sciences, knowledge in its wider context instead of narrow disciplines, he felt Academia Vitae should provide the perfect grounding for all that follows. On completion of the Freshman Year, you become an Academia Fellow. And may return throughout the rest of your life to participate in the other Academia Vitae programs.
>
> (Academia Vitae, 2007, p. 4)

The discovery of this niche followed two years of searching for a model, a location and a format for the new institution (since the idea grew out of an interdisciplinary PhD seminar in which I had participated, I could follow successive transformations of the original idea quite closely[43] over the period of four years). The birth of Academia Vitae also signals an attempt to create a new platform for permanent education by cultivating a customer relationship and welcoming back the alumni of their freshman year in the future. The present wave of transformations of educational services thus opens windows of opportunity for more academic entre- and intra-preneurs. It is only a matter of time, for instance, before intrapreneurial conclusions are drawn from the recognition of a difference in the quality of two bachelor diplomas currently available on the Dutch educational scene. As most academic teachers in master programmes have noticed, there is a difference between a holder of a bachelor diploma obtained in a post-secondary vocational school (HBO in the Dutch context), and a holder of a bachelor diploma obtained from a university. Some universities have introduced compensatory courses for students of master programmes recruited from non-academic BA diploma providers,[44] which they have to follow before starting their master programme on a par with their more academically educated colleagues. Academia Vitae Bis, or another, yet unknown platform to be imagined and created by institutional intrapreneurs or creative entrepreneurs from outside academia, could help those students bridge the gap and also acquire a broader humanist outlook, further improving their chances for academic success. Offering an upgrading programme could increase the number of high quality graduates within a BAMA[45] framework of higher education. The Bachelor + Master (BAMA) formula standardized European institutions of higher education, but also created new bottlenecks. It did so, for instance, by allowing less academic post-secondary vocational schools to grant bachelor diplomas without prior upgrading of their teaching staff and methods. Meanwhile the Academia Vitae experiment continues. Having obtained permission to run Academia Vitae in Deventer while enjoying a reduced workload at the Erasmus University in Rotterdam, Klamer is working on a new educational 'product', a new 'service' between secondary and higher education and promising competitive advantage in cultural capital accumulation:

The Freshman Year is a year of liberal arts and sciences with a core curriculum designed to introduce students to worldwide intellectual, artistic and cultural traditions. At the Academia Vitae the very best professors from many esteemed universities teach you to think, read, write and argue on an academic level. The Freshman Year is comparable to the first year at an excellent American Liberal Arts College or University in Europe, it serves as a pre-academic year, in which students lay the groundwork for further disciplinary studies at any university in The Netherlands or abroad.

(Academia Vitae, 2007, p. 4)

Although the words 'competitive' or 'competition' do not appear in the above fragment, they are bound to echo in the captive minds of readers of the above exhortation to follow Academia Vitae's freshman year programme. One can foresee the 'star breeding' freshmen programmes proliferating if Academia Vitae succeeds. Nor is the star system confined to education. The star system introduced by the ERIM research rankings, for instance, leads to complaints, which can be summed up as a resistance against a fencing of the intellectual commons in the service of the star system (some platforms – periodicals, semi-secret conferences, luxurious retreats in old castles – are selected for, gated and protected). Academics are articulate in their complaints against academic bureaucrats. The most frequent charges against the ranking dictatorship include arguments about bureaucrats trying to distort the academic non-zero-sum game of winning new knowledge. In the idealized self-image of the academic community every individual's share in research and teaching is presented as a cooperative contribution to knowledge understood as 'humanity's commons'. To manage academic professionals as though producing and disseminating knowledge was a zero-sum game on a competitive market clashes with this – idealized but affectionate – self-image. If successful, this shift, this fencing, this competitive ranking would result in a situation in which there would have to be a few winners and many more losers. The import of star-ship into the academic world is not an isolated phenomenon. The appearance of stars (researchers who publish in top journals, business schools that top the rankings) and celebrities (academic power holders who open ceremonies, and academics regularly invited by the media or chosen as key-note speakers, the alumni of top schools who are head-hunted for prestigious jobs) is supposed to be guiding our choices in every area – food, clothing, music, cinema, visual arts, leisure, research and teaching. The guiding role of this stardom is intimately linked to the consumer pattern of choice and market exchange and to the extension of this to all choices:

The phenomenon of stars exists where consumption requires knowledge … As an example, consider listening to music. Appreciation increases with knowledge. But how does one know about music? By listening to it, and by discussing it with other persons who know about it. (We are) better off patronizing the same artist as others do . . . Stardom is a market device to economize on learning.

(Adler, 1985, p. 208)[46]

Thus we arrive at the paradox of increased rationality breeding the irrational cult of stardom. Bureaucratic professionalism coupled with the economic exchange matrix prompts corporate strategies understood as a quest for 'excellence'. The ultimate end of the benchmarking, ranking and scoring is to improve the commercially exploitable position of an institution or a part of an institution among other suppliers and to become preferred suppliers of knowledge products to an increasingly diversified variety of clients. Stars glitter in the rankings and can help upgrade their institutional home to a higher, more expensive market segment, even if there is no independent evidence supporting institutional claims to their excellence. In some cases being a celebrity substitutes for excellence and those celebrities are famous for . . . being famous. Independent evidence of merit is not always sought, nor is any alternative to the ranking and popularity contests that make a celebrity a celebrity.

What would have happened, for instance, if instead of establishing the rankings of top periodicals for researchers and instead of listing the rankings of top universities for students, university officials and public authorities, NGOs and community organizations – deans and rectors, ministers and activists – had started discussing the impact of graduates and students, researchers and teachers on society at large? What if we had some alternative to rankings that allowed us to see whether the graduates of one university or another tend to play a more prominent and creative role in the political, cultural and social lives of their respective communities? Such an impact would have to be measured not only in the number of hours spent in consulting for business or government nor in the number of hours spent by academics in city hall meetings or in expert hearing sessions. It would also have to be measured in the quality of expert contributions to citizens' debates and in the ability of experts to assist underprivileged groups in local communities, enhancing their opportunities for participating in deliberative democracy. On this scale, Bourdieu might have emerged as much more relevant than Derrida, or Sen than Huntington, Sloterdijk than Habermas, Burawoy than Sahlins, Sennett than Putnam, Wolin than Fukuyama, Wallerstein than Huntington, and so on. Such judgements would have to be made in a more qualitative and interpretative way. For instance, the research value of a hypothesis by Sennett that the lower classes in the 1950s made better use of educational channels of upward social mobility from city slums than the lower classes of the 1980s could have been judged superior to the ideological claim of Huntington in *Who Are We?* that Spanish-speaking and Catholic US citizens with a Mexican background are unable to sustain deliberative democracy, which legitimizes anti-Mexican stereotypes in US policies towards illegal immigrants. The superiority of Sennett's sociological hypothesis on different approaches to upward mobility would be linked to the explanation of one of the most serious roots of failure of social integration policies. Huntington simply stigmatizes Spanish-speaking immigrants from Mexico and Latin American countries as not 'waspish' enough; he does not help us understand why they cannot be integrated and legalized into fellow-citizens and fellow-employees.

An attempt to side with the public instead of with the producers and professional associates or fellow-experts has already been tried in a different area, namely in wine tasting. Wine tasting was traditionally a domain of very narrow groups of influential critics and top professional specialists (sommeliers). Both these groups were wined and dined by the producers of wine. They had also developed an ideology for the justification of differentiated prices. Price rankings were based on differences of taste as defined and tested by sommeliers and influential critics, a small elite with professional training in wine tasting, catering to the richest clients. They linked their evaluations to the unique composition of soil (*terroir*) and the characteristics of grapes. The introduction of the Parker system of 100 points was based on an assumption that taste can be experienced by everybody and that one should have a right to select one's own combination of taste components independently of the verdicts of top clients' advisers. Consumers, instead of producers, were asked to apply the scoring tests and price rankings were expected to follow demand. One might claim that Robert Parker, whose influential bimonthly newsletter, 'The Wine Advocate', has a circulation of 45,000 in 38 countries, has broken free of the producers' and experts' club and led a popular consumer uprising. He has empowered consumers and educated his public – providing every single individual with a do-it-yourself navigation system (and allowing them to select wines to the 'star' class) at the expense of the producer-made navigational charts of vineyards with their own 'star' hierarchies. The overall result of these changes has been an enormous growth in global wine markets. Could Parker's empowering success in wines become a paradigm case for subverting the commercialization of education and provide insights for empowering students? Unfortunately, the revival of a consumer liberation ideology did not prevent wine businesses from driving prices up. Self-taught competence among wine consumers, resembling the 1968 student claims to self-government presented to academic bureaucrats, did not lead to the weakening of the commercialization of the wine sector. Under the wine tasting sloganizing, revolution does not seem likely. The long-term consequences of Parker's success had been moderated by the awareness that:

> He argued for the democratization of wine, and yet became the very symbol of the elite expert pronouncing on unobtainable wines. He wrestled the legitimization of wines from the merchants, but put it in the hands of the media. Though he insisted on individual taste, the would-be consumer advocate became the supreme judge. He railed against high prices, but whenever he anointed a wine its price went up ...
>
> (see McCoy, 2006, pp. 298–9)[47]

If a revival of consumer, student and citizen democracy does not immediately follow the actions of a subversive expert, perhaps we can use this case as a heuristic device – to measure the level of 'ripeness' of a commercialized domain of activities for a possible transformational change. Can similar developments be observed in other areas of social activities? One should ask if 'expertise' is – or is not – increasingly questioned and put to legitimizing and justifying tests. Are professional expert monopolies being questioned anywhere? They certainly seem to be being challenged.

For instance, the medical profession has been severely criticized for excessive reliance on high-tech surgery and low overall success rates (debates around therapies in the case of prostate cancer clearly demonstrate that diagnosis turns out to be correct in less than 50 per cent of cases and that – more often than not – surgery does not appear justified; see Krugman and Wells, 2006). Academic professionals are not left in peace, either. Repeated attempts to introduce 'intelligent design' into institutional education, discussed in Chapter 3, clearly demonstrate that a public (of 'parents of school children') is trying to renegotiate the educational curriculum in order to break the monopoly of academic professionals as suppliers of legitimate knowledge. This particular public of mobilized parents is motivated by religious sentiments, but a renegotiation of curricula may continue as other 'publics' become more aware of their responsibility in co-deciding what should be taught in schools. Academic professionals may yet be held accountable for monopolistic practices and arbitrary decisions. After all, Paul Feyerabend, an 'academic professional' and a certified expert in the philosophy of science, has written a book entitled *Science for a Free Society*, in which he condemns the new quasi-religious dictatorship of the academic producers of knowledge. Even mainstream academic stars have their doubts about the ranking system:

> The ultimate danger inherent in any ranking scheme is that by enshrining the language of competition and uniqueness the rankings themselves corrupt both student and college. The former arrives for his or her freshman year with the wrong expectations. The latter engages in a process that devalues education. Nobody wins in the rankings game.
>
> (Zemsky, 2008, p. 8)

However, not all mainstream, quantitative approaches to comparisons and rankings have to be avoided (although our trust in them should be much more qualified). Simply keeping track of the positions and salaries of graduates of particular business schools in order to check their progress in corporate and public bureaucracies would furnish much more interesting information than any ranking of a university's popularity among its academic peers or students, whose decisions influence the ranking results. Such information could also be verified and compared, although this would be a more complex and difficult job than is the case with the present system of rankings.[48] Such knowledge would add to a self-reflexive awareness among academic professionals, which, in turn, might focus their attention onto the non-conformist and potentially creative (if subversive from the point of view of some elites) images of a political mobilization. More modestly: these longitudinal comparative studies might have helped counterbalance the rankings drive, which had been outsourced to various professional, business, government and media establishments and platforms. These 'ranking' establishments reflect pecking orders in institutions producing academic knowledge. Viewing rankings as the basic criterion of success seriously curbs – even stifles – creativity by reducing the spontaneous readiness of researchers to share their 'internal conversations'[49] with peers. Replacing this spontaneous readiness, this voluntary contribution to the collective *esprit de corps* of a community of practice, with a routine of competition for 'tenured track', 'top talent', 'high potentials', 'the best and the brightest' does not improve the 'organizational climate', does not enrich the 'organizational culture' and usually leads to an oligarchic quasi-monopoly (as in the classic bureaucracies of trade unions studied by Michels at the beginning of the twentieth century). There are limits to market analogies, there are limits to the commercialization of educational activities. Copying market segmentation (according to price ranges and customers' purchasing power) on to academic segmentation (according to selected rankings and celebrity effects) has to be counterbalanced by attention to broader cultural relevance, social impact and civic relevance checks.

Ironically, it is precisely in this period of increasing commercialization in university education and research that academic professionals have realized that they need not remain passively over-determined by their structural position within the university bureaucracy. Their political choices do not have to be limited to voting for political parties according to an analysis of their budgets for higher education, but can and should be linked to broader issues of deliberative and participative democracy (for example, access of local communities to self-government processes). At the same time they also recognize that they cannot perceive themselves as individual representatives of a universal scientific rationality, as individual rational agencies representing *the* 'state of science'. They cannot pretend to be local ambassadors of universal wisdom, rational actors trained and professionally formed to subjectively reproduce and locally apply the universal rules for acquiring valid knowledge. Had they done so, they would continue playing the privatizing and marketizing games with the educational and research activities at the university without scruples or resistance. They would have mistaken their academic careers for the march of progress and the completion of the unfinished project of the Enlightenment married to the revived mercantilist ideology. Had they done so, they would not criticize 'distance learning, sweetheart deals with bioengineering corporations, marketizing admissions' (Burawoy, 2005, p. 524). Those who had not succumbed to the temptation to identify their bureaucracies with the embodiment of the only true rationality might try to increase their social relevance and turn towards 'the very publics we serve' (as Burawoy put it):

> As producers of knowledge and thus of ideology, we have a particular responsibility to produce a reflexive knowledge that, on the one hand, enters a critique of professional and policy knowledges for, among other things, imprisoning the imagination, but that, on the other hand, forges relations with publics, generating dialogue that calls into question the directions of society. The more university loses its autonomy and the more it is colonized by the market and the state, the more desperately it will need to engage with publics that share a similar fate.
>
> (Burawoy, 2005, p. 524)

The language in which Burawoy expressed his conviction that self-reflexive analysis is a moral and political duty of professional producers of 'knowledges' (that is, of academic professionals) has been influenced by critical theory. It reflects a Habermasian view of the world of individual experience (*Lebenswelt*) as being colonized by states (which impose bureaucracies to monitor and control what one does) and markets (which impose commercial exchange matrixes to control how one does it). Burawoy is a sociologist and a 'global ethnographer' (he started with analysing Zambian copper mines, worked incognito in US and Hungarian heavy industries, established a critical research centre in Berkeley and more recently studied Siberian cities with closed-down post-communist industrial sites) and mentions two effects of the scarcity of reflexive knowledge, namely:

- 'imprisoning of imagination'; and
- lack of 'relations with publics'.

The former means that intellectuals, by not engaging in a search for answers to the deeply felt problems of unmanageable inequalities, imprison the imagination in ideologically biased choices, which flatten political and moral worlds, turning them into stages for enacting consumer decisions. Among relevant questions, the answers to which could guide promising research projects, one could mention the following:

- Why did postcolonial southern power elites fail to deliver to their constituencies in the third world?
- Why did contemporary western political elites fail to integrate the new underdogs in market democracies in the first world?
- Why did the disappearance of the second world (eastern in the sense of non-western and non-capitalist) fail to generate a study of consequences for all three worlds?

Imprisoning the imagination should be countered by liberating the imagination and granting it more power as in the 1968 slogan 'Power to Imagination!'. '*Imagination au pouvoir*' is worth imagining, because it feeds social imaginaries. The latter would enable academic professionals to initiate a dialogue about the course of social life outside the safe compounds of politically correct group ideologies. The idea of a dialogue free of the dominating influence of the colonial masters – states and markets – can also be traced to Habermas's *The Theory of Communicative Action* (Habermas, 1984, 1987), but with the author of *Knowledge and Human Interests* it remains a normative ideal, since the colonization in question had also invaded the very language in which we articulate and express our attempts to emancipate ourselves from these 'colonial powers' and it was only recently that Habermas began to notice the religious and communitarian roots and guarantees of 'coercion-free dialogue'.[50]

In really existing academic life at the end of the first decade of the twenty-first century, faculty members are using language that is prepackaged with market-oriented meanings and saturated with business-friendly phrases and terms. They do so even as they try to wrestle free from the velvet cages of the commercialized factories of knowledge. This is especially clear in the increasingly frequent attempts to insert liberal arts into the professional bureaucracy of universities and – more broadly – into the academic educational system of institutions.[51] For instance, when arguing for the establishment of the new chair in the economics of the performing arts in the faculty of history and arts of the Erasmus University Rotterdam (within the department called 'the capacity group Culture', which offers courses in the economics of art and culture and in the organization of artistic and cultural institutions), members of the proposing committee pointed out the growing importance of the social consumption of art and culture, quoting – among others – the growth of 'the creative industries' and global competition with respect to city planning. These developments, and the subsequent need to generate research and teaching about the economics of the performing arts, are presented as the consequence of broader social processes. A causal explanation of the increased public consumption of art and culture links this increase to the presence of art and culture in school curricula, and to a rising level of education among increasingly broad sectors of population. In other words – the more is taught about art in all types of schools, colleges and universities, the more individuals are exposed to educational services in their lifetime. While becoming aware of artistic and cultural products and services, these growing numbers of potential audiences, spectators and publics also have to deal with a growing number of hours of free time, which can be devoted to leisure. Masses are better educated, hence they can experience more sophisticated cultural products and services. Going to a concert, visiting an exhibition or participating in a film festival requires financial and cultural resources, plus some capital, both financial and cultural, in the background. The masses are also more mobile, hence they can increase the range of options as far as cultural consumption goes (for instance travelling to distant festivals or performances, making use of special arrangements with travel, accommodation, restaurants clustered around cultural consumption, of, let us say, a 'museum night' in a city). Last not least, the masses can afford differentiated and much more sophisticated forms of cultural consumption, since these forms are less expensive than ever before and the publics are more affluent than ever before (the above sounds like a worn cliché of British prime minister Macmillan – 'you never had it so good' – but living standards did improve in absolute and relative terms in the last three decades of the twentieth century).[52]

In outlining the domain that should be covered by research and teaching supervised by the new chair holder, the committee report pointed out the necessity to understand and stimulate cultural entrepreneurship and to study the consequences of further commercialization of the performing arts, singling out the following research themes:

> mutual exchanges between culture and market, the effects of the financing modes, subsidizing, sponsoring production and consumption of performing arts, business models, pricing strategies, technologies, management of theatre stages and localization of theatre groups, the market for performing artists, the impact of the new multimedia, cultural entrepreneurship, marketing and management of theatre groups and theatres, both in the Dutch and in the international context.
>
> (Klamer, 2008)[53]

This proposal to establish a chair in the economics of performing arts was premised on the financial contribution of large companies from the world of stage and media entertainment. Their interest is much more clearly reflected in the name of the chair in Dutch, where one speaks of '*podiumkunsten*' or 'stage arts'. The proposal followed from the recognition of a new demand for expertise in financing, managing and disseminating cultural goods and services. How, for instance, to run an economically sustainable and culturally creative theatre in a middle-sized city? In order to become recognized and legitimately accepted, this expertise must be based on a legitimate knowledge produced within the university (or at least co-produced, as in the case of practitioners coming to academia to crown their experience with a PhD thesis).

We are dealing here with a double commercial helix (the genetic code of the commercialization of culture); on the one hand, the social practices of producing and disseminating art and cultural experiences are becoming rapidly commercialized and are being managed as material production and services used to be managed in the past. On the other hand, the way in which we design the construction of legitimate expertise – in this case, on the performing arts – consists of assigning knowledge-producing (or knowledge legitimizing, gentrifying, upgrading) tasks to culturally and artistically competent economists, sociologists, representatives of managerial sciences and other related researchers of managing and organizing. The commercialization of performing arts generates demand for sponsors and managers, while academic legitimization of their expertise – by economists and organizational scientists – justifies and facilitates further commercialization of 'creative industries'. The general academic reading public in the social sciences and the humanities first encountered this legitimization with Lash and Urry's *Economies of Signs and Space* published in 1994 and announcing the arrival of 'cultural goods' (designed to generate associations and to guide sensemaking) and a growing fashioning and aestheticization of daily, mundane, banal products and services (for instance, cooking gurus or hairdressing celebrities, do-it-yourself gardening skills toolkits or lifestyle clothing schools, the theoretical legitimization of popular music and wines, hermeneutics of 'gaze' in tourism and fan-community building in sports).[54]

Neither does the cultural twist in commercialization happen in a communicative vacuum. The accessibility and mobility of individualized communication technologies make it possible to open up transparencies to an extent that was inconceivable before. These new transparencies may be greeted with distrust, as was the case with Brin's (1998) *The Transparent Society: Will Technology Force us to Choose between Privacy and Freedom?* More recently, Nigel Thrift noted that the radical restructuring of office spaces in Accenture's Paris offices reflected a new self-image as a flexible, ambidextrous, creative and agile company. Accenture looks 'tasteful, participative and community-oriented, responsible', but may in fact reproduce the old European imperial domination over the third world – this time not on the basis of race, but using other, more artificially imposed values of culture-intensive commercialization. After all, one can discriminate not only on the basis of race, gender, religion or ethnicity. Political correctness might do as well. Segregating according to the criteria of individualized and professionalized, ranked and advertised educational merit and according to organizational and commercial success in creative industries may offer a sophisticated instrument for re-legitimizing old (and persistent) inequalities:

> Now, perhaps, a new great map of personkind is coming into existence, a map based on other attributes of personhood and, most specifically, potential for innovation and creativity. On the border of this map we would see a frieze of particular creative types, no doubt with Homo Silicon Valleycus in the evolutionary lead. And instead of maps of climate or characteristics like skull type, there would be major airports and educational systems. Yet the net result might, I suspect,

be surprisingly similar to the old map – with a few exceptions made for the new entrants like the Japanese and overseas Chinese.

(Thrift, 2002, p. 225)

This is a notably ironic, but at the same time powerful and compelling vision, because it suggests that new inequalities of wealth and knowledge may become – politically and economically, perhaps also culturally – unmanageable. They may become unmanageable by crowding out too many individuals and communities (none of which will be marginalized into invisibility because of the intensity of the new media and increased competition between potential alternative elites for the role of champion of the underdogs). They may become unmanageable because defending the privileges of the established elites depends on flexible alliances and ambidextrous policies. Moreover, attempting to prevent the freezing of new inequalities into old patterns also makes us aware of the increasingly important role that communication technologies play in our sensemaking processes.

The use of images as historical evidence[55] facilitates comparisons across time and space making them much more feasible and persuasive. Images of inequality and unfairness become dramatically expressive. 'Creative industries' make ample use of the new transparencies and accessibilities of communications. They produce (and reproduce) their own evaluation procedures shifting the attention of consumers and intermediaries with their symbolically saturated products and services and measuring the scope of these shifts. Measurements are performed with the assistance of academic knowledge producers (from marketing researchers to critical scholars such as Vance Packard in the 1960s and Brins or Thrifts and cultural economists now). The gradual evolution of new multimedia has not only facilitated the individualization and segmentation of cultural consumption, it has also increased the mobility of consumers, multiplying the reproduction and dissemination capabilities of cultural industries. This gradual evolution of new multimedia has made clear to a growing segment of culture, knowledge, communication and media professionals (let's say artists and writers, scientists and scholars, journalists, editors and presenters) that:

> commodities and commoditization practices are themselves embedded in more encompassing spheres or systems of producing value. Such systems not only recognize the existence of distinct regimes of value but combine and reorganize the activity from these various contexts into more complex mediations.

(Myers, 2002, p. 361)

It is to these intermediate mediations of social communication in multiplied contexts and within more complex mediations that the chapter now turns. We will ask about the emergence of multimedia landscapes, environments, realities, links, networks and connections, and the influence this emergence has had on the reconfiguration of social and individual agencies.

(c) Patterning the sensemaking processes 3: reconfigurations of agency and the emergence of multimedia communications

Bureaucratization and commercialization are not the only patterning clusters of sensemaking processes emerging at the beginning of the twenty-first century as dominant in our increasingly complex and change-addicted societies. The construction, maintenance, transmission and transformation of individual and organizational interactions involves most individuals who are not locked into isolated communities in increasingly frequent, more far-reaching and more sophisticated communications. Communicating (as in organizational meetings and circular emails, as in team sessions or brainstorming events, as in expressing our 'selves' and in pursuing lifestyles) is sometimes considered part and parcel of organizing, managing, doing. Some researchers go so far as to suggest that organizations exist mainly through their continuous communications, which are co-constitutive for them. The same argument has been made for managers, whose activities and functions display a growing share of time spent on 'communicating'. When the management of highly educated and trained employees in knowledge-intensive organizations requires more 'consulting' than 'ordering them around', communications become much more sophisticated and crucial.

> A large portion of everyday life consists of interlocking social interactions most of which are communicative ... The stabilization of communication patterns and their fusion into distinct genres serves the same purpose as institutionalization of social interaction: it liberates from the need to improvise when facing recurring communication problems.
>
> (Luckmann, 2008, p. 285)

Communications are part of the flow of processes (streams) of social life that takes place in real and virtual spaces. Every classroom in a school and every meeting room in a company becomes a virtual space when exercises in applying knowledge and skills are organized. Most training simulations and virtual learning environments allow participants to rehearse and instructors to prompt, involving feedback and coaching, and thus extending communications beyond the simplified scheme of sender plus message plus medium plus receiver. In prompting our students and in rehearsing in front of our coaches we are increasingly often surrounded by media, mediators and intermediaries. The popularity of simulation games, which allow us to rehearse communications in different contexts, indicates our awareness that communications are relevant, salient, important, and should be skilfully performed, with many factors and contexts taken into account (thus when we hear about organizational 'climates' or 'evolving organizational cultures', we adjust our communications accordingly, as public performers do when prompted and guided by the anticipated audiences' expectations):

> Moving imagery ... can obviously serve a multitude of agendas, from the documentation of scientific experiments, the analysis of movement, security surveillance, animal studies, the diagnosis of football strategies, ballistics testing, and weather forecasting to producing video and computer games, advertising, political propaganda, the delivery of the evening news, and, of course, fictional movies.
>
> (Carroll, 2008, p. 224)

Thus, the third patterning cluster of our sensemaking processes emerged with our increasing submersion in multimedia communications, which became simultaneously globally widespread, dense (they grew in both intensity[56] and frequency) and 'intimately' individualized.[57]

Communication multimedia became capable of inflating themselves all around us and tucking us in. Imagine each of us as a communicational cocoon, closed and private, but with busy terminals and active links. Imagine each of us as a 'monad' but online, a sovereign individual with our mobile phone always on. We are submerged in images and narratives. Providing information and entertainment, multimedia are at the same time blinding us to the world 'out there' (or at least not entirely here, not only within the self). They prevent us from becoming too aware of those individuals and groups who have not been recorded through images nor given a standpoint to express their views in communication flows. Viewed uncritically, these media offer security and comfort within their tight embrace. We do not need to open a morning newspaper in a mock prayer to the gods and fate. Our prayer is delivered by multimedia connections. Nice voices flow into our ears, streamlined images fill our eyes. These multimedia are our airbags in the moment of a car crash or the heated water of a swimming pool as we plunge into it. Captivating most of our senses most of the time, they influence the way in which we articulate, format and determine our navigational routes through the world by supplying formatted knowledge and flavoured emotions. We standardize through ever increasing individualization – the more our customized ways in the world of consumed knowledge and information are unique, the more they become similar to one another, affiliated, synchronized. Following Flaubert, one is tempted to say that contemporary multimedia offer a 'sentimental education'; not just the 'news that is fit to print', but also 'feelings that are fit to feel'. This ongoing sentimental education has important political and economic consequences, because it provides individuals with a repertory of responses to all forms of social communications, for instance political mobilization or commercial marketing.[58] The 'educational' influences of multimedia depend on the 'instrumental arrangement' of communications by those such as sponsors, creators, executors, media specialists, critics and journalists who offer guidance to mass audiences.

The structuring of media communications is a complex process that can be compared to the flow of interactions between a composer creating a musical score and a listener in the concert hall hearing the orchestra performing the composer's piece. Very much in the same way as composers or conductors 'split' the musical score between various instruments and then assign and coordinate the musicians, so many professionals involved in media communications participate as intermediaries. They channel messages through visual, audio, live and recorded 'carriers' or media, but they also manage feedback, audiences' acclaim, and the critical responses to particular mediated 'cultural events' or 'artistic products'. The term 'creative industries' is sometimes used in order to describe clusters of producers in media communications – for instance the Hollywood or Bollywood film industries, with their networks of specialist suppliers of services, half-products and creative designs, or the performing arts industries (music, theatre, the visual arts given a performative turn and in relation to the re-conquest of urban spaces and so on). Entrepreneurial strategies in these industries are being studied with the aim of 'unzipping' back-stage (and behind the screen) interactions and explaining why individual entrepreneurs succeeded or failed in floating their complex creations (let's say, feature films or large-scale theatre productions) into the stream of multimedia communications.[59]

The amount of information channelled through particular senses varies with time and changes with the ongoing re-designing of communications. For instance, traffic jams, which lengthen the time spent in cars, also swell the ranks of radio listeners with a potentially captive audience. The growth of air travel feeds the consumption of recorded films, TV programmes, news and music. Local radio made an unexpected comeback in spite of the visual overkill of the televised and computerized communication environment (at the same time local radio stations started playing an important part in some African countries where they fill the media gap caused by the relative inaccessibility of the printed press[60]). The comfortable multiplex cinema for feature films remains a strong media contender in spite of the growth of video/DVD rental and television channels specializing in recycling movies. There seems to be agreement among thinkers as diverse as Ivins, McLuhan, Debray and Jay (who published their studies of 'mediascapes' between the 1950s and the 1990s) that eyes, eyesight, vision dominate the other sensory portals in socially and culturally determined communications.[61] However, this domination is not complete. Listening to the radio is compatible with typing at the keyboard of a computer, driving a car or reading a book, while watching TV is not. Future combinations of proportions granted to each of the senses in mediated communications may still offer a few surprises. Media became capable of not only being – as in McLuhan's formula – the messages massaging our senses. They are also capable of producing: ' "factishes": new syntheses of the orders of scientific, technical factuality on the one hand and of fetishism, totemism and idolatry on the other' (W.J.T. Mitchell, 2005, p. 26) .

Multimedia have also gone small and swift, personal, portable, mobile. The dissemination of the 'walkman', of a mobile phone, of an iPod, of a TV set and of a personal computer (increasingly often it is also a mobile computer – a laptop or a notebook or another, still smaller, portable device combining the functions of previously distinct gadgets of connectivity) is changing the way we grow and prepare ourselves for future social interactions. However, 'changing ways' is not a one-way street on which technologies push and interacting humans respond by accommodating – by simply adjusting their interactions to new technological instruments. 'Changing ways' is a two-way street, in which new technologies, for instance new media for communication, meet interacting individuals and groups. Out of the interplay between pushing technologies and pulling individuals and groups a changed mode or pattern of communication or connectivity can emerge. Connectivity can be tested with different degrees of 'distance' and 'immediate presence' built into new mediated communications.

For example, a written letter did not require an immediate response. No instant answer was forced upon a receiver, and the sender did not know when and if an addressee had received the communication sent.

The telephone required an instant answer, and if somebody picked up the receiver, he or she could only either put it down again or speak. Communicating via text and email does not require an immediate response (as a matter of fact we have also added the answering machine option to phones, which makes a telephone call similar to an exchange of typed and recorded letter-like messages)[62] although they resemble traditional telephone communication in so far as in most cases a sender can see if the message got through, adding an element of instant connectivity, as in phone conversations or registered letters, but no obligation to respond at once, as in written letters. Modes of connectivity can fluctuate and designs can travel in time. The distance and time characteristic of epistolary communications can translate into telephone answering machines, and picking up a phone can translate into instant confirmation of a receipt of a text or of an email message. The popularity of the internet in general and of email in particular has reinvigorated the writing skills – no matter what users of ready-mades such as 'asap' or 'thnx' may think about the level of sophistication and literary value of emailed written messages.

One of the first observations made by researchers studying the dissemination of multimedia was that they are bound to influence the processes of socialization, of bringing up children in multimedia saturated communicational environments. In talking about changing patterns of socialization, we tend to think primarily of the young (family socialization, school socialization) and the deviant (as in re-socialization of juvenile delinquents) – as if socialization was not an indispensable part and parcel of all our interactions and as if socialization was not carried out through communications at all ages, not only during our childhood and adolescence. The old slogan of 'permanent education' (enshrined in INSEAD's 'Centre for Permanent Education' – CEDEP – for 'top managers') rightly stressed the ongoing nature of organized learning managed by professional institutions, but with the multimedia we are also facing a less focused kind of learning managed by less pedagogically and academically minded (and thus less responsible because less accountable to professional peer controls) professionals. 'Sentimental education', for example, as mentioned above, is the project of a lifetime. After all, 'emotions are primarily relational processes that shape and are shaped by our relations with other people' (Mosquera et al., 2004, p. 187).

The wide dissemination of TV sets, laptops, mobile phones and other electronic devices, coupled with universal literacy in the societies of the developed world, has hugely increased the penetration of individual life by instant communications. Multimedia offer – and their offer increases in size and sophistication with every technological invention – an alternative 'school of seeing' (but also of hearing, imagining, perceiving, of categorizing, of clustering, relating, comparing, interpreting, speculating and negotiating – of making sense). This school of seeing (or, rather, these schools of seeing, which for brevity's sake we shall reduce to a singular) does not have a curriculum and enrols individuals through activities that are not implemented according to a preconceived 'intelligent design', but which have emerged as a result of disseminating new technologies of communication and by individuals bending them to their benefit, often at the expense of the original desired destination.[63]

The ubiquity of communicative multimedia in our lives increases our instant, intuitive, tacit awareness that they are here to stay and will further shape the idioms of our interactions. The growing popularity of internet dating typifies this awareness – and the mixed theoretical feelings that accompany it, particularly fears of the alienating, reifying and standardizing effects of these new modes of symbolic negotiation and material, including sexual, interaction.[64]

The third patterning of sensemaking processes, which accompanies bureaucratization and commercialization, can thus be viewed as a process that might be labelled 'ongoing re-media-ting (of communications and "connectivities")'.

In fact, there are many different processes, which tend to be bundled together as 'electronic re-media-ting' or the saturation of all relations and social interactions with electronically mediated (tele)communications. The multimedia clustered in information and communication technologies play an important role in reinforcing both bureaucratization (since tele-multimedia require professional bureaucracies to run them) and commercialization (since tele-multimedia require differentiated sources of sustainable financing). These supportive and noisy acts of presence behind our backs and before our senses – 'the modest but constant hum of connection and interconnection that they make possible' (Thrift, 2005, p. 212) – are relatively less frequently chosen as a focus of theoretical attention. Refocusing theoretical attention and institutional embedding – resulting in research projects and the growth of knowledge[65] – could help us better understand how to recompose and re-network our academic specializations in hot pursuit of tele-multimedia as teachers of the masses. What prevents us from recognizing theoretically the need to account for the media as the mature partner of markets and bureaucracies? One of the first causes should be sought in the consequences of a social ontology inherited tacitly from historical materialism, which places multimedia communications squarely alongside political ideologies, religious doctrines or artistic expressions and reduces their ontological status to a secondary reflection of much more profound and fundamental, powerful economic (base) and political (superstructure) forces. Steel mills and ministries supposedly weigh more than TV networks (though TV stations were contested much more often – in the sense that they were what insurgents wanted to capture first – than the other two).

It is as if some remnants of the old superstition inherited from historical materialism lingered in the theoretical memories of social scientists in general and organizational researchers in particular. According to this lingering tacit assumption, commercialization is about the economic base, bureaucratization is about the political structures perched on this base, while media are ultra-light. Media apparently belong to the ideological sphere, a kind of a super-superstructure topping the other clusters as icing on a cake. This super-superstructure tops the cake of society, it is an embellishment on a society viewed as a layer cake. Economy is material and feeds societies by making us work (hence it merits the label 'base' as in 'basic'), politics is violent and coordinates societies, making us obey and distribute (hence it merits the name of 'superstructure' built on the economic base). The super-superstructure of symbols and persuasions is less palpable and less fundamental, less primary, always secondary or even tertiary (or worse – as the label 'the fourth estate' for the media following parliaments, governments and courts indicates). Acting entirely according to this superstition, the communist state authorities paid teachers, lawyers, architects and actors less than industrial workers. In the super-superstructure one deals with ideologies. Ideologies inspire and guide individuals and groups through visions and dreams, because in dreams begin responsibilities and because socialization implies enculturation. Enculturation is usually conceived as a systematic and organized exposure to knowing and evaluating in their relation to potential future actions (at least this is what we hope education is all about, when it works). In the superstructure one deals with precise theories (which deserve support) and with cloudy ideologies (which deserve criticism), both of which legitimize visible relations and interactions occurring in real life (which merit reflexive examination).

Both theories and ideologies can be used to justify collective and individual projects but both may themselves remain far away from the real life of social and individual projects and their implementations. An abstract theory that has not yet triggered the joint efforts of researchers, investors and designers, that has not yet led to a successful dissemination of nuclear weapons or mobile cell phones floats in the super-superstructural high altitudes of social geography without triggering the rain of practical implementations that leave material, palpable traces. Theories and ideologies and the other inhabitants of culture/super-superstructure are supposed indirectly to reflect what happens in market economies (nicknamed the material basis) or in state bureaucracies (power relations, political superstructures), but – and here the burden of the tacit traditional legacy becomes visible – they can also trigger technological revolutions, political movements and unpredictable transformations of societies as if they were primary and core components of social agencies, as if they were 'cannons hidden in flowers' (which is how Marx characterized the 'revolutionary' Fifth Symphony by Beethoven). They may thus – tacit ontological assumptions about 'lightness' notwithstanding – become ontologically 'heavier' than mere reflections of more basic processes. They may turn out to be not just mere reflections of more basic forces, which presumably dictate the blueprint of historical evolution by determining which evolutionary stages should be reached, but may acquire the status of contingent and emergent but crucial and unpredictable moulding forces of social development in their own ontological right. At the time of writing, the world's media are tracing the Olympic holy fire on its global journey to Beijing where it will illuminate the opening ceremony of the 2008 Olympic Games. All along the route of the symbolic journey individuals and groups protest against the Chinese government's harsh repression of Tibetan demonstrators.[66] In spite of the world's leaders assuring the Chinese that they will attend the ceremony and in spite of the national Olympic committees confirming their desire to participate, the protests prompted the International Olympic Committee to consider cancelling the rest of the holy fire's journey for fear that further protests – their impact multiplied by the media – could have palpable effects (in sports, politics and economics). Eventually, cancellation turned out to be unnecessary as a result of other contingencies and media responses – we shall return to this case later on.

Not all the inhabitants of the super-superstructural realm are equal. While scientific theories are rigorously produced within a professional community of academic researchers (total quality management of competitive peers according to self-congratulatory professional common sense) whose channels of communication to the general public through the media are systematically regulated, political ideologies have a much more differentiated pedigree and are more hastily assembled by varied and more flexible teams, networks and interest groups, then to be channelled through less regulated and less predictable media to different segments of general publics (or to the publics of the future which have yet to be invented and assembled). In the case of art, communications lie somewhere between those of science (art is professionally and institutionally regulated), politics (there is a social acceptance of radical and extreme experiments) and of religion (the ultimate justification of aesthetic experiments or social transformations in art refer to values – both codified and created). The paradox of historical materialism was that two incidental decisions of its classic manifestations, namely to reduce the explanation of the history of human societies to the interplay of forces of production and political violence and to grant Marxian ideology the status of a privileged scientific theory making all previous theories obsolete (but itself never decaying into obsolescence), have solidified into dogma. Has the shadow of an assumption that bread comes first and then morality follows (the Brechtian slogan about morality being relevant only for the well fed, while the hungry may use immoral means to get fed) survived the breakdown of communism? Did the intuitive feeling that ideologies weigh less than incomes and should be analysed as 'distorted reflections' of economic and political relations linger long after historical materialism was gone? Perhaps it has. Among the possible symptoms of this lingering survival of the remnants of the old layer-cake ontology of society two stand out.

- First, the remnants of a passionate atheism among the intellectual left. A personal vendetta against 'religion' or 'God' as the source of intellectual blindness ('leap of faith') and of violent wars and as an alibi for economic inequalities may follow from this tacit assumption that religion is a core element of the super-superstructure. Religion is perceived as the primary ideological illusion, which would disappear if people stuck to 'clear vision' (unencumbered by any ideological 'opium' for the masses) and 'rational analysis' (unclouded by irrational religious and tribal loyalties). They would thus be capable of understanding commodities and power struggles.[67] One might call this attitude of the media intellectuals – the *leftist puritan* attitude. Leftist puritans claim that the social world should be cleansed of the crown jewels of all ideological collections – of religions – so that market and state powers can be exposed to public view without their softening lenses and become transparent for social actors. This leftist puritanism blinds researchers to the fact that although churches are not the only ideological 'banks' for depositing and investing higher values, religions still provide the idiom in which most individuals carry on their internal and external conversations. Our internal moral evaluations still follow the route of sin, redemption, atonement and other signs of the religious past. For example, in the case study in the previous chapter, the rector sinned against gender equality, was punished by the media, regretted his sin and produced a pro-feminist brochure as a gesture of atonement. He redeemed himself and his university. Thus, entering into a complex game of mediated communications we are in fact – and the 'we' includes the present author picking a religious term a few lines before – also using a language full of 'puritans', 'orthodoxies', 'heretics', or 'sects', not to mention 'charismas'. Thus even the most leftist intellectuals are prone to admit that: 'I had no target, no wish, and no discipline to worship, ni Dieu ni Maitre, in my work (in my intimate life I do believe in some kind of spiritual force)' (Castells, 2003, p. 149).

- Second, the reluctance to undertake the analysis of new information and communication technologies as heavy duty clusters triggering complex consequences for economic and political actors. This reluctance prevents scholars from appreciating the fact that media communications have become much more fundamental and primary than they were in the apparently forgotten and rejected but still tacitly present social ontologism of historical materialism. Old superstitions die hard and elements of super-superstructure (culturally generated social communications, transmissions and receptions filtered through and flavoured by theories or ideologies) remain safely isolated as part of an inventory of alibis for agents and agencies already pre-shaped by power and wealth. If our social ontologies were based on flows and events and not objects and locations, perhaps we would avoid problems in linking interdisciplinary research methods in order to account for technological-economic, political-managerial and cultural-ideological aspects of these transformational processes.[68] Perhaps we would be able to avoid partitioning the research area into academically defined domains and outsourcing parcels of research questions. There are some signs of theoretical hope. There is, for instance, an ambitious project of 'network society studies' of the 'information age' by Manuel Castells, which is based on an ontology of 'flows' and 'networks'. Castells's theory of network society appeals to sociologists and political scientists, but academically, he remains lodged between technology and society studies on the one hand and urban studies on the other.[69] Fencing multimedia flows according to an academic division of labour reflects the tacit assumption of their somewhat ideological, super-superstructural location in social ontology, hence a refusal to see them as the *spiritus movens* of social evolution and change. One might call this attitude of academic professionals – the *leftist reified essentialism*. It is a belief in the incredible lightness of media, whose messages are mere ideological reflections of the powers that be, reducible to states and markets. The consequence of this belief in the economic and political essence of mediated communications is an inability to see media professionals and stakeholders as increasingly unpredictable constellations of a fourth estate meriting attention as an increasingly sovereign actor (Clinton's Lewinsky affair, Princess Diana's death and funeral, live broadcasts from international Olympic Games and other similar cases signal this emergent role, which can hardly be reduced to a passive reflection of economic or political interests).

Puritanism and reified essentialism in the above senses are harmful because they prefabricate our attitudes even before we start articulating professionally our research topics. Researchers publishing studies of visual cultures and the new media with MIT Press, with academic depth (going beyond the lingering theoretical assumptions of historical materialism mentioned above) and political courage (identities are constructed as in 'flows' not given as in 'places', and some of these 'flows' can be conceptualized – after Appadurai – as 'mediascapes') might help produce a potentially more robust academic output, and there are some signs that this may happen. For instance, the vice-rector of the Open University of Catalonia in Barcelona, Imma Tubella, advocates the re-thinking of the communications-identity nexus, adding that:

> Today, classical elements of collective identity definition, such as language, territory, religion, common past or common future, are still relevant but there are other important factors to be considered, like the capacity for connectivity, cooperation and interaction ... and the ability to present and represent themselves ... It is very important to remember that collective identity is a collective consensus, a symbolic project, and shared interests, and that media in general and the Internet in particular are powerful tools to build it.
>
> (Tubella, 2004, p. 398)

Within the US academic context one should mention David F. Noble's *Forces of Production: the Social History of Industrial Automation*, which became a contemporary classic in the study of new technologies (and their sociopolitical scaffolding) with a clearly indicated interest in tracing the effects left by managerialist ideologies (CAD/CAM manufacturing) on material processes in economics and politics (the 'robotization' of car manufacturing and frequency of industrial strikes in Japan and the USA). Noble observed that one should reverse the old assumption about the priority of the material base and the secondary role of ideologies. The emergence and establishment of an ideology of top-down manufacturing design at the expense of organized labour had been – according to him – causally prior to 'material' effects. Choosing to ignore the human operators of machinery and to exclude them from a role in re-designing industrial robots had been a purely ideological decision prompted by frequent strikes in times of full employment. Exploiting this approach and investigating comparable linkages could lead to rapid growth in the production of both relevant and salient and academically 'respectable' knowledge on ideological media communications.

However, Noble (1986) has been marginalized in the academic community as a 'leftist' or a 'Marxian' – the labelling being a result of the 'traditional' (that is, 'originated in Cold War mobilization'), latent and tacit anticommunist streak in US academic HR policies, aggravated by the neoliberal and neoconservative backlash after the 1968 student movements.[70] Noble did strike back – with *Digital Diploma Mills* (2005) – but had far less influence upon research agendas than his academic merit, status and significance would have commanded if it had reverberated through academic bureaucracies (he is presently in Canada, not in the USA, which may be considered a mild form of academic exile). Communications, including mediated visual communications were thus academically fenced in – pushed close to 'cultural studies', 'art theory and history' and the 'cultural turn' in academic studies of visual rhetoric.[71] Appadurai himself complained bitterly about the effects of such fencing and marginalization. He is a professor of anthropology and South Asian languages and civilizations at the University of Chicago, hardly a marginal position within the US academic establishment, but he complained about difficulties in accounting for the voices from below in a public debate on globalization:

> Critical voices who speak for the poor, the vulnerable, the dispossessed, and the marginalized in the international fora in which global policies are made lack the means to produce a systematic grasp of the complexities of globalization. A new architecture for producing and sharing knowledge about globalization could provide the foundations of a pedagogy that closes this gap and helps democratize the flow of knowledge about globalization itself. Such pedagogy would create new forms of dialogue between academics, public intellectuals,

activists and policymakers in different societies . . . it might help even the playing field.

(Appadurai, 2001, p. 20)

Interestingly enough, attempts to break out of the academic corral have occasionally been made by researchers trying to make sense of the ideological sensemaking of the underdogs as reflected in artworks produced with mass media technologies, for instance feature films. Thus, for instance, discussing Bollywood's film melodramas, Bhaskar Sarkar observed that:

> The neoliberal transitional model of development relegates the post-colonies to the peripheries of history, casting them as underdogs – even victims. But victimhood is a deeply ambivalent subject position, for it comes equipped with a remarkable moral authority. Marginality, poverty, suffering have been tied to a moral stance, be it in the proto-Catholic humanism of Italian Neorealism, the revolutionary rhetoric of Third Cinema, or the telenovelas of Latin America. I argue that a melodramatic mode, which allows the underdog to have a moral upper hand, often comes into play when a wounded or marginalized subjectivity is the object of representation, whether in developed societies or in the developing world. And since melodrama as a genre provides a space for the symbolic negotiation of social contradictions through formal delays and deferrals, it is not surprising that the genre remains particularly popular in societies that find themselves forever in the waiting room of history.

(Sarkar, 2008, p. 48)

The author teaches at the Department of Film and Media Studies at the University of California in Santa Barbara, hence he is academically fenced *into* new media and artistic film studies, but he asks questions about the influence of these artistically mediated film messages on our awareness of economic inequalities and political asymmetries within the context of the third world gaining a voice through the creative use of the new media. He contributes to a refocusing of our knowledge about new media as powerful patterning influences upon contemporary sensemaking (for instance by articulating the ideologies of the underdogs). Likewise, an associate professor of English at Ohio State University (where she teaches feminist theory and transnational literature and cinema), Katarzyna Marciniak, also asks questions about ideological distortions – very much disseminated due to the tele-multimedia – of the image of the so-called 'Second World' after the end of the Cold War. Again, she is fenced in academically – teaching about literary and cinematographic works of art, defending the feminist point of view, publishing in *Obscura, Cinema Journal, differences* and editing a philosophical volume on postmodernism. From this academic periphery of mainstream political and ideological debates she tries to provide a theoretical analysis of an ideologically sophisticated masterpiece coming from the former Yugoslavia and giving a voice to those who had been turned into exotic barbarians by the mass media (she is discussing Manchevski's *Before the Rain*):

> I am specifically interested in the formal challenges that cinema faces in order to perform the Balkan conflict without reproducing the familiar impulse to binarize Europe (the civilized West versus the barbaric East). How can a critical tribute be paid to the region without falling into the predictable pattern of portraying the Balkans as 'the Other of the West' and 'the madhouse of thriving nationalisms' (Žižek, 1994, 212–213)? What textual strategies might be effective in subverting either a xenophobic or xenophilic illustration of the Balkan struggle or in representing violence against the usual scheme of sexualized entertainment or sublimated, sentimentalized brutality? How to enunciate the workings of the logic of ethnic violence without either demonizing or exoticizing the inhabitants of the Balkans? These are important questions, because they involve opening up representational practices that would allow for more complex registers of cinematic signification. In this context, these registers might give voice to the critique of the logic of ethnic cleansing, propelled by the idea of privileged and authentic citizenry.
>
> (Marciniak, 2006, p. 130)

Sarkar and Marciniak are not the only cases in point, but they are fairly typical. Media, artistic creativity and the reconstruction of ideological links to economic and political struggles all point to a growing awareness that under-investigated media links in sensemaking patterns deserve attention. Closer to the mainstream of US academic life, significant attempts to break out of this academic fencing had also been taking place within the MIT Press circle of authors and a growing literature on 'creative industries' produced by academic researchers in London and Copenhagen. Let us begin with the MIT Press, which was the earliest site of multimedia studies. Jonathan Crary's dictum – 'so much of what seems to constitute a domain of the visual is an effect of other kinds of forces and relations of power' (Crary, 2001, p. 3) – is the starting point.[72] Will his and others' efforts trigger a major shift of institutionalized academic research on the media patterning of sensemaking? To put it in a nutshell: responding to the fact that the media are becoming the messages, and that the competence of professional intermediaries running the media incorporates their economic links and political bonds (which flavour and colour multimedia communications and shape their connectivities, but do not turn media communications into mere 'effects' of economic and political pressures) is long overdue. When will multimedia communications gain more mainstream attention than has been granted so far by academic professionals within their institutional frameworks? Should we try a more multidisciplinary approach to the 'fourth estate'? If so, what platforms could trigger this shift? Can a tele-multimedia turn follow the 'linguistic turn' in social sciences? What is the best strategy for organizing research around the third cluster of patterning which co-shapes our sensemaking processes, carried through with numerous media and intermediaries? How to reverse the consequences of excessive academic fencing for relevant research?

Having corralled communication inside 'cultural' practices, researchers discovered that in the context of culture and art, social communication became 'lite'. Compared to the theoretical efforts of economists and political scientists, the role of symbolic communication in re-organizing economies and in re-engineering politics, studied as 'cultural practices', remains poorly rated. Politicians are interested in expertise in the field of political PR, hence the proliferation of spin doctors (a new professionalized domain of consulting services), but not necessarily in employing public research resources for the sake of future informed citizens. Business managers are interested in the expertise of commercial marketing and advertising companies with their total image and total experience designs, but not necessarily in vaccinating the general public against contagious commercial persuasion. If not them, then perhaps 'symbolic analysts' (the most critical segments of intellectuals, including academic researchers, media journalists, press critics and creative writers) will offer an alternative, more balanced, disciplined and critical approach? Kurt Tucholsky may have said that an image speaks more loudly than a thousand words, Susan Sontag may have said that every picture tells a story (adding 'or does it?'[73]), but an interdisciplinary, multifocal approach to multimediated communications is not particularly popular, and intellectuals themselves may also be blind to their own intoxication with the media. Thus critical research on mediation is not aided by academic bureaucracies or commercial interests and it does not appear as a priority on lists of projects undertaken by critical intellectuals. Some researchers have even found out that the most knowledgeable segment of the media public – professionals with higher education displaying political sophistication – are actually highly susceptible to media influence, especially as concerns 'swallowing', taking over media prejudices. For instance, Bolce and De Maio discovered in their study of media reporting on Christian fundamentalists, evangelicals and the religious 'right' (all of whom had been bundled together in the media as intolerant, extremist, violent and anti-feminist 'silent majorities' behind the electoral victories of conservative politicians – a powerful negative stereotype) that this stereotyping actually bred a tacit belief in the sinister rise of a fundamentalist Christian right ready to subvert democracy and plotting a crackdown on affluent and decadent lifestyles. Bolce and De Maio conclude that:

> Because cultural liberals are significantly more likely than traditionalists to stress that tolerating people with value systems different from their own is important, the prejudice these individuals expressed towards fundamentalists indicates either that they are unaware that this specific case (i.e. that the moral values of Christian fundamentalists are different from their own) and the general principle (i.e. 'tolerating moral values different from one's own is very important') belong in the same belief system, or that they are unwilling to extend this norm to at least one prominent group with value orientation different from their own. This phenomenon could represent a contemporary example of Allport's 'militant tolerance', a form of out-group prejudice driven by intolerance towards groups labeled as being intolerant, a syndrome that embodies the same 'overcategorizing and ... hidden psychodynamics' as classic forms of racism and anti-Semitism.
>
> (Bolce and De Maio, 2008, p. 175)

There was no particular economic or political interest behind the media mobilization of anti-Christian sentiment through negative stereotyping and overcategorizing – both had been initiated entirely in the media, an image created solely by media professionals involved in symbolic communications and appealing primarily to the better educated public. Target audiences were able to access and understand the most sophisticated media messages (hence the title of the research paper quoted above refers to 'a prejudice for the thinking classes' and to 'anti-Christian fundamentalists').[74]

But such studies are few and far between. Even if sophisticated multimedia communications are being analysed, the analyses usually cluster around a narrower, more specific aspect of visual anthropology or the ethnographies of television (see Derrida and Stiegler, 2002) or around a niche provided by a theoretical school. It may be the 'anthropology of image', 'visual anthropology', 'visual sociology', 'visual consumption' or 'visual culture', but it may also be a segment of 'contemporary art theory', 'theory of the new media', or 'communication theory'. Analyses often cluster around a selected aspect of multimediated communications – for instance, around political PR and the use of the media in organized politics, around commercial advertising and the stimulation of the consumer market by not always hidden persuaders, around the artistic avant-garde and the uses of mixed media such as photography, film, video and TV,[75] and around other articulated media contexts. What most critics and researchers seem to agree is that technologies of multimediated communications can – and sometimes do – lead towards a reconfiguration of agencies and agents involved in mediated communications. Reorganizing activities into more complex mediations with the matrixes of spheres or systems of producing value often assumes the form of reconfiguring of agencies. Interestingly enough, this reconfiguring had been noticed by one of the authors of *The Social Construction of Reality* (Berger and Luckmann, 1966). Thomas Luckmann was one of the first to comment on these processes of the re-engineering of the social communication of knowledge at the expense of past legitimizing criteria (Wikipedia is less reliable than Larousse or *Encyclopaedia Britannica*, because no systematic and yet open procedures have been agreed upon by both professional associations and user communities, but it is also much more accessible and in most cases provides sufficient initial information for most users):

> The rapid expansion of the Googles, Yahoos and Wikipedias shows that electronic media are taking an increasingly larger share in dissemination of knowledge, half-knowledge and bunk, largely uncontrolled for inaccuracy in capitalist and more or less democratic societies, and controlled for, or rather, against accuracy for narrow political and ideological purposes in autocratic regimes.
>
> (Luckmann, 2008, p. 288)

Wikipedia is slowly becoming an object of more systematic academic attention, though most of this theoretical reflection is still a chronicling of constitutive events (often written from a highly partisan participative point of view) and single case analyses (which are rarely framed within a more abstract theoretical explanation). There are signs that Wikipedia's most frequent users and suppliers are leaning towards the development of a professional oligarchy of those user-governance communities that tend to supply most of the entries and to control and select the others.[76] It remains to be seen if Wikipedia follows the iron principle of oligarchy, which Michels detected in early twentieth-century trade unions and whether these new professional oligarchies and oligarchs (if they try to capitalize on business opportunities) will engage in power struggles and succession wars similar to those which prompted Pareto to speak of 'the circulation of elites'. If indeed we witness the oligarchiza-tion of the self-appointed rule-making gate-keepers of Wikipedia, there will be an opportunity to trace the emergence of a new social agency out of the flows of tele-mediated communications (and, let us add, from among our peers in academic communities – privileged in their access to knowledge and quick to capitalize on it).

Let us try to reconstruct this re-engineering of actors and agencies under the influence of the new electronic communication technolo-gies (usually abbreviated as ICT – Information and Communication Technologies) and in relation to well established messages in social communication – for instance political stereotype-forming with over-categorizing, and artistic stereotype-breaking through performances and installations. In connection with such well-established genres, we have to be critical about classifications that are based on the 'content analysis' of media communications. One reason for caution is that neither a shift in mediated communications nor an overall re-making of agencies have to follow content, but can result from a transformation of the medium, the invention of new forms and the evolution of different contexts. Elec-tronic telecommunication media often appeal more to individuals and groups because of the enhanced connectivity (or chances for establishing new connections) that they offer than because of the increased volume of contents. As some critics have observed 'people tend to spend more on connectivity than on content'.[77] This restructuring of agencies has been the topic of some research, but mostly with respect to the reconstruction of the past. For instance, talking of the emergence of printed media in France around the time of the French Revolution, roughly from Diderot and the authors of the *Encyclopédie* to Balzac and an explosion of popular novels, Debray writes:

> It is in the eighteenth century that there comes into being a breed of authors who are not yet journalists but are forced to busy themselves with what it means to make a book, to compose it, get it into print, sell it, live from it. There are men of letters who head toward (whether or not from a directly interested business angle) the literal manufacture of the letter – the papermaking industry, foundry casting and the print trade – who are concerned as professionals with the business of the book trade, with literary property and copyright infringement or the pirating of copies ... This is why I cited Diderot in *Teachers, Writers,*

Celebrities as mediology's great-uncle and Balzac as its founding father. The genealogy exaggerates of course the literary aspect of mediations, but the two of them explored the three sides – political, technological, and cultural – of the mediological triangle. The essential correlation of the three poles did not escape notice of these honorable ancestors: powers of opinion over governments, networks of circulation of the sign, and the typology of the literary milieu.

(Debray, 1996, pp. 99–100)

Today's 'mediascape' (the term is attributed to Appadurai, who also introduced the term 'symbolic analysts', meaning 'intellectuals, artists, journalists, diplomats, businessmen and others ... as well as academics'; Appadurai, 2001, p. 9) is less transparent to us. One possible reason for this lack of transparency can be found in our relatively late and frag-mented attempt to understand the 'rituals of mediation' (see Debrix and Weber, 2003). When the US media conflate a raft of hostile prejudices against Christian communities – that they are traditional, rigid, dog-matic, rightist, violent, even antediluvian as far as women's right go – they are not mediating between any 'really existing' world of Christian communities 'out there' (that is, in front of the TV cameras and the editors writing comments and selecting recordings) and a 'really perceiv-ing' world of cultural liberals in front of the TV sets. They are doing much more, they are conveying a negative stereotype of an out-group that became particularly visible – and attracted stereotyping – when the media themselves focused on issues that set them against 'cultural lib-erals'. Sometimes these issues involved important social problems, such as abortion or euthanasia, sometimes relatively less pressing social issues (for example, the recognition of the rights of homosexuals to adopt chil-dren), but whether or not the issues were of a kind to attract modest attention from the public, with the intensified negative stereotyping of opposing groups the professionals servicing the mass media were able to articulate the 'news' in a much more dramatic manner. The hidden social costs of the media gain of increased attention lay in the increased negative stereotyping and the potential that lay therein for inciting acts of intolerance (symbolic or physical violence) against individuals either openly declaring religious affiliation or associated with fundamentalist Christian communities.

A self-reflexive critique of the hidden costs of the 'dramatization' of the news (firing the emotions with negative stereotypes that linger in the public mind long after broadcasts and issues are gone), of this on-going 'theatricalization' of social processes as they are being converted into media messages, could result in the introduction of indispens-able checks and balances of the media's tendency to stereotyping, could indeed open the often tacit stereotyping to public debate. It could help us to understand the in-built biases and prejudices of tele-mediated communications.[78] For instance, we could understand why Rocco Bottiglione's remark that 'homosexuality is a sin' prevented him from becoming a European Commissioner (with justice in his portfolio) in 2004, even though he declared that as a European Commissioner for Justice he would not act to criminalize homosexuality. He was still feared by the leftist members of the European Parliament whose anxiety was that his belief in the wrongness of homosexuality could lead him to discriminate against this sexual minority, even though he had made a clear-cut distinction between a sin and a crime and had no record of discrimination of any kind. He was 'purged' (Barroso had to with-draw his candidature from the list of proposed commissioners) because he had honestly presented his moral point of view. The anti-clerical and anti-Christian witch-hunters wanted personal moral views publicly streamlined into convergence with the politically correct cultural lib-eral dogma. The punitive approach of the deputies to the European Parliament towards Bottiglione contrasts with their refusal to take action a few years later when journalists discovered an article written in the 1970s by one of the leftist members of the European parliament, the German 'Green' party's Daniel Cohn-Bendit. Cohn-Bendit rode out a public admission that he had enjoyed sexual contact with five-year-old children in a 'progressive' kindergarten he was running in Frankfurt am Main. Rather than being condemned for paedophilia, he was admired as a cultural liberal exploring challenging lifestyles and pioneering extreme experiences for broader segments of the European population. Both the 'punishment' of Bottiglione for his public endorsement of his church's point of view and the 'forgiveness' of Cohn-Bendit for his public confes-sion of sexual adventures with children in his care[79] are closely related to media prejudices, which frequently boil down to black and white distinc-tions. Being associated with the Catholic Church, which is allegedly bad for impartiality and signals potential discrimination makes one black. Being associated with the leftist liberal political camp, which is sup-posedly good for impartiality and signals universal tolerance (well, not universal, because there is no tolerance for religious and rightist groups, but this is somehow defined as a 'lighter' sin) whitewashes one instantly. Leftist liberals are also associated with the socially progressive left, work-ing to increase the happiness of the masses, which is good for historical correctness and objective impartiality (after all, we are all progressives and believe that all chains should be broken, so objectively the liberators are closer to a historically correct point of view)[80] – so having sexual contacts with kindergarten children is exciting and charming, and opens up challenging lifestyles. These prejudices are built in to the reporting on both cases, built in to 'rituals of mediation', and produced mass effects (constituencies did not rise in support of Bottiglione, nor did they respond to the admissions of Cohn-Bendit – which would put them in the awkward position of having to revise the principle of unconditional liberation of all forms of human sexuality). Mediated negative prejudices pushed the leftist members of the European Parliament against a candidate for political position, while another mediated prejudice – positive this time – prevented any punitive action against a self-declared paedophile. The media succeeded in framing Cohn-Bendit's allegedly suspect activities within the larger leftist project of liberalizing and legalizing new forms of social interactions[81] In each case the communication process was one of persuasion, of contextualization within stereotypes and of networking for social action (or for refraining from action). By evoking ideological antipathies (for the Catholic Church) or sympathies (for leftist reformers in the name of the pleasure principle and for the good of reducing 'superfluous' repression wherever possible), professionals manufacturing messages communicated their preferences and shaped political outcomes.

Tele-mediated communications are obviously important for politics and politicians learn how to address their constituencies and how to try to create new ones. Politicians speaking to their constituencies make use of numerous professional intermediaries, including spin doctors, public relations firms and image creating companies. Some cynical observers go as far as to claim that the 'political effects of international events lie more in the pictures produced than in the agreements reached' (Brown, 2003, p. 154).[82] Politicians on both left and right have to devise a strategy for identifying a potential audience and turning it into a constituency through the manipulation of coordinated and arranged – and skilfully mediated – communications. Critchley articulated this as follows:

> The political task, then, is one of inventing a name around which a political subject can be aggregated from the various social struggles, through which we are living. This act of the aggregation of the political subject is the moment of hegemony. More accurately still, following through on the thought of the multiplication of social actors in the contemporary world, it is perhaps a question of inventing situated *names* for that around which politics can hegemonize itself and

then aggregating those names into some sort of association, common front or collective will.

(Critchley, 2007, p. 104)

However, media-induced, biased decision-making processes are not limited to politics. They are equally frequently encountered in the arts. Like politicians, artists communicating with their audiences make use of professional intermediaries – museum directors, exhibition curators, gallery owners, press and TV critics, academic theoreticians of art – through whose mediations works of art become commodities and in whose services these commodification processes are both embedded and professionally (ideologically) legitimized. Legitimization is sought by enacting 'rituals of mediation', networking (which social spaces, processes, timings, exposures and 'flows' can be instrumentally arranged) and value listing (which values and from which domains can be helpful in appealing to the audiences) and by searching for theoretical justifications of dominant artistic communications:

After the area of relations between humankind and deity and then between humankind and the object, artistic practice is now focused upon the sphere of inter-human relations, as illustrated by the activities that have been in progress since the early 1990s. Now the artist sets his sights more and more clearly on the relations that his work will create among his public and on the invention of models of sociability.

(Bourriaud, 2007, p. 48)

An artist who is often cited by critics and theoreticians focusing on creating novel ways of social communications by inserting critical self-reflection into social communications (not only critical reflection on others, which exempts the artist from examination, leaving him or her free to evaluate everybody else) is the Polish artist, living in New York and teaching at the Interrogative Design Group of MIT's Center of Advanced Visual Studies (of which he is also head), Krzysztof Wodiczko. His installations, exhibitions and public projections take place all around the world. He has become known for his 'Interrogative Design' projections, which beam images onto city buildings, turning them into giant screens and inviting passers by in urban spaces both to rethink social or political issues and to question the architectural language of power radiated by the same buildings during the day (the most famous projections have been installed in New York, London, Washington, Berlin, Boston, Krakow, Hiroshima, Basel, Warsaw and Caracas).

On the dome of Tijuana's Centro Cultural Wodiczko projected an image of a Mexican worker with his hands clasped behind his head, as if he was an illegal immigrant to the USA, about to be arrested by the US border patrol during a foiled attempt to cross the fences or by 'La Migra' during a search for illegally employed immigrant labourers on a farm or in a sweatshop. Inside the theatre's auditorium under the dome, audiences can watch a film on Mexican civilization, which is presented daily. When evening comes, Wodiczko's projection on the outside of the dome suggested a narrative in order to open a public debate about contemporary Mexican civilization – where Mexican migrant workers are writing contemporary history. Subject to negative stereotyping, exploitation and administrative repression, victims of crimes that both the US and the Mexican authorities are eager to suppress ('missing women') but nonetheless indispensable for the US economy, these migrant workers are writing an important chapter in the contemporary history of the underdogs. (Illustration 4.2 shows part of the projection on the dome of the Cultural Centre in Tijuana.) In Kassel, in 1987, Wodiczko came to a city that had been rehearsing the evacuation of its inhabitants because of the extent of the potentially hazardous pollution from the industrial sites that surround it. He projected an image on the tower of the Martin Luther church of a worshipper praying to God while dressed from head to toes in a protective anti-chemical and anti-radiation suite and wearing a gas mask. In Madrid, soon after the outbreak of the first Gulf War in 1991, Wodiczko beamed images onto the triumphal arch constructed to celebrate Franco's victory in the Spanish civil war. He projected two giant hands onto the columns of the arch and beamed a word followed by a question mark across the top. One of the hands held a machine gun and the other a gas pump nozzle, while the word was 'Cuantos?' ('How much?'). No wonder in his book on 'Public Addresses' Wodiczko speaks of attacking buildings at night, when they are 'asleep' and their 'bodies dream of themselves' (Wodiczko, 1992).

His 'Homeless Vehicle' a shopping cart redesigned according to the suggestions of its homeless users, the city poor in New York, could be used as a mobile shelter. It has subsequently become part and parcel of the homelessness project realized in many social spaces. The vehicle and the project made city dwellers aware of those whom the vehicle would protect. That it is not produced on a broader scale is due to the artificial 'invisibility' of the homeless. We see them, but fail to register the necessity to account for them in our thinking of social progress, economic improvement, political emancipation, and the like. They become invisible when we dream of the 'good life' and the satisfaction of our needs,

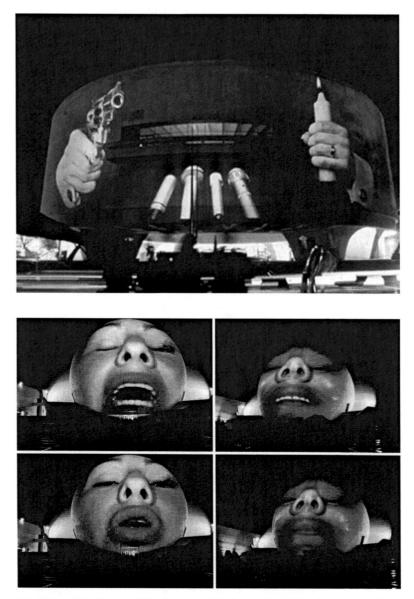

Illustration 4.2 Krzysztof Wodiczko, Public Projections, Hirschorn Art Gallery, Washington DC (above) and Cultural Centre in Tijuana, Mexico (below) (courtesy of the artist)

because any anxiety that the survival of the most vulnerable members of our communities is at stake could introduce cognitive dissonance into our ideological daydreaming.

In his 'Alien Staff' project Wodiczko sent foreign immigrants carrying staffs to walk the busy New York streets and to confront passers by. He mounted miniature TV monitors on the staffs and while the immigrants themselves remained silent their recorded faces spoke from the monitor screens and told their stories, which otherwise would have remained untold. Interpreting Wodiczko's artistic project from the borderland between art criticism, political theory and communication in re-arranged media, Debrix (who teaches political theory at Florida International University) notes that:

> As a ritual of representation, Wodiczko's 'Alien Staff' may be taken as an allegory for the impossible passage of some individuals in democratic political systems from the status of alien to that of citizen. Similarly, 'Alien Staff' could be interpreted as a ritual of transformation that denounces the unequal status of some individuals in a society vis-à-vis others and thus calls for the change of condition ... Wodiczko provides a pluralizing model of mediation ... What Wodiczko's plural approach to the manipulation of the medium and to the use of mediation wants to avoid is not the fact that mediation is being used to produce social meanings. This, Wodiczko suggests, is inevitable and in a sense, desirable. What it wants to avoid and what it protects against is the idea, prevalent among proponents of mediation as either representation or transformation, that desirable social meanings are decided and often established before the method of mediation even has a chance to deploy its cultural and political effects.
>
> (Debrix, 2003, p. xxxix)[83]

The last comment is particularly important because it reflects an idea that a creative artistic intervention in contemporary urban space requires a certain self-reflexive and self-critical refusal to except oneself as a privileged participant in mediated communications. If we place ourselves in a privileged position (the best and the brightest experts, the best and most sophisticated creative artists and the like), we distinguish ourselves from other participants. We are granting ourselves a privileged status. Every critical discussion is allowed, except the one in which our status is questioned, even if it was questioned by those on whose behalf we allegedly perform.[84] Wodiczko does not 'speak up' for the immigrants of New York, he does not replace them in public debate nor represent them before politicians and constituencies. He creates a new mix of media, he confronts New Yorkers with immigrants and immigrants with New Yorkers, rearranging mediated communications and giving the voiceless immigrants a voice through electronic media which provide a starting point for a public debate about selected underdogs (in Wodiczko's projects these might have been illegal foreigners, inhabitants of a city threatened by industrial pollution, homeless or voiceless immigrants).

Examples from the domains of arts and politics should allow us to trace the transformations of the concepts of 'charisma' and 'aura', and to trace them specifically from the point of view of the pluralizing model of mediated communications. The pluralizing model of mediated communications would not reinforce negative stereotypes but would help us strive for the joint creation of a more inclusive categorization of 'others'. The concepts of 'charisma' (in politics) and of 'aura' (in art) have been in popular use since Max Weber smuggled the former into social sciences and Walter Benjamin smuggled the latter into art theory and the philosophy of the mass media.[85] (Weber wrote at the beginning of the twentieth century, Benjamin mostly in the 1930s, but their influence spread beyond the academic world after 1968.) Would it be possible to trace the role of the media in the long march from *charisma* (in politics), and *aura* (in art) to *celebrity* (political as well as artistic; the category of celebrity is more inclusive than the former two) in multi-mediated communications? Can some important media campaigns be interpreted as attempts to return to a re-engineered and media-repackaged re-enchantment? Re-enchantment as communication process re-engineering? With celebrities 'magically' (re)turned into the imagined 'charismatic leaders' and artists (re)composing a lost 'aura' of aesthetic experiences – are we witnessing and co-producing this re-enchantment? Are contemporary multimedia producing sequences of (re)enchantments taking us back to 'charismatic leaders' and 'auratic art experiences', this time multi-mediated, globally standardized, virtually re-packaged and 'glocally' adapted and adjusted versions of mobile and mobilized symbolic images?

First, let us try to see what constitutes 'charisma' and how it travels through historical transformations of sensemaking processes in order to end up conflated with 'celebrity' status (the granting of which is not entirely transparent). How do we recognize a charismatic person or an 'auratic' artistic experience? What made John F. Kennedy or Mohandas Gandhi, Lech Walesa or Nelson Mandela 'charismatic' leaders in the eyes of their followers and of the audiences of the world media? What turned Leonardo da Vinci's 'Mona Lisa' or Andy Warhol's portrait of Marilyn Monroe, a live concert by the Rolling Stones or a live performance of

Bach's Goldberg variations by Murray Perahia into 'auratic' experiences for viewers and listeners? A vast majority of the viewers and listeners of these experiences had neither seen nor heard the un-mediated physical originals. Most of their experiences were through recorded, re-heated and tele-digi-communicated 'copies'. Nevertheless, one does not have to be in the physical presence of the original (a person or a work of art or an arranged experience) in order to experience them as charismatic or auratic or to discuss the aura with others, both those who have had physical contact with the original and those who have not. But how does one recognize charisma or an aura?

Do we recognize charisma and aura because our attention has been turned in a premeditated way towards a particular person or a singled out performance by the media? Are we conditioned through repetition? Do we start to value some people or performances above others because of their framing and frequency in the media? In other words, do we perceive objects or persons in the media and value them favourably because the media have smuggled in a tacit evaluation matrix under the guise of frequent favourable representation? Are we the victims of media reiteration of manipulated, pre-shuffled stocks of knowledge and traditional interpretations (shaping our tacit expectations)? Or do we value first[86] and then focus on particular aspects of mediated communications, demanding their more frequent media presence? If frequency precedes valuation, we would start noticing charismatic persons and auratic objects or events *after* valuation had already been performed. Or do our knowledgeable and informed senses first fish auratic experiences out of the ocean of images, and value them later? And could it be that both processes take place simultaneously, that we zigzag from value to frequency and from frequency to value?

Moreover, the statement 'we value' is profoundly ambiguous: it is not clear who 'we' are: consumers, experiencing audiences, critics or promoters, theoreticians or media intermediaries, art exhibition curators or gallery owners or lovers and buyers of art works? Research on Wikipedia found that a very small minority of all contributors supply more than 80 per cent of all the retained entries (Baker, 2008). Are they the prospective oligarchy of Wikipedia, the new elite among the free and equal contributors to the creative commons? Or perhaps we are all real and virtual *flâneurs* – but only a small minority of us take notes when walking along and make sure others read them. Perhaps we are all virtual passers by – waiting to be provoked by a creative artist to a salient debate and the performance of the responsible role of concerned citizen (a debate on illegal immigrants, glass ceilings for women, manageable inequalities?)

The problem remains: while we want to participate in a democratic forum in which meanings can be produced (for instance, the development of a just integration policy for immigrants), how can we best detect and disarm prejudice, especially our own, if producers are not keen on granting us a right to talk back to their tele-mediated messages and sponsors and journalists have their own agendas?

Let us return to aura and charisma. Do we judge the charismatic persons and auratic objects first (because they are, for instance – respectively – brave and beautiful) and start noticing them later, because we are searching for work under responsible political leaders and for rewarding experiences with aesthetic values? Or are we initially surprised and attracted, persuaded to fish something special out of the media flows, to focus on it and to force the media to report on it particularly frequently, and only later come to ascribe to our chosen objects the 'second best' type of charisma and aura – celebrity status, which seduces us with the appearance of higher value? If my leader is not what I would expect, at least his or her image is more successfully projected in mediascapes than the images of the others. If my aesthetic experience is not a very sophisticated one, at least the artists who provided it are popular and their images are frequently broadcast. Warhol sensed exactly this junction of media receptivity and growth of aesthetic attention and turned to the media, betting on growing aesthetic attention afterwards. Today's great artists of the multimedia in public spaces – Krzysztof Wodiczko, Bill Viola, Edouardo Kac or Christo and Jeanne-Claude – use the media in their work, but do not advertise themselves as celebrities; they do not require the biennials, the fashionable galleries, the in-crowd critics, because they are not on their way to becoming superstars of the visual arts. They prefer to step aside in order to leave space for the individual imaginations of their audiences, they prefer gently coaching communities' creativity. They advise and persuade others to reflect on possible responsible civic actions. Wodiczko's projects demonstrate to us the need to safeguard a certain flexibility within the media and a degree of interactive feedback, and an in-built self-reflexivity of communications (the latter should reflect our values, valuations and tastes, all of which should be up for negotiation in pluralist spaces and not up for grabs by oligarchies and monopolies).

The paradoxes of attention deficit have been well observed by critics of *Homo sapiens* and the damage caused by omnipresent commercial advertising have also been recognized, although less frequently subjected to systematic analysis. For instance, Georg Franck, an architect and urban planner from Vienna, studied the 'political economy of attention' and 'mental capitalism'[87] and noted a disturbing circularity around the political economy of attention and ambiguity about the acknowledgment and ascription of value. Do we pay attention to what we value, or do we value what we pay attention to?

Franck does not discuss Christo and Jeanne-Claude, Kac,[88] Wodiczko or Viola, but we may try to see how these artists prompt us, their audiences, into a more reflective, interactive role of 'talking back' in urban media-filled spaces. The Wrapped Reichstag in Berlin or the Wrapped Pont Neuf in Paris, a mobile shelter vehicle for the homeless in New York or a public projection in Hiroshima – all these experiences are meant to help audience members to think along new lines. There is no coercion; no clasping of hands, no aesthetic homage are expected. Critical reflection and the possible sparking off of a civic initiative are appropriate responses and the artists' rewards. When we see these artists' installations and participate in their performances, we are already graduating from higher classes in media literacy – and the metaphor of graduation is not innocent. It assumes teachers who grant us the grades and decide if we pass or fail. When we positively evaluate our experience of these artistic creations – performances, installations, paintings, sculptures, happenings, interventions – do we recognize that we are choosing them over others (we are not choosing Koons, Dali, Spielberg[89])? Our choices are guided and confirmed by those to whom we listen – by critics, reviewers, journalists, reporters – but also by less 'visible' (at least to the mass audiences) opinion makers – theoreticians, academics, 'authorities' mobilized by the media or responding professionally to new artistic phenomena. The lurking suspicion is that we are much more finely tuned to their whispers, their prompting than we are aware of or would admit to. Are we not pre-programmed by all those assembled media professionals – the critics, curators, gallery owners, media journalists, art teachers, researchers and theoreticians and other professionals – who make us notice some art works more frequently and in more auratic context than others? When do we begin to value as they do, to accept their valuations as if they were our own, and when are we aware of their influences? Some authors come up with the concept of weak ontology in order to explain that those influences are mediated by our individual ability to feel 'awe, wonder or reverence' (White, 2000, p. 9; Bennett, 2001, p. 163) and thus we ourselves are responsible for 'filtering' them. Moreover, the critical artists are re-enchanting social spaces without putting a 'spell' on us (as the Dalis and Koonses and Spielbergs do) and without imprisoning us in passive 'captive audience' roles.

Wodiczko's oeuvre, composed of public projections, tools, vehicles and installations, wearable communication instrumentations ('Alien Staff', 'Porte-parole', 'Aegis', 'Dis-Armor') is one of the finest examples of a remediation, of redirecting and rearranging mediated communications so as to experiment with new intermediated matrixes for the democratic patterning of our sensemaking practices. His artistic use of contemporary electronic communication media (beaming images onto buildings or using monitors on staffs) illustrates an opportunity for a 'paragrammatic' approach to tele-multimedia. Not only visual artists are capable of taming tele-multimedia. Creative uses of new communication media are potentially accessible in all walks of life, which includes the academic professions. We do not have to act on a large scale, with major buildings and large city centres as our stages. Creativity, like charity, can begin at home and in the office. Yiannis Gabriel, who proposed the term 'paragramme' in order to describe 'flexible routines, allowing users to improvise, innovate and reconfigure' (Gabriel, 2002), recently applied this concept to the uses of PowerPoint by academic teachers, arguing that:

> instead of replacing arguments, theories, narratives and stories with images, lists and graphs, PowerPoint can open up the possibility of juxtaposing and comparing arguments with lists, enriching narratives with images and adding to the clarity of theories with graphs ... it can provide a learning and teaching experience in line with the visual sensitivities and skills of our times.
>
> (Gabriel, 2008, p. 272)

Gabriel is right: patterning matrixes for sensemaking processes in contemporary settings require us to be paragrammatic, that is to be artificial by nature, to rely on flexible routines in performing our balancing acts. We have to learn how (please note the PowerPoint bullet points pointed at you):

- to question our bureaucratic shells, but rely on them for managing complexity (so that new, reconfigured agencies can emerge in a predominantly bureaucratic environment);
- to question our commercial exchanges but to rely on them for increasing connectivities and segmenting exchanges (so that new modes of interacting can be sustained);
- to question our tele-multimediated communications, but to rely on them for broader and more sophisticated dissemination of knowledge and skills (so that hyperconnectivity can give rise to new modes of mobilization and identity forming).

5
Case in Point: Scaffolding for a Critical Turn in the Sciences of Management

The arrival of a critical turn in the contemporary sciences of management was not unexpected and prompted one of the established gurus of the managerial sciences, Henry Mintzberg, to proclaim that MBA programmes were dead. Based on narrowly dogmatic but institutionally privileged (it is tempting to label them 'barren') paradigms and irrelevant research, they were less than useful for future managers. So said Mintzberg during the Academy of Management annual conference in Honolulu in 2005. A critical attitude towards mainstream managerial sciences has subsequently become a permanent feature of the AoM publications.[1] By reconstructing critical incidents in the recent history of research communities we can track some of the individuals, ideas, events and processes that provided the scaffolding for this critical turn. For example, we might ask, when did the first get-together of researchers who later shaped critical management studies take place? When were the basic ideas that led to this meeting first articulated? Flows of ideas and the emergence of schools and research topics are still easier to track through the memoirs of retired researchers and by following their informal chats than through openly accessible information sources on research communities and their outputs. Members of research communities are not particularly eager to provide detailed lists of the social events and personal relationships which became relevant to the construction of networks, platforms, templates and other elements of scaffolding for a school, a movement or a twist and turn of their output. They are reluctant to cooperate because a rational legitimization of new schools, trends and fashions in social sciences requires referencing. References direct researchers to an accepted model of 'scientific rationality', which presumably does not 'mutate' in response to contingent and emergent contextual and temporal differences. The same holds true for politics (even though politicians differentiate their communications depending on the audience that they are addressing and their currency is legitimacy not rationality) and art (even though artists offer different rationalizations of their performance vis-à-vis sponsors, clients, critics and professional colleagues and their currency is the quality of aesthetic experience, not the rationality of insights offered). Hence the booming market for memoirs and other personal documents of 'history in the making'[2] in politics and in art. Science and scientific communities are no exception. Only indirectly can one reconstruct the emergence of patterning clusters by sifting through the official records of conferences, congresses, seminars, meetings, or the contents lists of journals and books. The narrative that follows a reconstruction of the emergence of a 'critical stream' or 'linguistic turn' or 'dialogic approach' or 'narrative school' is usually a critically reconstructed story told about a certain theme, which can be distinguished by names, events and ideas.

Such a narrative could be constructed on the influence of the Frankfurt School's critical theory on managerial sciences. Some authors are pessimistic:

> Critical thought is aestheticized and privatized, stripped of any political implications. There can be no politically relevant critical theory and hence no theoretically informed critical practice. No place is allowed to those large-scale theoretical accounts of socio-structural change that are basic to any politics which aims at restructuring social institutions. We are prevented from even thinking, in any theoretically informed way, the thought that the basic structures of society might be inherently unjust in some way, that they might work to the systematic disadvantage of certain social groups.
>
> (McCarthy, 1990, p. 122)

Others, however, are more hopeful. The story of critical theory in the social sciences in general and in the sciences of management in particular could be told from the point of view of a participant and fellow-traveller who had something to do with the triggering process, and who took part in some of the constitutive events that can now be perceived as stepping stones in the construction of the emergent stream of research around the 'critical theory' theme ... It is hard to keep on talking about myself in the third person, so let me add that the story about to be told 'ended', as of the present writing, when I became, along with David Boje and Yiannis Gabriel, a convener of a track at the most recent, July 2007, Critical Management Studies (CMS) conference in Manchester. In the nineteen years between November 1988 and July 2007, the CMS research community grew and gained recognition in and on mainstream academic institutions and platforms. This particular reconstruction will take us back to the end of November and the beginning of December 1988, when the scaffolding for the revival of critical theory was set up and some of the main characters in the revival were assembled on the (academic) stage.

The origins of the 1988 Rotterdam conference were formal, bureaucratic and contingent. In 1988, Erasmus University Rotterdam celebrated its seventy-fifth birthday (dies natalis). I had contributed to these celebrations by organizing (together with Frits Engeldorp-Gastelaars)[3] an international conference entitled 'The Frankfurt School: How Relevant is it Today?' (30 November–2 December 1988). In the introduction to the first book of proceedings published after the conference, the scientific supervisors – Engeldorp-Gastelaars and Magala – claim that:

> The idea of the congress was conceived independently by both scientific supervisors. Dr van Engeldorp-Gastelaars thought about it during his year at the NIAS[4] in Wassenaar (1984–1985) and during his conversations with prof. dr J.S. Folkers, operations research specialist at the Interfaculty of Business Management in Delft, and dr Otmar Preuss, professor of sociology of education at the Bremen University who studied at the Frankfurt Institute of Social Research (the Bremen University was founded in 1971 with a focal point being education and the scientific understanding of many professors based on the Critical Theory of the Frankfurt School). Dr S. Magala conceived a similar idea during his 'Habilitationsschrift' post-doc research in Frankfurt am Main in 1981 and 1984 as a Humboldt fellow of Alexander von Humboldt Stiftung from Bad Godesberg, and during his discussions with the youngest generation of critical scholars of the neo-Habermasian brand, Axel Honneth and Helmut Dubiel in Frankfurt, Bonn, Stuttgart and Dubrovnik.
>
> (Engeldorp-Gastelaars et al., 1990, p. 7)

We wanted to convey the impression that critical theory was not only relevant to the academic community, but that it was also important in many other non-scientific domains of culture, particularly to art (visual arts, media arts and literature) and we therefore designed a 'halo' of cultural events around the scientific congress itself. The conference was thus consciously framed by a series of cultural events preceding, accompanying and following it from September to December in many of Rotterdam's cultural institutions (museums, exhibition halls, theatres, concert halls and lecture rooms). These events included a series of public lectures on social engagement, which had been directly associated with the legacy of the Frankfurt School. Speakers debated the legacy of the student protests of 1968, discussed the evolving nature of the 'green' movement from the Club of Rome to green parties in national parliaments, speculated on future forms of feminism and on transformations of the university as a multifaceted institution subjected to new pressures from multiple social agencies. Some of the speakers at those public events made a political career within national and European political frameworks in the following years. A discussion of the legacy of student rebellions opened with a public lecture by Pim Fortuyn, who went on to become a populist political leader and might have become the prime minister of the Netherlands, had he not been shot dead during the electoral campaign on 6 May 2002.[5] A discussion on price tags for fresh air and clean water was opened by the chairperson of the Green Party fraction at the regional parliament in Hessen, Germany, Joshka Fischer. Fischer went on to become the first Green minister of foreign affairs in the ruling coalition of German social democrats and the Greens (1988–2005), and from January to June 1999, he was chair of the Council of Europe. Another participant – my fellow Humboldtian[6] from Serbia, Zoran Djindjic – became prime minister of Serbia in January 2001 (he was assassinated in 2003).

The accompanying events included exhibitions illustrating 'Frankfurter Zeitgeist' and Frankfurt's post-Second World War cultural rebirth, as well as ballet, theatre and film performances from Germany (one of the visitors, Anselm Kiefer, went on to become one of Germany's best-known painters, while another became an extremely idiosyncratic film director in Munich: Hans-Jurgen Syberberg made a dreamlike, six-hour long film on Wagner entitled 'Hitler: a Film from Germany' and wrote a public intellectual's essay on the 'spiritual diagnosis of the times'). One of the most unusual artistic events was organized together with the Rotterdam Philharmonic Orchestra, which performed – for the first time ever – six short pieces for the orchestra composed by Adorno (in a programme with compositions by Adorno's admired composers – Schönberg, Berg and Hindemith). Habermas did not come, but Luhman and Sloterdijk, Jay and McCarthy, Honneth and Arato, Howard and Erasaari, Dubiel and Forester did – together with about 250 other active participants. Leo Loewenthal – one of the original members of the Frankfurt School, residing in California at the time – had agreed to come, but was ultimately prevented from travelling for health reasons (he was 94 when the invitation was issued).

Not all participants shared our point of view – some questioned the identity of 'critical theory' as a product of the Institute of Social Research.

Martin Jay, himself the author of a significant contribution to the making of this identity in contemporary social sciences (as the author of 'Dialectical Imagination'), warned – quoting himself from the book on dialectical imagination – that 'identity may best be understood as the product of a force field of untotalized and sometimes contesting impulses that defy any harmonious integration' and concluded that:

> In the case of the Frankfurt School it is precisely the dynamic intersection and overlapping of discrete context that provided the stimulus to their work. Their constellation of tensely interrelated ideas, themselves never achieving a perfectly harmonious synthesis, was thus enabled by the irreducibly plural and often conflicting contexts of their lives ... The Frankfurt School's favorite phrase *nicht mitmachen*, not playing along, thus comes to mean more than just a defiance of conventionality and political camp-following; it defines instead the very conditions of their intellectual productivity, and perhaps not theirs alone.
>
> (Jay, 1990, pp. 142–3)

From our point of view, that is, from the point of view of our focus on the potential applications of the critical theoreticians' insights to the sciences of management and organization, the following participants merit special attention: Barbara Czarniawska, Mats Alvesson and Hugh Willmott, Risto Erasaari, Thomas McCarthy, Peter Sloterdijk and Dick Howard.[7] I will focus on the first three, since they were most successful in orchestrating movements within the research community. Alvesson and Willmott contributed to the creation of a new network of critical researchers under the rubric of 'Critical Management Studies', which forms a relatively flexible, relatively established and relatively '*salonsfähig*' (respectable), versatile community assembling once in two years (as if following the example of the most famous biennials in visual arts – Venice and Kassel – but not the model of the Academy of Management or the European Academy of Management, both of which meet annually[8]). The representatives of this cluster of researchers have their roots in the 1992 publication by Mats Alvesson and Hugh Willmott, *Critical Management Studies*. The book grew out of the original paper for the Rotterdam conference. Back in 1988, Alvesson and Willmott announced in their paper 'Critical Theory and the Sciences of Management' that:

> Through critical reflection upon knowledge and practice, such as that associated with a narrow, technocratic conception of 'management' and 'science', CT [critical theory] is seen to expose their connection

with the material, historical contexts of their everyday reproduction. In doing so, CT also offers an alternative account of why so much 'science' of management is found to have limited applicability. For, in disregarding the inescapably political and ethical (communicative) dimension of social reality, it generates theories and prescriptions which are excessively idealized. The understanding of the complex and contradictory quality of the contemporary labor processes is so superficial within mainstream MS [managerial sciences] that its abstractions often have little relevance for the complex, politically charged, problems of organization encountered in the office or on the shop floor.

(Alvesson and Willmott, 1990, p. 24)

This manifesto was followed by an analysis of contemporary developments in critical social sciences, especially of the Habermasian theory of communicative action and of the applications of insights derived from this theory in different domains – for instance, in Forester's approach to organizational planning practice (John Forester of Cornell University also participated in the conference; I had invited him because of the Frankfurter-Habermas connection). In conclusion, the authors point out the need to be relevant to those, who 'are actively engaged in shaping the contours of the "real world"'(ibid., p. 68). Commenting later (2008) on this paper, the subsequent book on critical management studies and the movement in the sciences of management, one of the authors, Hugh Willmott, said:

CMS [critical management studies] draws together disparate elements into what, from the outside, can appear as a unified counterweight to the established template-in-use. Positively, the sprawling and ill-defined nature of the CMS constituency makes participation and association comparatively easy, with low barriers to entry (but also exit). Nonetheless, from the outside, it might be assumed that CMS is a rather doctrinaire, sect-like movement where only converts or supplicants feel comfortable. Tellingly, however, self-defined Mainstreamers who have ventured into CMS meetings report a different story.[9]

Willmott points out that since the first critical management studies meeting, which took place in the UK in 1989 and attracted about 25 participants (ten years later, in 1999 the bi-annual event attracted 350 participants and this number had doubled by 2007), much has changed in terms of legitimizing the movement professionally. Participants have been offered professorial positions in business schools of major universities, research agencies have financed projects and seminars, and mainstream academics are not afraid of associating with the CMS participants. As an editor of a journal devoted to organizational change, I can confirm this diagnosis. Thus the latest call for papers for a special issue of the *Journal of Organizational Change Management* ('Movement of Transition 20 Years on: Identities, Ideologies, Imaginary Institutions') is signed by Marianna Fotaki, Steffen Böhm and John Hassard. In this ad hoc editorial team, Fotaki is characterized as a member of the Critical Management Studies Interest Group at the Academy of Management meeting in Philadelphia in 2007, Böhm as open-access journal and open publishing press co-editor and co-founder, while Hassard is a professor of organizational analysis at the Manchester Business School and Judge Business School at Cambridge University and a board member of the Society for the Advancement of Management Studies. This combination indicates a degree of recognition and professional acknowledgment of CMS within the broader academic community. Since many personal memories of the scaffolding events tend to exaggerate the contribution of the author, let us add that Willmott also duly notes that the Rotterdam event of 1988 would not have had the effect it had if there was no tradition of stand-alone, self-funding conferences in the UK, which offered a template for further action and legitimization within the academic institutional environment. Willmott mentions the Labour Process Conferences, which have been around for the past 25 years and adds that: 'experience gained in organizing these conferences was crucial for the design and delivery of Critical Management Studies Conferences' (Willmott, 2008, p. 3).

Let us note Willmott's conscious use of religious vocabulary in an ironic self-definition of a 'sectarian' climate for converts and supplicants, which might deter 'normal' researchers. This is echoed in the Wikipedia entry on 'critical management studies', where questions of inclusion and exclusion are mentioned as central issues debated by the participants, as is the high number of members of the CMS Interest Group within the American Academy of Management (800) – higher than the membership of many more established associations within the AoM, which are also less international in their constitution. While acknowledging the pioneering and founding role of Alvesson and Willmott, with their stress on the Frankfurt School and Habermas, the authors of the Wikipedia entry add, as influences, 'Foucault, Derrida, Deleuze, feminism, queer theory, postcolonial theory, anarchism, ecological philosophies and radical democratic theory'. Once again they are quoting Alvesson and Willmott, this time from *Studying Management Critically* (2003) and they also mention a reader edited by Grey and Willmott in 2005. Thus they broaden the list of the influences shaping the present theoretical frameworks and methodological sympathies of critical researchers of management. Legitimizing the ideology of the professional institutional scaffolding for CMS takes a less 'religious' and more 'political' turn of phrase in Wikipedia:

> Wider impatience with market managerial forms of organization is common enough outside the business school, from anti-corporate protest to popular media presentations of managers. What CMS attempts to do is to articulate these voices within the business school,[10] and provide ways of thinking beyond current dominant theories and practices of organization.
>
> (CMS/Wikipedia, 2008)

Self-referential aside: perhaps a reader could gain a better insight into the ambiguities of CMS's recognition and embedding in professional academic environment when reading the following brief exchange of self-ironic emails between Hugh Willmott and the present author:

Original Message ——

From: *Slawek Magala*

To: *Hugh WILLMOTT*

Sent: *Saturday, March 22, 2008 9:39 AM*

Subject: *RE: RE: cms*

Dear Father Hugh,

first of all thanks a lot. Second, two remarks on my main points of interest

a) the religious language of cms seeing themselves as a sect comfy for converts and supplicants (quite right, we do formulate our evaluations of clusters and interactions in religious idiom)

b) the paradox of our closest allies in criticality and progressiveness contributing to the most dogmatic rankism and rankophilia as a result of their merging into bureaucratic landscapes of academic institutions (quite right, rankings are seen as a level ground, where no sympathies or paradigmatic feuds will mar the picture, but they do bring about even more blindness and randomness) will send you what I did with it in my forthcoming book with a plea for Christian forgiveness if chopping you down into a quote

your humble co-believer

father Slawek[11]

Van: *Hugh WILLMOTT*

Verzonden: *do 27-3-2008 18:05*

Aan: *Slawek Magala*

Onderwerp: *Re: RE: cms*

Dear Father Slawek

Your abbey must indeed be cosier than our cells in which we do try to squeeze as many sinners and outcasts - such call us 'critters'- as we can.

As a high priest of the sacred order of research assessment I could not possibly comment on rampant rankophilia. I can only hint at the exquisite masochistic pleasures derived from the evaluation rituals.

Your fellow cross carrier,

father Hugh

Cardiff Penitentiary

End of personal aside

Another interesting development that was signalled at the Rotterdam event and subsequently considered significant from the point of the later theoretical developments for which it had provided the scaffolding is the 'narrative turn' in management studies, exemplified by the brilliant Polish-Swedish researcher, Barbara Czarniawska, who was torn between increasingly prestigious roles within academic institutions (she was an associate professor in Stockholm School of Business at the time of the conference, and is currently a member of the Swedish Academy of Sciences and a professor at Goteborg University) and her critical designs linked to broader cultural interests. As a true European, she writes in English and Polish, speaks fluent Swedish and Italian and invites broader humanist exchanges of ideas. She does so by participating in conferences such as 'The Role of the Humanities in the Making of the European Elites', organized by Pascale Gagliardi at the Cini Foundation in Venice against the background of the visual arts biennale, or in small, elitist humanist seminars requiring a passion for the novel as an art form and an area of research, for instance, 'Novel and Organization' organized by Martyna Sliwa at Essex University.

In 2008, it is possible to claim that Barbara Czarniawska, along with David Boje and Yiannis Gabriel, is a founding parent of the narrative turn in the sciences of management.[12] In 1988 this was – obviously – not yet evident. Czarniawska's major contributions to this research stream came later, but her *Ideological Control in Non-Ideological Organizations* appeared in 1988, and 'Narratives of Individual and Organizational Identities' in 1994 (as a chapter in a book edited by Stanley Deetz; see Czarniawska, 1988, 1994). Her mature works, *Narrating the Organization: Dramas of Institutional Identity* and *Writing Management: Organization Theory as a Literary Genre* were published in 1997 and 1999 respectively. Back in 1988, as a participant in the Rotterdam conference, Czarniawska presented a paper on 'Rationality as an Organizational Product: on Multiple Rationalities and Organizational Learning'. She tried to define organizational realities as man-made realities in physical, symbolic or political 'space', claiming that organizations should be perceived as 'complex, systematic actions of construction' and, referring to her 1988 book, described them as 'systems of collective action undertaken in an effort to shape the world and human lives'. She said in her 1988 paper for the Rotterdam conference that:

> rationality is a product of an interaction between people who use it retrospectively to legitimize what has already been taking place ... Rationality, then, is the crucial product in every organization and the key accomplishment in everyday organizational activity.
>
> (Czarniawska, 1990, pp. 116–17)

Closing her discussion with a broader analysis of the implications of her research programme for social sciences in general and the sciences of management in particular, Czarniawska evoked Rorty's concept of rationality as 'civility' and Habermas's concept of an ideal communicative situation (in which a coercion-free dialogue between individuals and groups becomes possible). She pleaded for an analysis of sense-making in organizations, which would focus on 'translating of values into goals and not goals into means' (ibid., p. 127) and urged social scientists to come up with a language allowing for more transparency in rationalizations of collective actions performed in organizations as they 'streamline' management of meaning, asking fellow researchers to focus on an interpretive and empirical approach and on rationality as the 'ultimate legitimation' in professional bureaucracies:

> More specifically, we could analyze how people engaged in a collective action decide what is rational and what is not. How is rationality produced and for what purposes, and how are the clashes between multiple rationalities handled in front of internal and external audiences? What is the politics of rationality?
>
> (Czarniawska, 1990, p. 129)

Since I had met Barbara Czarniawska (then, Barbara Czarniawska-Joerges) at the SCOS conference hosted by Pascale Gagliardi at the Catholic University in Milan in 1987, we might say that the historical tracks of the Critical Management Studies, Standing Conference on Organizational Symbolism and Standing Conference on Management and Organization Inquiry can be reconstructed – ex post – as crossing each other in Rotterdam at the end of 1988 in not entirely predictable ways. Looking back, it is tempting to say that meeting at the critical theory conference made sense, but the senses we were making of it at the time were not entirely clear even for us as participants. Some of us, however, also working within the critical theory track inspired by the Frankfurt School – for instance Risto Erasaari (then at the University of Jivaskyla, and now at the University of Helsinki) – had already been toying with the idea of a 'network society' (he had derived this from Helmut Dubiel's concept of societal 'inner cultures' such as family, neighbourhood and social networks), which was to gain popularity in the late 1990s: 'Network model is one conceptual and sociopolitical means with the help of which contemporary society is being transformed both from above and from below – following the motivational idea that this actually happens from within' (Erasaari, 1990, p. 107).

There are more themes that could be traced back to this conference, but a complete inventory would distract us from the main theme here. Let us thus return to the management of meaning, to the rationalization of the meaning of meaning. What did this conference mean for the construction of meaning in the sciences of management and organization? From a distance of twenty years, we can see that all three elements of the 'past tense of meaning' inherited and embodied in the 'present tense of meaning' were criticized from the point of view of a postulated 'future tense of meaning'. Thus the universalist concept of manageable rationality (embodied in professional bureaucracies) was criticized within the critical management studies research community as well as by the representatives of the 'narrative turn' in organizational studies (where critical research conducted in business organizations from alternative methodological standpoints has often been labelled 'organizational ethnography' and is associated with Czarniawska, Denzin, Van Maanen, Burawoy, Gabriel and Boje among others[13]). The liberal concept of a marketplace as the matrix for shaping organizations (of exchanges, of interactions, of ideas and influences) was criticized from several directions:

- *Alternative methodologies.* If organizational rationality and commercial accountability are achievements rather than blueprints imposed from above and valid until CEOs and Nobel Prize winners in economists announce their change, then these achievements should be studied *in statu nascendi*, as Rorty studied 'achieving our country' and not as frozen and immutable 'iron rules', 'universally valid exchange converters' or 'principles with a re-enchanted aura'.[14]
- *Within the ideological articulations of new social movements.* If early twentieth-century social sciences were burdened with the original sin of working within the framework of a middle class, which feared 'unruly working class mobs' and thus developed knowledge for policing rather than emancipating the underdogs, then alternative globalists, environmentalists, feminists and counter-culturalists try to compensate for this with self-reflective balancing act and with re-inventing democracy.[15]
- *Through the countercultural components of socialization in the network societies.* Social scientists specializing in comparative intercultural studies of work organizations – of whom and for whom Hofstede is the most influential example – assumed that individuals are socialized in three consecutive 'matrixes'. Family is the first – children are influenced by parental authority and religion. School comes next – teenagers are influenced by national educational curricula. Workplace comes last – young employees are influenced by managerial sciences offering HRM policy suggestions. Critical social studies trace and trigger the emergence of alternative identities and clusters within professional bureaucracies, networked communities of practice and mobilized clusters in public domains.

The increasing critical focus on tendencies towards rationalization and commercialization manifested within the institutional arrangements of self-reflexive research communities was accompanied by a growing awareness that 'every picture tells a story'; and this is especially true if the main stream of an aspect of social communications acquires overwhelmingly visual characteristics as it reaches individuals in their mobile multimedia cocoons. Thus the multimedia connection is criticized in relation to both hidden[16] and less hidden persuaders ('no logo day', Naomi Klein) and with the aim of arming the audiences with the means to 'talk back', to 'feedback' to the media co-authors and to co-shape the mediated telecommunications. We have are witnessing a growing awareness of the need for new concepts of increasingly complex multimedia communications. We would like to see media allowing for a much more rapid recycling, renegotiating and dissemination of meanings. Particularly valued would be access to interactive feedback, especially from the point of heretofore excluded minorities or other 'silent' members of societies 'talking back' to those images that speak out more loudly than words. The underlying tacit expectation makes us look for a chance to break the code of ideological domination orchestrated for and through contemporary multimedia.

6
The Future Tense of Meaning (Cultural Revolutions, Social Transformations and Media Rituals)

Can comparative studies of fundamental transformations in such domains of culture as science, art and religion help us recognize the contours of changes to come? Can the patterned clusters of change processes perhaps best be described as 'socio-cultural revolutions' and as 'socio-cultural transformations'? Or should they be seen as series of clandestine plots and underground deals between various domains of culture and society? Since the development of mobile individualized connectivity and the emergence of telecommunicational infrastructure, we can also speak of a qualitative leap forward in the 'theatricalization' of daily life. Even a relatively marginal public order disturbance at an open-air rock festival or an outbreak of aggressive behaviour by football fans at a regional game can immediately be amplified and presented in the media as a major threat from sinister 'angry mobs'. Charles Baudelaire and Walter Benjamin had to look for the shape of the future among middle-class *flâneurs* in the well-lit and crowded centres of Paris or Berlin – our contemporaries have instant access to illuminated virtual passages, linkedIns, wikipedias and 'second lives'. It might be said that our contemporaries have transcended the selected spaces and 'illuminated passages' of concrete, palpable, material cities functioning as metropolises for social imaginaries (Paris, Berlin, London, New York). We have moved into a multidimensional space of online arrangements, simcities and instant utopias. At the beginning of the nineteenth century a French avant-garde dramatist, Alfred Jarry, wrote a grotesque and absurd comedy *Ubu Roi* which opens with the information that the 'Action takes place in Poland, which is nowhere.'[1] If it were written today, it could open with 'Action takes place in virtual space, which is nowhere.'

> In a dictatorship 'what is shared' is imposed; it rules because its subjects are not allowed to act otherwise. 'What is shared' rules also in a

democracy, but not because its citizens either cannot think and act in any other way or because they have been forbidden to think and act in any other way; 'what is shared' rules because the citizens have decided to orient their public actions (*not* all their actions) temporarily (*not* forever) around a simple program (*not* around a 'rational foundation' or a 'humanitarian ideal' – though either can play a role in the choice of the program). The program is conceived by individuals, it rests on their idiosyncrasies, and it disappears when they do.

(Feyerabend, 1999, p. 263)

Past cultural revolutions – those inspired by the invention of writing or the reinvention of print in Europe, the dissemination of literacy and numeracy and the like – are easier to trace than the cultural revolutions that might emerge out of the invention of the internet. The very format of 'cultural revolution', the very emotion of 'Sturm und Drang', the generation of 'the young Turks' might twist and turn and change. Contemporary programmes of the management of meaning cannot be taken for granted when we discuss the future tense of meaning. Some or even most of them will become extinct or may undergo far reaching transformations. Programmes are mortal. They can be articulated as business projects, community initiatives, 5-year plans or as scientific research methodologies, but they are bound to involve imagined continuities and clandestine exchanges with other domains of cultural creativity and the 'creative industries'. Christianity's programme for the individual salvation of all members of a community or the Enlightenment programme of collective progress and individual development are cases in point. Christian communities stress continuity in spite of transformations inside and outside of them. The Enlightenment is defined as an 'unfinished project', evolving as do our rationality and social order projects. Even if programmes promise immortality to individuals who implement them – eternal salvation, for instance (or market expansion, or a classless society, or more satisfying experience, even more truth discovered per square inch of lab floor . . .) – they may still decline and be replaced, reinvented, redesigned, rejuvenated and re-engineered. Equally mortal are the institutions in which programmes are articulated and pursued, embedded, supported and killed off. Even if organizations claim longevity beyond the lifetime of a human individual ('a thousand year Reich', an 'invincible Soviet Union', a 'royal academy with an unbroken tradition of scientific progress', the 'continuity of the apostolic church', a 'medieval university devoted to the eternal search for Truth and equipped with state of the art laboratories'), they are still liable to break down, fall apart, disintegrate, disappear – and thus, metaphorically speaking, to die.

When programmes are being designed and their institutional implementation is being organized there can be no foreknowledge of their potential mortality or resurrection rates. Resurrecting a programme is sometimes described in terms of long-term 'sustainability' rather than 'immortality', since the contemporary secular idiom is not compatible with the reinsertion of a religious mode of thinking into the mainstream of social life. The programme of building a strong party-state to prepare for world revolution and a global classless society ruled by a single party representing the proletarian masses died – not only metaphorically – when the Soviet Union dissolved in 1991. A new style Soviet Union seems neither a candidate for resurrection (nor a sustainable prospect) in the near future. The communist party of the Russian Federation might still be capable of protesting against the depiction of communist rule in the latest Indiana Jones movie, but it cannot win a majority of votes in elections nor attract a global following with its programme for constructing a classless society (nor can it prevent the disputed film from being shown in 200 cinemas throughout the Russian Federation). However, it should not be forgotten that the successes of communist and socialist parties in the past (the memory of which will influence our management of meaning in the future) depended crucially on the ability to mix a scientific theory of industrial economy with a political ideology of shifting power to the powerless. The management of meaning was linked to knowledge produced by academic professionals (for instance Marx, who linked capitalist profits to the exploitation of labour) and by trade union organizers (who linked improvements in the wages and social status of workers to the success of socialist parties in parliaments and communist parties in revolutions). Making sense when talking about the future tense of meaning may depend on:

- our ability to avoid both reification of methodological research programmes (and their equivalents in other domains of culture – for instance aesthetic schools in artistic communications or political ideologies in social governance games) as if they were immortal and 'fixed' (the fate of the 'historical materialism' of the communist parties provides a stern warning against such fixing); and
- our ability to avoid the anthropomorphization of individual organizations or collective institutional contexts[2] (as if they were resurrectable 'carriers' or even 'saviours' of worthy programmes and causes), which is what happened to political parties (notably the communist ones)

and business corporations (most notably the multinationals) when they designed policies to make themselves 'immortal' (at the price of putting themselves above the law).

Neither programmatic contents nor institutional embeddings can or should be taken for granted. When Feyerabend wrote *Against Method*, he was treated as an *enfant terrible* of the Popperian school, both because he considered himself as a methodological anarchist (escaping the academic dictatorship of professional research communities and their unholy alliances with the powers that be) and because he drew an analogy between his anarchistic scientific methodology (which he had designed on the margins of the Popper-Kuhn-Lakatos-Musgrave debate)[3] and the Dadaist anarchism of early twentieth-century avant-garde art. Both anarchism and Dadaism merit attention, because they influenced the course of history by broadening the spectrum of possible and imaginable choices.

The Dadaists were trying to escape the trammels of artistic conventions linked to aesthetic tradition, market promotion and political ideologies (although the irony of history placed Tristan Tzara and his Dadaist co-founders in a Zurich café – 'Club Voltaire' – also frequented by Lenin, who had little sense of humour or ironic distance between himself and his cause[4]). While the Zurich Dadaists met under the leadership of Tristan Tzara, a French Dadaist in New York had changed the history of both contemporary artistic practices and aesthetic theory. Marcel Duchamp's defiant work of art, 'Fountain' (signed 'R. Mutt'), was submitted to the Armory Show jury but never actually exhibited. It had thus never actually been accessible to the gallery-going public in New York. Nevertheless, it was duly chronicled in Alfred Stieglitz's photographic documentation of the Armory Show. Documented, listed and illustrated in the catalogue of the show in spite of its physical absence, it had become virtually accessible to critics, historians, curators and theoreticians and everybody else studying the US avant-garde. It has since become the most significant, relevant and salient component of the show and the single most creative contribution to the management of meaning in artistic practice and aesthetic consumption. For all practical purposes (except those of the original visiting public, especially if visitors failed to purchase the catalogue) it had 'really' been there. Duchamp's urinal has also become a cause célèbre, a clear example of a work of art without intrinsic properties, like *A Man without Qualities* (to quote the title of Robert Musil's novel describing the same period). Duchamp triggered a re-evaluation of the concept of the artistic avant-garde in artistic communications; pointing out to critics and audiences alike that the intrinsic properties of the work of art were not decisive in shaping our judgement and experience. His submission to the Armory Show had been purchased from a warehouse and signed in the false name of 'R. Mutt'. The artist's signature and the exhibition's context determined experience and judgement, the value and appreciation of audiences and publics. Nobody would have noticed the urinal had Duchamp been a construction worker and painted 'R. Mutt, the fountain' as graffiti on one of the stacked construction pieces on a building site. The context (art show) and legitimizing procedures (selection by a professional jury) mattered, while the material constitution and the fabrication procedure did not. The idea of an artistic creation mattered more than the material, palpable object representing or embodying it. It was these contextual positionings ('we are making an art show') and these legitimizing procedures ('everybody who submits a signed work and pays five dollars can participate') that determined the value of the aesthetic experience, not the material components of an object called a work of art or the artistic techniques employed to produce it. Duchamp's urinal had been mass produced by a construction company supplier, but it was signed by him and put inside the artistic exhibition space to be seen and experienced as a work of art, not as part of a sanitary installation.

Emergent re-evaluations of the great debates in the philosophy of science will probably also result in an upgrading of Feyerabend's contribution to our understanding of the matters of rationality. Methodological research programmes disguised as universal norms are open to criticism and cannot be dogmatically protected from it.

Some attempts at dogmatic protection have been made by particularly conservative sociobiologists calling for a universal recognition of 'consilience' at the expense of the diversification of research communities and programmes, or by critics of postmodernist methodological and theoretical 'promiscuity', writing parodies of hermeneutic texts and publishing them in *Social Text* (the article, entitled 'Transgressing the Boundaries: Towards a Transformative Hermeneutics of Quantum Gravity', was followed by two books, namely *Fashionable Nonsense* and *Beyond the Hoax*: Sokal, 1996, 2008; Sokal and Bricmont, 1999). However, such attempts to protect established boundaries in academic communities are quickly forgotten. Academic institutionalism cannot be ideologically protected from a free debate on sociopolitical power struggles disguised as modernization or the defence of rigorous knowledge production – they have to remain open to political renegotiation and cannot be isolated from it (at least not everywhere and not in the long run).

Due acknowledgment of Feyerabend's significance may take longer than the rise of Duchamp's reputation. A contemporary art critic can call a book *Kant after Duchamp* (de Duve, 1998), but contemporary philosophers of science do not yet write books entitled *Popper after Latour* or *Kuhn after Feyerabend*, because science lags behind art in recognizing, acknowledging and accommodating change, due to the pressures of 'imagined continuity'. When an art critic wants to understand Duchamp's significance, relevance, salience for contemporary aesthetic communications, s/he writes about the twentieth century, a century of political disasters and artistic breakthroughs, with two world wars, two industrial-scale genocide programmes (Soviet Russia and Nazi Germany) and a string of scientific and artistic avant-gardes. The latter stretch from Duchamp to Warhol, from Picasso and Dali to Bacon and Beuys. The former include the quantum and relativity theories in physics, biochemical theories of genes and dynamic flows and emergent theories of local and thick knowledge (for example, behavioural finance). De Duve, who wants to re-read Kant after Duchamp notices that the *critical function* (moral and aesthetic) introduced by the early twentieth-century avant-garde to art separates it from the art of the past. For this art critic (and he is not alone) the future tense of meaning is thus linked to expected breakthroughs and he confidently predicts that an avant-garde artist, for instance Rodchenko, will still be considered an artist when we change our criteria, while a more traditional, figurative painter, for instance Bonnard will not, simply because Rodchenko was part of a cultural revolution of the European futurism, and Bonnard was not:

> critical function had to be absent from artistic production prior to the historical emergence of the project of humanity's emancipation, a project that dates from the Enlightenment and marks the beginning of modernity ... Once it appears in the artworks, the very function of critical vigilance – precisely because it is new – radically severs them from the past, it further forbids anyone to valorize art forms that failed to make the same break on their own. The only modern art of significance and quality is avant-garde art, and any art that is satisfied with exerting functions that predate modernity (placating taste, for instance) loses its value as well as its critical function simply by being retarded, retrograde. When push comes to a shove, Rodchenko is an artist and Bonnard is not.
>
> (de Duve, 1998, p. 432)[5]

Feyerabend's theoretical pamphlets, although too passionate and too free-floating between different domains of culture for the conservative academic fashions of the late twentieth century to allow them to enter the mainstream of academic discourse, may guide us towards a better understanding of cultural revolution, drawing their energies from 'translations' and analogies between science, art and morality. These analogies should be studied, especially if we want to understand the future tense of meaning. After all, to understand the future tense of meaning, one should ask why 'we', our professional group of academic professionals, closed ranks and praised Feyerabend's wit and brilliance, while at the same time making sure that he did not acquire an institutional foothold in research communities. One should ask why the author of *Against Method* remained an academic nomad, wandering between Vienna and Berkeley, between his 'Popperian' peers and his young disciples (who found 'Dadaist' theoretical reflections useful in legitimizing their post-1968 attitudes), between artists and scientists, between leftists and conservatives, between traditional intellectual professions and emergent media professionals? Or, perhaps, one should ask, after the contemporary representatives of critical anthropology analysing 'science wars', if the blocking of the appointment of Bruno Latour by the mathematicians at the Institute for Advanced Studies in Princeton (Latour's status and impact in research communities was far higher than that of his enemies) did not signal the resentment caused by:

> the expansion of the humanities curriculum to incorporate work and research agendas from cultural studies, media studies, postcolonial studies, feminism and gender studies. The claim of those reacting against any expansion of perspectives or questions was that these new initiatives constituted attacks on intellectual foundations of knowledge.
>
> (Fischer, 2003, p. 5)

Fischer linked this hostile response to the frustration of the representatives of exact and natural sciences (especially nuclear physicists) after the US government refused to finance the Texas elementary particle supercollider and he attributed the shameful treatment of Latour to their misguided outburst of anger against humanist 'softies'. The ire of the mathematicians was misguided, because they assumed that the humanist 'softies' were the main threat to science as they know it. However, humanists accept the rigours of organized and systematic inquiry and question only the dictatorship of the neopositivist vision of science, which often combines logical analysis of the language of science with stern empiricism. Meanwhile a true enemy of scientific pursuits looms large somewhere else. Fischer pointed at the creationists in Kansas scheming to remove the Darwinian theory of evolution from the school curriculum and called them the real enemies of researchers' status and prestige in society. He also pointed out that:

> the real action in the 1990s and the first years of the twenty-first century was not in these minor academic skirmishes. Rather, it was in the growth of social movements demanding transparency and public accountability for work done in the technosciences as crucial to the development of more complex civil society in the twenty-first century.
>
> (Fischer, 2003, p. 6)

While I disagree that these kinds of conflicts within research communities are necessarily minor skirmishes (somehow less real and relevant than the large-scale processes of civil society's pressure to make the alliances of researchers with politicians and corporate leaders more transparent), it is hard not to agree that for most members of our societies it's not the methodological arguments but the accountability and transparency of the entire research community (and its dealings with government funding and corporate sponsorship) that matter most. This is what will determine the future flow of knowledge creation and technology development, and knowing the professional, personal and political pedigree of knowledge 'bites' (legitimizing public spending) makes sense. This is what will be decisive in the future tense of meaning. But the methodological arguments also matter, because the inputs of academic communities, frequently divided on vital issues, may change the course of large-scale mobilization by shaping and framing public opinion, which – in turn – might be mobilized to press politicians and business leaders to action.

The future tense of meaning is much more difficult to discuss than the past or the present tenses – not only because we have by definition not yet experienced it within our own realities and not only because we have not yet processed it within our 'memory manufacturing' systems. The future tense of meaning is also more difficult to envision because of the sheer quantity of possibilities for institutional and geographical outsourcing of the manufacturing and servicing of values and meanings in our contemporary over-connected[6] and hyper-communicative (one is almost tempted to say 'garrulous') societies; hence we do not know where the new clusters of agencies and new socio-cultural transformations will be coming from. Moreover, it is much easier to predict possible ideological inventions and political interventions if we assume dogmatic continuity – whether of a church, a party or an academy – all of which have been questioned. The most recent witticism on this subject – 'causa locuta, Roma finita' (see Žižek, 2008, p. 1) – captures the historical reversal of roles in the management of meaning. In the last millennium of European history, the ideological domination of the popes interpreting the world once meant that if they spoke (from Rome), the case could be considered closed, because they were the ultimate authority. Hence – *Roma locuta, causa finita*. The most famous Slovenian public intellectual wanted to stress the fact that the general public no longer accepts a single authority. Cases are tried, considered, discussed, and, if necessary, decided upon, in a way which dispenses with heretofore dominant authorities by ignoring or disobeying them and by refusing to consider a given case in light of their doctrines. Hence the fate of a cause in a free debate may result in 'finishing' with Rome – the control of meaning moves towards the local, the concerned, the involved, away from ultimate and solid authorities, distant but dominant.

It is much more difficult to predict the outcome of any particular case of the management of meaning if we are dealing, as Foucault rightly observed of the Enlightenment, with *fidelity to an attitude rather than to a doctrine*. Bourdieu quoted Foucault and Bakunin, not Feyrabend and Tzara in his essay on 'How to Effectively Establish the Critical Attitude',[7] but he could have quoted Feyerabend and Tzara as well, had he considered them to be public intellectuals on a par with Foucault (who managed to stay within the academic establishment while sponsoring the causes of the underdogs) and Bakunin (who was marginalized by the mainstream Marxist ideologues and growing working class movements in the late nineteenth and early twentieth centuries but managed to remain within the political discourse of anarchism and anarchosyndicalism long enough to avoid obscurity).

Choices between patron saints – Foucault and Bakunin and not Feyerabend or Tzara – and the possibility of their prompt reversals (in an ongoing re-evaluation of all results of the management of meaning in societies, in which 'people must be told everything'), are symptoms of future social and cultural choices, which will not easily be decided by existing social actors and clusters of agencies. Let us mention three cases in point.

First, there is growing concern among academic communities, primarily in the agro-sciences, that world food production should be protected from multinational corporations. The latter allegedly prey upon local agricultural markets and decrease the overall efficiency of food production (although not the profitability of their operations in the eyes of their shareholders). Mantras on economies of scale may well turn out to be no more than ideological deceptions – if we ask 'whose scale?' and 'whose economies?' often enough. Will the corporate giants further increase the risk of world food shortages or will the danger of food shortages be averted by an alliance of ideological programmes (exposing neoliberal fictions and fuelling less fictitious explanations) and networked political and economic institutions (holding the Parmalats and Walmarts at bay)?

Second, there is a growing trend for lifestyles with less conspicuous consumption and more spiritual depth. Will the new chastity movement among European Christian youth – no sex before marriage – influence our lifestyles (and birth statistics) more than the more permissive sexual morality implied in the yuppie vision of a 'single's paradise' (after all, it is not only internet promiscuity, but also the 'generation of John Paul II' or 'Generation Benedict' that attract millions)? Such unanticipated expeditions from one domain of culture (youth lifestyle) and from one social walk of life (generational cohort's subculture) to another (religious community, social movement with religious inspiration influencing individual and public sexual morality) abound (bulky treatises entitled such as *A Secular Age*, see Taylor, 2007, notwithstanding).

Which brings me to the third case. Media specialists have apparently taken over some of the tasks of the judicial and executive branches of governments. Investigative journalists have replaced private detectives and public prosecutors in finding out 'whodunit', while media campaigns present thrilling true-life crime stories directly and immediately to the public, bypassing legal due process and allowing emotions and biases to explode on screens, pages and over the radio waves. The splendid isolation of jury members in locked rooms is a thing of the past and so are the former norms of privacy or clear distinctions between emotionally 'cosy' private spheres (family, household, intimate erotic relations, old boys and girls networks, in which one is authentically 'at ease') and an emotionally 'cold', calculative workplace, where an alienated, reified individual kills time and makes money, playing out his or her artificial, instrumental, temporarily assumed, social and organizational roles.

We do not see these changes as they happen, because we still tend to perceive them according to past ideological associations to which we have linked them. We can work with laptops, notebooks and iPhones, but we still pretend that a screen is a page, even if it is a webpage and the persistence of bookish associations remains a charming anachronism and a purely artificial convention. Medical professionals still behave in their contact with patients according to codes of conduct based on unquestionable authority and superiority – but patients have access to second and even hundredth opinions and no longer blindly accept the authority of their doctors. Patients have become more active in soliciting second or third opinions and collecting relevant information; but the entire institutional arrangement of health-care (most significantly insurance policies) rests on this authority and has not yet been modified. Since patients and students are huge populations serviced by the two fastest growing multiform professional bureaucracies, any cultural revolutions or social movements among these two categories of individuals are bound to have significant consequences for the future.[8]

The future tense of meaning is also less accessible to analysis and more difficult to present analytically because it is hidden behind 'smokescreens' (formerly known as 'ideologies' or 'opium for the people and for intellectuals' or 'shared illusions') of our own making. How can we clear these smokescreens in order to see what is to come? So far, we have learned that the first step towards detection and reduction of smokescreen effects requires a critical self-reflection.

Self-reflection – individual (does what I take for granted in being myself make sense?), social (does what we witness in transparent interactions make sense?) and professional (does my community of practice actually follow what it preaches or does it preach only to legitimize choices post hoc?) – within an ethnic or a religious, gendered or generational reference group is one starting point. In the European academic and philosophical tradition this self-reflective mode of analytical re-engineering had been traditionally associated with Descartes, Kant and Husserl. This was, is and still would be the basic choice of acknowledged authors associated with self-reflection in the broadest sense and acceptable to all paradigms. However, this allows for only a very rough and approximate 'image' of self-reflection; and we do not want to set readers off in hot pursuit of Husserl's disciples and the many different tracks taken by their numerous followers and critics. The disciples would include, for instance, Heidegger and Arendt, Ingarden and Stein, and the French prisoners of war who first read Heidegger in early 1940s in their Oflags – Sartre, Levinas and so on.[9] We are thus mostly concerned with reconstruction of the past, preferably relatively recent ways of 'worldmaking', and with exploring some analogies, even if our declared intention is to research the future ways of sensemaking and meaning management. The recent past and the present are our preferred research periods. We have seen the attempts to reconstruct the sensemaking and management of meaning by architects 'behind the postmodern façade' (Larson, 1993) and we have noticed how they employed aesthetic criteria to increase the economic value of their services. We have also seen the attempts to reconstruct critical management studies within the business schools tucked inside the academic institutions geared to service business corporations and public authorities. Business schools were designed to produce skilled middle and upper level employees, not critical and creative individuals capable of changing the course of institutional histories and triggering cultural revolutions, but their status within the academic and business communities often depends on their ability to trigger critical and creative reflection. This triggering role requires tapping the margins of the academic world (as was the case with the Frankfurt School) or enlisting strangers to the business community (as was the case with Foucault or Bourdieu, the numbers of whose followers are growing, as reflected by the number of tracks and papers at the annual conferences of the established academies of management).

In Chapter 4 we outlined this development within a professional community of academic researchers specializing in the sciences of management and organization. We reconstructed the roots of critical management studies on the basis of the self-reflective memories of networked researchers involved in the launching of this movement within the professional communities of academic specialists. There emerged a 'social space' enabling academic researchers with a critical twist of mind and with a certain distrust of latent managerialist ideologies to come together, to articulate the programme and to shape a part-time movement, which became accepted by a larger academic community. Feyerabend remained an isolated theoretician, who triggered the self-reflection of fellow-professionals with his extremist idiom, himself leading the bohemian life of a self-declared anarchist on the margins of the broader scientific community. Alvesson and Willmott embedded self-reflection in a new social movement within the professional community, interacting from within the mainstream networks of researchers.

But for the fact that the author of the present reflections was placed within the network of personal relations that came to constitute the 'founding fathers' generation (as a result of a slightly irregular international conference that contributed to the articulation of ideas that were apparently waiting to be born), this reconstruction would not yet have become possible, and communications would still be being made behind the ideological smokescreens of academic communities. These smokescreens deserve our attention.

Our ability to predict some of the properties of the future tense of meaning depends to a large extent on our ability to pursue the analysis of three particular smokescreens that slow down our understanding of 'what do we do when we mean what we mean'. This is an awkward formula, but expresses a self-reflective attempt better than, for instance, the question 'how is an academic (political, religious, aesthetic and so on) discourse articulated and justified?', because it allows both for more distance to discourses and for a broader view of the academic and non-academic contexts in which they are embedded. These three smokescreens are:

- The smokescreen of controlled communications of professional academic communities, which appear to imitate the medieval guilds by enforcing the quest for quality as a professional monopoly on legitimate knowledge production. By securing this monopoly through bureaucratic control, but stumbling over issues of the legitimacy of institutional arrangements and the broader relevance of monopolistic services, academic communities create fertile ground for dissidents, rebels and heretics. New research movements like that of critical management studies are cases in point and so are the matrices of 'cultural revolutions' or 'new social movements' or 'fundamental reforms' as socio-cognitive constructions facilitating the breakdown of temporary monopolies.
- The smokescreen of spectacular and inevitable commercialization, which seems to be a historical necessity. Commercializing the political activities of the public authorities in post-welfare states in order to 'sell' them to the constituencies perceived as consumers of political PR follows a vision of democracy as a sequence of consumer choices. New consumer movements, such as the 'slow food' movement, 'no logo', 'buy-nothing-day' and emergent constituencies reinventing participative/deliberative democracy with 'virtual commons' are premonitions of things to come. They might render the conspicuous consumption of political PR less glorious and promote more difficult, labour- and commitment-intensive participative-deliberative alternatives, making them more attractive in the eyes of the post-consumerist beholders.
- The smokescreen of tele-mediated social communications with the in-built inequalities and disproportions that guide the attention of receivers, educate the mass public in sophisticated visual code-breaking and coach audiences towards attitudes and preferences hampering the recognition of significant and relevant problems. The existence of this smokescreen slows down individual and collective focusing on our reflexive and self-reflexive analysis and derails the negotiation of public choices (dramatized rituals for identifying possible, feasible, desirable action and mobilizing for it in 'converted' public spheres are cases in point).

Before we examine these smokescreens individually, artificially separating them from one another, let us add that in real life they all work together and their influences upon our cognition, perception, analysis and design of actions are inevitably intertwined. Thus the policies of academic research communities shape expert opinion, which has a dominant influence on the making up of the 'public mind' and its appearance in the theatre of political life. Rituals of political communication (packaging soundbites, manipulating imagery) prepare the ground for the media to report on what the experts think and to determine what their audiences should see and hear. The education of media professionals moulds their minds according to the political expectations and preferences of academic professionals (who train media specialists and supply them with expertise). Note that the public interface of all research communities and to a large extent of all political organizations is formed by an 'expert' or by units of 'expertise', which are usually determined by individuals with academic credentials, who further continue the dissemination of acquired preferences, sometimes dogmatically frozen into stereotypes. The pro-female professors brochure of the EUR was prepared by academically credited professionals. Expert opinion is produced within the institutional context, of which little is known (the general public does not examine the 'inner life' of expert communities – hence the need to reconstruct the origins and dissemination of schools, trends, movements, if we are to judge the relative merits of differing expert opinions).

What is known is not easily traceable nor accessible for the general public, which is presented with 'expert opinion' wearing a 'halo' of legitimacy. Moreover, all expert opinions are framed under the influence of the institutional centres of political decision-making. This institutional embedding precludes some choices and strongly favours others. Thus, only some political choices are presented in public as rational, realistic or feasible, in much the same way as consumer choices. Others remain 'unrealistic' in the same sense in which it would be unrealistic for me to try purchasing an item which is not on sale in a supermarket I shop in. Very much like consumer choices, political choices come with price tags – but these price tags reflect 'political market' forces and not the hopes to which constituencies might have held during their seduction by political spectacle. These choices are formulated within institutions in which inequalities are neither recognized nor accounted for. Hence the persistent silence about the underdogs; focusing on the underdogs would mean articulating a political agenda for redressing wrongs and diminishing inequalities. Hence also the persistent silence about essential byproducts and side effects that might not be immediately detectable;

studying them could mean revealing the hidden costs of implemented projects. It is, after all, no coincidence that the most egalitarian of four elementary relational models of social organizing constructed by Fiske, namely 'equality matching', is derived from the 'desire for equality', of which we learn only that it is 'insufficiently studied' (Fiske, 1991, p. 45). The other elementary relational models – communal sharing, authority ranking and market pricing – are more readily explicable on the grounds of motivation for intimacy, power and achievement and are, according to Fiske, systematically studied and discussed in public.

Hence, to quote one of the latest symptoms of this unquestioned expertise underwriting social agendas by prefabricating public opinion, the bitter inadequacy of debates about 'integration into a multicultural society' in the Netherlands. While 67 per cent of white Dutch adults have paying jobs as opposed to 37 per cent of Moroccans and 46 per cent of Turks (Schmidt, 2008), there is no coherent approach towards amending these disproportions. The statistical data are potentially available – but one has to be able to reach them and they are not readily quoted by experts (and even less so by the media), especially if the experts have been commissioned by the government institutions or given a chance to appear in the media. An expert on a popular TV show or in the news mentioning structural discrimination would not be well received by the 'native' audiences. Facing the data would require acknowledging the inequalities, which in turn would provoke the question of whether immigrants had been given a fair chance on the job market. And how to deal with the demonization of some minorities in the media? Mexicans are depicted as 'stealing health-care benefits' from legal taxpayers in the USA by media professionals who must recognize that they are inflating racist bias to make their broadcasts more dramatic – at the expense both of dissenting expert opinions and the targeted minority. Moroccan youths are perceived as forming aggressive street gangs and terrorizing the ageing population in Dutch inner cities. Muslim communities are often suspected of harbouring terrorist 'fifth columns' inside western societies, which heaps insult upon the injury of a systematic discrimination and exclusion from educational and job opportunities.[10] Media professionals are slow in defusing such popular sentiments with more carefully calibrated expert knowledge, especially when experts themselves disagree on diagnoses and predictions. When it does appear, expert opinion is too easily canonized in the media, which rarely pit the rival research schools against one another. Afraid that disunity among experts might undermine the trust in their message, media usually present experts as a unified front – unless the debate calls for the representation of opposing, more extreme views.

The institutionalized policies of major parties are also legitimized by the media, which show them as available, realistic choices duly presented by the main political actors to future constituencies. Thus, for instance, the Dutch media continue to engage in the public debate about the integration of new immigrants into a multicultural society, but often by presenting their audiences with a choice between, say, an extreme right nationalist politician (a former minister for integration famous for anti-immigrant policies, leader of the 'Proud of the Netherlands' party) and a representative of the ruling coalition of Christian Democrats and the Labour Party, which does not have any coherent policy towards predominantly Muslim and non-white immigrants, except that it would like to have a less white-racist and Dutch-nationalist image ('proud to be cosmopolitan and European'). The experts do not provide promising insights into the immigration and integration processes, the politicians do not go beyond the limited choices prompted by their institutional commitments, the media do not apply their investigative skills to critically analyse expert voices and politicians' options and – last but not least – they do not actually give a 'voice' or a 'face' to the underdogs themselves. The media follow their own rules; they try to present both experts and politicians as part of a thrilling spectacle, to keep the audience 'captive' (on behalf of their advertisers), not necessarily in order to make it more educated and informed. If a conservative and populist politician launches a slogan 'Proud to be Dutch', the media pick it up, because it has a fascinating (if slightly suspect) affinity with the racist 'white supremacy' ideologies of the past. When a former minister of foreign affairs launches a counter-slogan 'proud to be European', politicians, researchers and corporate leaders applaud, but the general public does not learn about it from the media (which consider it too obvious, too subdued and thus too boring).[11]

Meanwhile the smokescreens – influencing the public in a joint, concerted action – prevent a more insightful and creative public discussion or render it more difficult by hampering access to relevant and salient knowledge and information sought by emergent agencies and actors. This is by no means an unusual situation: for instance, in Germany, Gunther Walraff, with his persistent unmasking of systematic discrimination against Turkish employees, stands alone against experts, politicians and media unable to deal adequately with the under-employed Turkish urban underclass. In the USA, the late Studs Terkel or Barbara Ehrenreich have stood almost alone against the mainstream media's demonization of Mexican and Latin American immigrants and media downplaying of the exploitation of female employees in service industries. The illegal Mexican immigrants and underpaid females are indispensable to the US economy, but they are under-researched by experts (the serial disappearances of young women in maquiladora factories located on the Mexican side of the border go routinely 'unnoticed' and 'unanalysed'), demonized by politicians and their ideologues (Huntington in *Who are We?* denies Spanish-speaking Mexican and Latin American immigrants access to the 'American Dream'; Huntington, 2005) and under-represented by the media (there are no interviews with the 'nickel and dimed' in the media unless they become 'exotic' enough to merit a picturesque journey of discovery into 'how the other half lives', which they usually aren't until they fall prey to violent crime).

Let us unzip the public debate about these smokescreens, one by one. Let us begin with the smokescreen of our professional community:

- First, can we, as members of this community, contribute to the thinning of this smokescreen, rather as we have worked to reduce smog in our urban centres?
- Second, can we resist the smokescreen of commercialization in contemporary social spaces? Can we look for non-commercial exchanges and contribute to the broadening of 'free spaces' for civil dialogues?
- Third, can we talk back to the media in order to reduce the 'smog' content and to increase the interactive contribution of the media to emergent public debates on significant issues that have been ideologically 'hidden' or neglected?

In order to reduce the smog of our own academic professions, we have to be able to go beyond the narrow specializations in which we have advanced through the ranks of the bureaucratic division of intellectual labour and to aspire to new attitudes and roles:

- First, we have to understand our colleagues and ourselves as 'the natives' and to try and transcribe our own real-life experiences in the 'anthropological voice', measuring the distance between our routine academic reports on our professional activities on the one hand and the natives' (our) real-life responses to their (our) realities on the other. In other words, we have to dive *below* the surface of official scientific communications. Once we have gone native, we can become our own professional ethnographers and should prepare to launch a critical report.

- Second, we have to ascend to the role of an 'intellectual' or 'public intellectual'. While acknowledging – after Bauman – that our ambitions have been trimmed and we no longer aspire to be the legislators of mankind, we can still harbour reasonable hope that we can at least turn out to be decent interpreters of relevant public issues, and that we are still able to perform critical analysis of broader social issues or deconstruct any ideological contamination of relevant policies. In other words, we have to fly *above* the surface of normal science and its scientific communications.

This means that we have to heed two principles at the same time; first, we need to turn our attention to the analysis of our academic organizations, primarily universities, which: 'are becoming transnational bureaucratic corporations regulated under the administrative metrics of "excellence" and productivity' (Fischer, 2003, p. 37).[12] And, second, we have to turn our attention to broader, culturally-embedded evaluations and procedures for public opinion forming, demonstrating to society at large that we are able to: 'rise above the partial preoccupation of one's own profession or artistic genre and engage with the global issues of truth, judgment and taste of the time' (Bauman, 1987, p. 2).[13]

However, even these modestly complex and sophisticated roles of 'critical native son' inside the academic community and of 'public intellectual' inside the public space of civil society are difficult to undertake within the institutional arrangements of the contemporary university. The role of 'critical native son (or indeed daughter)' is problematized in professional communities where 'native-ness' is a matter of formal certification and thus subjected to bureaucratic controls, which limit the space for experimenting with anarchist, Dadaist and other non-conventional displays of creative deviation from a tacit or explicit norm. 'Intellectuals' become public only when they are visible, audible or readable in the media – which may prefer to avoid difficult or controversial academic experts altogether (and anyway have their favourite 'gurus', chosen independently of their actual expertise) or to stick to their limited circle of superstars, leaving most academic professionals unable to access public debates.[14] If we hone our critical faculties and exercise them not only for domestic debates within a circle of immediate colleagues or friends, but also for interdisciplinary discussions with peers, for open lectures, for inspiring students and for broadening the agenda of public debates, we can overcome some of the difficulties linked to access to the 'public agora', which may be related to our own lack of confidence in the validity of our contribution. This lack of confidence was observed in 1987 by Wayne C. Booth in his Ryerson Lecture at the University of Chicago on 'The Idea of a University as Seen by a Rhetorician': 'even for the most learned of us, the circle of what we might call participatory understanding does not extend very far' (Booth, 1987, p. 23).

All of us experience the sense of a reduction in our professional competence as we witness development and cooperate in the growth and dissemination of knowledge. All of us have second thoughts about the narrowing down of our knowledge in the context of an ongoing specialization of skills and a declining ability to evaluate issues in a broader perspective of symbolic culture. We are packaging our expertise in the much more instrumental toolkit of a more narrowly defined 'expert bag'. We are becoming providers of expertise packaged either as an educational, research or consulting commodity. All the more reason then to cherish critical self-reflection when it is successfully expressed in the course of our professional communications, for instance on turning the dominant English of our professional communications into the language of empowerment for the rank and file rather than an instrument for maintaining US hegemonic power in academic knowledge factories:

> While one accepts English as the hypercentral language of transnational and transcultural communication, it might be prised loose from its native speakers. 'Il faut desangliciser l'Anglais', Pierre Bourdieu exclaimed in a public debate on European language policy: English should be de-anglicized. Europeans might develop their own variety, the way Indians did, for example. Native speakers of other European languages, trained in English at the language academies of the Union, could become authoritative editors and judges of style for the emergent European English...If English is the language of the powers that be, it is also the language of empowerment.
>
> (De Swaan, 2001, pp. 192–3)[15]

The questions of empowerment and of manageable inequalities are among the most important issues in new social movements. Even among modest clusters of researchers at regular academic meetings, congresses and conferences linked by critical topics, tracks and research interests, these questions may trigger discussions that may reach non-academics. Empowerment matters as much among migrant labour as among the highly trained employees of knowledge-intensive organizations and companies. Will a movement around empowerment emerge in the universities in the next decade? Empowerment matters because it is quite clear that the smog of neoliberal ideology advocating *alignment* (of the universities in general and business schools in particular) with business corporations is getting thinner. It is becoming clear that business schools remodelled as strictly commercial ventures either do not work or involve too many hidden costs (borne by the universities). Politically relevant issues are rarely visible in the daily life of academic professionals. They do not necessarily figure close to the top of personal priority lists. Promotion is unlikely to depend on belonging to an exciting seminar or participating in a creative workshop or co-founding a standing conference on a politically relevant issue, nor for criticizing one's university's authorities. One does not get rewarded for belonging to: 'a group of heterodox critical scholars...who have a common interest in studying how the contemporary world has come to be organized as it is, and how it might be re-imagined' (Williams, 2005, p. xii).[16]

Nevertheless, the self-reflective project of becoming a 'heterodox critical scholar' capable of public critical assessment (of new world orders and powers that be) does contribute to the reduction of the academic professional smog that conceals the details of knowledge production from outside observers (as well as from the producers themselves). There are also opportunities for creating spaces, zones, events and communications that can sustain the elective sub-communities (for instance, researchers linked to the diversifying critical management studies of the future) and can lead to the emergence of interesting alternatives in sciences of management and of organization. Even calls for track proposals for the European clone of the US-based Academy of Management, EURAM (the European Academy of Management) manifest a similar tone in announcing the conference theme for 2009 – 'Renaissance and Renewal in Management Studies':

> In management research too, there is an emerging concern with the recovery of people and people-focused procedures in organizations...Are firms exploiting human potential in the service of one set of commercial needs? Is freedom of choice empty if there is little on offer to choose from? The human body, virtual reality and even the future have become the scene of trading and hence managed activity. Are there limits to such a pervasive spread of managers and the managed, and should there be?
> (EURAM 2009 – Call for Track Proposals, 2008, p. 2)[17]

This also signals uneasiness about the second of our smokescreens: the authors speak of the spread of a professional bureaucracy ('managed and managers'), commercialization ('trading') and corporatization of all walks of life and all domains of activity ('are there limits?') Let us thus turn to this second smokescreen, the one which makes us apply the logic of a commercial contract, the model of market pricing (associated with a glorified dream-world of 'conspicuous consumption', to which we have been mentally attuned by ubiquitous commercial advertising), to our professional activities. I will begin with an anecdote that illustrates the spread of the commercial patterning of activities even among the student population. A few years ago I realized that only one student would appear at the re-sit of a multiple-choice exam prepared for 50 individuals and thus cancelled it. The student in question failed to read his email and duly came to the test hall. Upon being told that the re-sit had been cancelled and that he would instead have a re-sit session a month later, he sent me a bill for €800, explaining that he had quit his summer job a week earlier and had been studying to pass the exam. Had he continued to work he would have made €800 more. I told him that he should shed his false modesty and the claim for a mere five days and sue us for the money he could have made instead of studying for BSc and MSc diplomas for five years. He failed to respond, but there was a certain charming logic in his reasoning, an intuitive *reductio ad absurdum*, which makes intellectual life at the university a very interesting adventure indeed.

However, it takes more than a frustrated student attempt to calculate the financial loss inflicted by his choice of educational (accumulation of cultural, symbolic capital of knowledge) rather than commercial payoffs (accumulating money earned as wages) to understand how the smokescreen of apparently inevitable commercialization[18] subtly underlies and penetrates our mode of conceptualizing our problems, imagining alternative solutions and deciding about preferred courses of action. In fact, my response was wrong: instead of criticizing his attempt at calculating the commercial value of the time 'wasted' on preparing for an exam, I should have pointed out that he was investing not only in his future professional job, but also in his future development as an informed and committed citizen. I should have repeated after Jeffrey Goldfarb that: 'What is most important about a free, liberal education is that it does have a critical component, even as it prepares the young for vocational positions in the established social hierarchy' (Goldfarb, 2006, p. 120).

The author of *The Politics of Small Things* also points out that both universities and the media are educational institutions contributing to raising informed citizens: 'The real promise and meaning of free institutions of higher learning and journalism is in the details: what goes

on between and among students and teachers, journalists and readers'
(ibid.)

This broadly educational role of both universities and of the media
can be best understood in relation to complex or controversial issues
where the media are obliged to rely on expert opinion in spite of the
fact that such opinion might be deeply divided and that strong political
ideologies have emerged on both sides of the argument. It is here that
we can actually try to make use of the rational economic calculation for
making informed choices in the public domain and in the general interest. Perhaps this is how we can balance the shares of experts, politicians
and informed citizens in making significant public choices. This seems
to be happening very gradually with the global warming debate, which
became an issue in public discussions in the following way:

1. Objective material reality 'out there'
   Emissions of carbon dioxide into the atmosphere had been measured for fifty years and the results clearly indicated an increase in
   these emissions as a result of growing (human) consumption of fuels,
   mainly coal, oil and gas.
2. The academic research community's theoretical response
   (a) A majority of researchers believe that global warming represents a
       grave danger for human societies
   (b) A minority of researchers believe that climate changes are smaller
       than predicted by theoretical models and looming dangers are
       exaggerated as a result of mistaken assumptions
3. Politicians' responses
   (a) The left and new left in Britain (democrats in the USA) believe that
       there is a looming danger which should be averted by immediate
       and drastic action – see, for instance, the Stern Report (House of
       Commons Treasury Committee, 2008) in the United Kingdom and
       Al Gore's (2006) book or film (*An Inconvenient Truth*) in the United
       States
   (b) Neoliberals believe that the minority opinion should be accepted
       and reduction of emissions should be achieved gradually, in a
       balanced way
4. Media responses
   (a) Left and new left environmentalist and anti-globalist mobiliza-
       tion includes alarming exhortations to heed the warning about
       forthcoming environmental disasters and to impose international
       restraint on emissions even at the cost of slowing the rate of
       economic growth

    (b) The liberal and conservative media message is that the economic growth of China and India are more important than slowing carbon dioxide emissions now and that hoped-for inventions of new biotechnologies (for example, carbon-dioxide-eating plants) will provide the best solution in the longer run

5. Emergent ideologies

    (a) Environmentalism based on both left (restraining the evils of capitalism) and right (preserving God's habitat for future generations) political views, which unite in the basic agreement on a necessity to work out policies to protect the environment and propagate this environmentalism through all educational and mass media channels

    (b) No clear alternative to a generalized scepticism in view of the failures of hasty environmentalist solutions dictated by political correctness (introduction of bio-fuels briefly eased the conscience of rich consumers but raised food prices for the poor)

6. The critical reflection of a public intellectual. Freeman Dyson's popular explanation of the views expressed by William Nordhaus (Nordhaus, 2008) in the *New York Review of Books*:

> If we can save M dollars of damage caused by climate change in the year 2110 by spending one dollar on reducing emissions in the year 2010, how large must M be to make spending worthwhile? Or, as economists might put it, how much can future losses from climate change be diminished or 'discounted' by money invested in reducing emissions now? . . . The main conclusion of Nordhaus' analysis is that the ambitious proposals, 'Stern' and 'Gore', are disastrously expensive, the 'low-cost backstop'[19] is enormously advantageous if it can be achieved, and the other policies including business-as-usual and Kyoto are only moderately worse than the optimal policy. The practical consequence for global-warming policy is that we should pursue the following objectives in order of priority. (1) Avoid the ambitious proposals. (2) Develop the science and technology for a low-cost backstop. (3) Negotiate an international treaty coming as close as possible to the optimal policy, in case the low-cost backstop fails. (4) Avoid an international treaty making the Kyoto Protocol policy permanent. These objectives are valid for economic reasons, independent of the scientific details of global warming.
>
> (Dyson, 2008, p. 44)[20]

This simplified review of the public debates on environmental protection and the dangers of global warming (which resulted, among others, in Cassandra-like prophecies of a deluge submerging the Dutch depression) makes clear that although there is (broad) agreement on facts (increases in carbon dioxide emissions are not in doubt) and on values (the protection of environment is everybody's concern), there is disagreement on the legitimacy of expert opinion (the expert community being divided) with respect to theoretical explanations and empirical predictions, disagreement and uncertainty with respect to implementable policies and their intended and unintended consequences, and disagreement on where ideological zeal transcends legitimate passionate commitment. Finally, there is disagreement as to which of the threats to the sustainable and inhabitable environment should be tackled first.

As far as the media smokescreen goes, the lesson of Brent Spar seem to have been forgotten (the public no longer remember – if they ever noticed it – that the Shell experts from Aberdeen were right and that their solution of sinking the platform was safer and cheaper than the 'green' alternative). Public opinion again appears to be on the Greenpeace side, because the environmentalist message seems to be a purely ethical one, hovering above political and economic conflicts of interest. Al Gore received a Nobel Prize for his warnings and dire predictions, and most PR and advertising messages (especially from the oil companies) include a politically correct acknowledgment of global warming with an indispensable assurance that the company in question contributes to the solution, not to the aggravation of the problem. The much less spectacular and cautious arguments of experts such as William Nordhaus – are usually published in the scholarly volumes of university presses. This means limited editions, narrow circles of potential readers and their virtual nonexistence in mainstream media terms. Attempts to insert these arguments into the public debate might result, as did Dyson's more popular and accessible 'translation' of Nordhaus's views, in their publication in a highly intellectual (though often opinion-making and intellectual trendsetting) bi-weekly with a limited circulation of its own. Is this enough to offer a counterbalance to the excessive focus on global warming and to help us design a more balanced process of public negotiation of meaning in future? We are talking about a process, which is still open and its outcome very difficult to predict, since unexpected events can change the situation prompting or delaying decisions about actions to be taken in national and international contexts. The most interesting forthcoming event in the globally tele-mediated public debate on global warming will probably come with the clash of three arguments:

- The argument that global warming forms an imminent threat to the survival of mankind as a whole and thus prompt and far-reaching actions have to be undertaken immediately, even if it means that the interests of some nations will suffer (Stern, Gore)(+)
- The argument that doom-laden prophecies about global warming are based on questionable assumptions and that therefore the rationality of actions advocated on the basis of these prophecies should be subjected to a critical and transparent discussion (Nordhaus, Dyson)(−)
- The argument that the richest capitalist countries, for instance the United Kingdom and the United States, have no moral right to prevent the developing countries, primarily the Indians and the Chinese (or the BRIC block if we add Brazil and Russia to the list) from enjoying their share of the planet's resources and from improving standards of living of their respective populations(−)

The first and the third arguments will fire the ideological passions, while the second may become the decisive third party, supplying arguments for rational debate. Whoever wins the argument by persuading public opinion to their point of view and triggering action by supranational networks and organizations will shape the new context for future choices, will influence the future tense of meaning. What will the majority of informed citizens all over the world consider a priority: to secure decent living conditions for the populations of former third world countries (and then devote attention to environmental protection) or to prevent further deterioration of our transformed environment, threatening us all with unsustainability (and then turn our attention to inequalities)? If we want to focus on compensating for the injuries of uneven development and unequal exchange, China and India might take the fast lane towards material prosperity. If we want to focus on policing the environmentally damaging side-effects of economic growth, we will have to explain what other measures of bridging the gap between the individual chances of a decent life in the first and third world are available. Needless to say, the entire course of this debate could be strongly influenced by an unpredictable critical incident, which may shift the moral weights. There are many instances of such contingent critical changes, which would have been extremely difficult to predict in advance. Let us illustrate this mechanism with a relatively minor shift in public opinion engineered to a large extent by intensive media coverage.

The earthquake of 12 May 2008 in southern China resulted in more than 70,000 deaths in the first month after the event, and had an unforeseeable influence on the worldwide mobilization of public opinion by human rights activists. The latter were trying to persuade sportsmen and governments to boycott the Olympic Games in Beijing in protest against Chinese government persecution of opposition leaders and the native Tibetan population. The swift, efficient and open response of the Chinese government and the Chinese media to the emergency (without any attempts to deny the extent of the disaster or to stonewall it and with a prompt distribution of army food reserves) and the immediate acceptance of international rescue and relief aid effectively silenced this protest. Before the earthquake, the symbolic global march of the Olympic fire had frequently and predictably led to demonstrations and clashes with the police, for instance in Paris. Solidarity with imprisoned opposition leaders and dissident intellectuals and sympathy for the Tibetan native population whose demonstrations have been heavily suppressed incited world public opinion. The newborn solidarity with the suffering victims of the earthquake reclassified the Chinese in the tacit and virtual global public mind from oppressors to victims. This dramatic reclassification provided governments and sportsmen and sportswomen with a morally acceptable alibi for dropping the protests against human rights abuses. In a sense, they were excused for having no qualms about taking part in the Olympics.

This may seem cynical; but media rituals can be used to purposes, which can appear cynical (a skilful use of media during a national disaster by a government whose human rights policies and suppression of political opposition arouse our suspicions is bound to appear cynical in the eyes of this government's critics). The problems of human rights and authoritarian rule did not go away, but the moral status of the organizers of the Olympic Games in 2008 was temporarily altered by detailed, frequent and urgent media reports on the unexpected, contingent large-scale event (the latest shocking news, images of a deadly natural disaster of planetary proportions). The problems of human rights and authoritarian rule did not go away, but sympathy for the victims of the earthquake gained – at least temporarily – the upper hand compared to moral outrage caused by oppression and maintenance of the authoritarian political system. This example of a shift in public sentiment and a different 'frame' for thinking and judgement is very telling – it brings us closer to the main conclusion of the present study. In order to reach this conclusion we have to go back to the vilification and demonization of crowds in early western sociology on the one hand and to the striking parallels in the development of the outsourced, pluralist management of meaning in arts and sciences, both of which resulted in a changed social stage on which the continuous drama of contemporary history will assume its future shape.

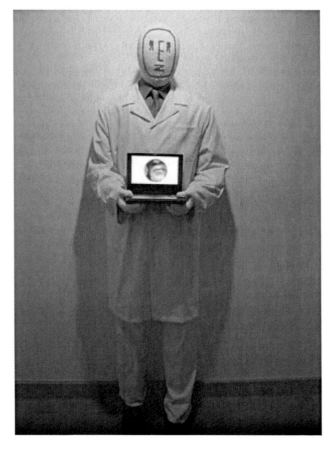

Illustration 6.1   Leszek Knaflewski, 'e-Flux' (courtesy of the artist)

7

Instead of Conclusions: the Revenge of Populism and the Transformation of Angry Mobs into Mobilized Alternative Social Networks

Public debates, for instance the ongoing discussions on global warming, make it increasingly clear that fundamental social choices cannot be indefinitely postponed. Let us hope that our decisions will not be distorted by our fears ('black spring') or media demonizing ('angry mobs'). These choices will influence all human individuals and it is essential that all people understand what the choices mean and that they are empowered actually to express their opinions. Turning the population of the planet into an assembly of informed citizens is certainly not going to be easy, but leaving things in the hands of incidental populists is hardly an option.

> Even though the recording and preservation of arguments tend to be biased in the direction of the articulations of the powerful and the well schooled, many of the most interesting accounts of arguments from the past involve members of disadvantaged groups.
>
> (Sen, 2005, p. xiii)

Large clusters of this population may be deprived of relevant knowledge and of a political say in decision-making processes, but leaving them to their fate is morally untenable. Living with the consequences of these choices will furnish the context for the future tense of the management of meaning. The most fundamental set of alternatives has already been mentioned, although this choice had not yet clearly been articulated by participants in contemporary environmental and political debates. Within the framework of these debates, however, the following alternatives can be identified (provided that political actors find it practical to clarify them rather than keeping in the background), in – respectively – global-political, political-managerial and academic debates.

1. The fundamental global-political difference of opinion with respect to the priority of either 'ecology' (prioritizing the environment) or 'sociology' (compensating inequalities first). In the course of a public debate along this divide, the negotiated construction of *meaning* in future tense will emerge:

    (a) Organized human societies have reached the point of a dramatic transformation of their physical environment and should suspend their economic and political differences until ecological sustainability can be secured for all. In concrete terms this necessitates a significant reduction of carbon dioxide emissions to the atmosphere. Given available global governance instruments, the Kyoto protocol should be ratified by all states. [*Tacit assumption: once we have secured sustainability for all involved societies and the entire population of the planet, inequality between various locations can be tackled and welfare spread more evenly.*]

    (b) Organized human societies have reached the point of a dramatic growth of inequalities and should suspend their present policies until an egalitarian, democratic correction is successfully inserted into the organized complexity of social processes. In concrete terms this necessitates large improvements in living standards and civic participation for significant numbers of the 'wretched of the earth'. Given the available instruments of national state policies, India and China should be assisted in continuing their present economic growth and urged to promote local democracy. [*Tacit assumption: once two billion human beings have secure access to water, shelter, food, education, health care, jobs and political decision-making – we can start designing more sustainable technologies for the future.*][1]

2. The fundamental political-managerial difference of opinion is a choice between a market unbound or a market bound. In the course of this debate, the future tense of *management* (and partly the preferred instruments of managers and leaders) will be determined:

    (a) Organized processes of complex exchanges can only be sustained within the capitalist market as the best available regulating mechanism for material prosperity compatible with the democratic state. Structural inequality is the precondition for this mechanism's functioning and has to be preserved by organized hierarchies. Inequalities of income, status and power are thus desirable engines of progress and should be carefully protected against rash radicals. [*Tacit assumption: professional managers are indispensable for the smooth functioning of complex professional bureaucracies and the growth of the global 'CEO' elite class is an unfortunate but necessary and in the long run negligible cost of progress. High salaries of top managers are thus a non-issue and can be safely ignored.*]

(b) Organized processes of complex exchanges can only be sustained within the capitalist market corrected by the democratic policies of welfare states and global organizations spreading material prosperity and securing inclusion for all citizens to counter the growth of inequalities and attain a balance between economic wealth and democratic justice. Egalitarian and inclusive policies should be applied to turn 'human resources' into responsible citizens. [*Tacit assumption: the iron law of oligarchy should be systematically broken on all levels and empowerment and self-managing teams are indispensable for the smooth functioning of organizations in market democracies. High salaries of top managers are thus a serious signal that oligarchization is in full swing and should be opposed.*]

3. The fundamental academic difference of opinion about the place of a university in contemporary society, the a choice between a competitive business-like unit of research/education/consulting services or a centre of learning (with research and teaching activities) which is also a dress-rehearsal for informed and responsible citizens. During public debates along these lines, the future tense of *the social construction of meaning* will be articulated:

(a) Universities are primarily knowledge factories producing human resources for complex professional bureaucracies and should be hierarchically managed to synchronize their output with the needs of corporate and state planners. [*Tacit assumption: utopian visions of academic self-government and the liberal arts model of education can be sacrificed at the altar of economic growth as anachronistic illusions.*]

(b) Universities are both professional training centres and spaces for individual rehearsing of the role of informed citizen capable of participating in public debates and willing to do so. [*Tacit assumption; charity begins at home and so does the upbringing of informed citizenry in democratic societies – empowerment of both academics and students is not a luxury but a basic necessity if relevant expertise and committed citizens are expected to sustain democratic affluent societies, those unfinished projects.*]

Those are the fundamental themes with which – as we have seen in previous chapters – public debates are already concerned, although participants in these debates are not always focused on the core dilemmas. In each case we see the choices that will have to be made, which may assume different forms and trigger a variety of movements, actions, initiatives or trends. In each case we see the fault lines along which the 'sentences' articulated in the future tense will signal the forthcoming attempts at the management of meaning in, respectively, global, national and professional arenas.

The future tense of the management of meaning is much more difficult to use than the past or the present, since meaning emerges out of the spirit of exchange in the course of social interactions and thus the underdogs, or the 'members of disadvantaged groups' (as Sen puts it) are likely to provide necessary but as yet unpredictable inputs. Unpredictability increases further because academic experts, when forging theoretical categories and researching the actors involved in management of meaning, smuggle their own biases into the exercise, in turn, influencing social actors articulating alternatives and making choices. This 'smuggling' (underground, illicit, clandestine, even unconscious at times) needs to be revealed, made transparent and negotiable. Otherwise relevant social actors – especially disadvantaged groups, the underdogs – can easily become stereotyped, labelled, excluded from public debate, limited in democratic choices and demonized in the media.

'Anti-globalists' on the streets of Seattle and Genoa were defined by the media as dangerous crowds and treated accordingly (regardless of whether they included pacifists and politically correct environmentalists). Demonizing them as angry mobs of anarchistic anti-globalists prevented a more manageable confrontation and a more constructive comparison of views. Human rights activists protesting against the symbolic travel of the Olympic flame to Beijing were defined as concerned citizens and were protected by the police on the streets of Paris (the police regulated traffic leaving empty space for demonstrators around the stadium to which the torch was eventually transported by bus, even though some of the demonstrators broke into shops). They were not demonized. It remains to be seen if excessive focus on global warming will freeze the stereotypes of the politically correct environmentalists versus reckless consumers instead of opening a public discussion – for instance on price tags and the long-term efficiency of reducing carbon dioxide emissions.

Participative and deliberative democratization of European universities in the wake of the 1968 student and faculty protests had been gradually but efficiently undone by the turn of the century. Faculty and university councils were reduced to rubber stamping the decisions of increasingly professionalized academic managers. Students ceased to be partners and became unruly crowds in lecture halls, subjected to standardized managerial control. Can this process be reversed and a democratic correction reinserted into academic life? Can we turn unruly student crowds into our co-responsible partners? If recent history offers examples of breaking through the bureaucratic stalemate within a much more repressive organization, then the spontaneous mobilization of 10 million citizens by an illegal trade union deserves attention. Horizontal networks of the broad anti-communist social movement disguised as an independent trade union – 'Solidarność' – emerged during the August 1980 strikes in Poland and managed to design a manageable dismantling of the communist rule in Poland. The emergence of 'Solidarity' – together with attempted reforms of the Soviet system by Gorbachev – triggered the breakdown of communism in the whole of central Europe, culminating in 1989, when the Berlin Wall came down, symbolically ending the era of the Cold War. While there are no signs that the academic communities are on the verge of revolutionary mobilization against excessive bureaucratization and unchecked commercialization, against professional deans and commercially active presidents, there are symptoms – even among mainstream researchers – of a growing recognition of the need to face the future with something other than a business plan and a professional bureaucracy to oversee its implementation. There is not yet enough for us to speak of the emergence of a new counter-culture, but there is enough to notice the change of climate in contributions by established academic authorities in mainstream publications:

> The new coveted degree might become the MBD (Master of Business Design) or the MBArts (Master of Business Arts), rather than the traditional MBA. Why? Because the challenges we face cannot be solved with our current level of knowledge. We can't get from where we are to where we want to go by using what we already know. The 21st century challenge is to create options worthy of choosing; and that type of creativity calls for innovative design skills. Not merely the continued application of increasingly sophisticated analytical skills that have until now defined most MBAs and their approaches to management.
>
> (Adler, 2008, p. 96)

Some terms are more heavily contaminated by smuggled biases than others – for instance 'creativity' (as in 'creative design'), or 'the people' (as in 'power to the people'). We noted earlier that fine arts are increasingly frequently evoked when architects as professionals or new individualists (sons and daughters of the 'organization men', but in a generational cohort) justify and legitimize their choices. The rise of 'creative industries' is linked to this new focus on creativity and is accompanied by a tacit ideology of upward mobility through creative sublimation of the resentment of the underdogs. Creativity is not only for the da Vincis and Picassos of this world. It should not remain a privilege of isolated 'superstar' geniuses, but it should become accessible to all members of our societies (hence the popularity of TV shows dancing with the stars or searching for young talent). Creativity should be omnipresent through designed artifacts filling social spaces and providing cultural contents for the multimedia (hence the gentrification of the designer's profession and the emergence of boutique eyeglasses and hotels, motorcycles and museums). In the above quotation, Adler comments on the growing role of creativity and thus of the non-scientific, artistic inputs. While research communities remain the preferred suppliers of socially valid knowledge, artistic communities are evolving towards the role of total designers of social experiences. Adler advocates a balancing act, a proactive restoring of a more nuanced, more humanist approach to the academic production of knowledge and the teaching of skills. This balanced approach would change a university as research communities understand it, but it would provide only a partial solution to the problems of excessive bureaucratization and commercialization. To change a university from the point of view of the students, to empower them as future citizens who should exercise their rights and political skills, another transformation would have to emerge.

The transformation in question would have to turn student cohorts ('angry mobs' filling the lecture halls) into socially conscious, networked citizens capable of public action (concerned and informed citizens making full use of their rights). Discussions about the shaping of responsible citizens through public institutions (such as universities) or new social movements (such as emergent 'green' parties or less institutionalized alternatives) have already been led by leftist intellectuals. For instance, Laclau pointed out that the construction of a theoretical concept of 'the people' had been contaminated by the fear of 'angry mobs' of working class rioters, as testified by the classic studies of Le Bon and Tarde (whose work influenced empirical research in the USA through Park and Blumer). Definitions of social actors are rarely innocent – and their innocence is further compromised when they are exposed by the contemporary mediated communications, where:

> dangerous crowds, ideal publics and isolated individuals continue to be features of discourses on audiences. Two centuries of representing

audiences in terms relevant to citizenship and evaluating the worthiness of audiences in terms of their social inequality indicate that discourses on audiences, whether academic, elite, intellectual, journalistic or popular, are neither innocent description nor private opinion, but are filled with political implications that sustain mainstream conceptions of citizenship and worthiness. Whatever our assertions about audiences, we need to be cognizant that we speak in the context of these long-term discourses and that our claims may be incorporated into and our meaning transformed by them.

(Butsch, 2008, p. 144)[2]

We cannot safely predict what inputs friendly crowds (as opposed to 'angry mobs'), really existing publics (as opposed to ideal and idealized ones) and dynamically interconnected individuals (as opposed to artificially isolated ones) will bring into public debates, either on fundamental or less fundamental issues. However, we can predict that if we fail to account for smuggled concepts, frameworks and political implications, if we ignore the underground, clandestine, illicit traffic in ideas and values, we will forgo a chance to make these debates more transparent and we will miss a window of opportunity in which we might make our organizations both more democratic and more sustainable. This is particularly true with respect to our academic organizations. The demonization of 'angry mobs' had taken its revenge and our ability to see students as partners in a democratic community has declined in comparison to the 1970s. So has the idealization of a single type of an imagined public; the segmentation of a market does not favour joint efforts to forge the public project of an egalitarian society. Last but not least, the standardization of research around the isolated individual as a sovereign decision-maker has prevented us from participative research in making more socialized models available and relevant. We have traced the origins of demonization (angry mobs versus rational individuals) to Cold War academic policies, which were developed against the background of history conceived as a sequence of never-ending sessions of single frozen protagonists routinely enacting, reiterating, copying, repeating the prisoner's dilemma and simply requiring superior analytical skills to win the future (as if it were a game of chess, a blockade of Berlin, a Cuban missile crisis, a war by proxy in Angola or Afghanistan) and to continue winning it over and over again.

There is no cunning passage within our institutional history, which would lead us to a city on the hill or to a single best option for which there is no alternative among a cluster of individuals who make choices as if there were no such thing as society. Values and meanings cannot be entirely outsourced; responsible citizens have also to be part-time 'economists of worth'. Withdrawal from participation in the public life of professional bureaucracies gradually ceases to be an option. Creative industries have already emerged, but creative political movements and institutions are still in *statu nascendi*, they are being born under our very eyes inside professional bureaucracies and between the high walls of social spaces, which can impede mobility but do not impede communications. In communications, especially in hyperlinked societies, meanings can be imported and smuggled and thus the unfinished project of democracy can be retrieved, reinvented, rejuvenated and retried. Meaning, as language, should be regarded as a mode of action, not just a frozen trace of a thought with value in the background.

Appendix 1: Track proposal for EURAM 2009, Liverpool 11–14 May 2009

Title:

Limits of Inequality: Citizens and Academies

Track convenor

Sławomir Magala, Rotterdam School of Management, Erasmus University, The Netherlands. Academic interest: cross-cultural competence, sociology of organizations, intercultural communication, management of meaning in networks and organizations, avant-garde literature, aesthetics of photography.

Track description

Major key terms:
Democratizing (professional bureaucracies)
Empowerment
Academic escapes

If universities are not business units for training managerial elites, they might become academic stages for dress rehearsals of civic duties. Are we contributing to the emergence of the latter? Could we do more? Ideological, sociological and political aspects of 'universities in ruins' deserve research attention. We are inviting papers, which deal with the following aspects of democratization of academic and other professional bureaucracies, especially through empowerment of the disadvantaged.

In discussing ideological aspects of democratization, we would like to draw attention to the following issues:

- the ambiguous return of the fortieth anniversary of 'May 1968' as generational symbol of counterculture and protest against authoritarian organizational structures and international policies frozen into Cold War.
- the decline of the neoconservative and neoliberal consensus symbolized by Thatcher-Reagan or Bush-Blair sync. Is the neoliberal ideological 'smog' providing political dust storm and ideologically legitimizing the reduction of the welfare state thinning down?
- The emergence of the environmentalist ideology as a crucial template for ideologies of the future. If frozen into dogma, this ideology might prevent a rational public debate on alternative options

In discussing the sociological contexts of democratization and 'Bildung' of informed citizens, we would like to encourage reflection on the following issues:

- the decline of the participative forms of managing universities and other professional bureaucracies and in particular the dismantling of the student and junior professional influences in consultative, participative forms of self-government
- the appearance of academic escapes from the velvet cage of bureaucratic division of labour into the humanization of managerial sciences – with philosophy, centres for art and leadership, coaching of creativity and innovation with traditional humanist inputs
- the development of a performative perspective on organizational learning and change, and the establishment of a critical canon of sociological analyses of organizational realities (e.g. Bakhtin, Foucault, Bourdieu, Habermas, Honneth, Burawoy)

In articulating political processes and struggles, we would like to invite papers dealing with the following issues:

- Is it possible to empower students or researchers? Why have we given up traditional academic liberties of an old professional guild, but failed to give up the dictatorship of academic CEOs?
- will the jargon and window-dressing of diversity management replace any dreams of empowered women without glass ceilings above them, students without ranking calculations in hand and retirees with full access to peer feedback instead of age-limit cut-offs?
- can we prevent developing multimedia infrastructures from following powers that be (or drifting aimlessly) when linking information, education, entertainment and commercialization in seamless web (Second Life is a case in point)?

We hope to be able to plot critical approach to the issues of cultivating civic virtues in academic professionals and to the issues of coaching civic virtues in students and young researchers. Inequalities are manageable if responsible and informed organizational citizens recognize them in a transparent process and negotiate them in specific contexts (speak up, social imaginaries). Palpable empowerment leads to real action, online access may contribute to transparency. Managing the transition to imagined and desirable organizations of empowered citizens may lead us out of the slavery of organizational pyramid building – towards perhaps a more democratic and egalitarian community, more skilled in dialogues than we are. Will alternative futures emerge and will they work, after all?

Bibliographical note

On core critical management studies approaches:
Alvesson, Mats and Hugh Willmott, 1996, *Making Sense of Management: a Critical Introduction*, London: Sage.

Arrighi, Giovanni, 2007, *Adam Smith in Beijing: Lineages of the Twenty-First Century*, London and New York: Verso.
Bourdieu, Pierre, 2008, *Political Interventions: Social Science and Political Action*, London and New York: Verso.

On the re-evaluated Frankfurt School scholars:
Honneth, Axel, 1995, *The Struggle for Recognition*, Cambridge, MA: MIT Press.
Jeffrey T. Nealon and Caren Irr (eds), 2002, *Rethinking the Frankfurt School: Alternative Legacies of Cultural Critique*, Albany: State University of New York.

From emergent academic dissent within the limits of law and order:
Michael M. Fischer, 2003, *Emergent Forms of Life and the Anthropological Voice*, Durham and London, Duke University Press.

Or in a more European vein:
Collin C. Williams, 2005, *A Commodified World? Mapping the Limits of Capitalism*, London and New York: ZED Books.

Further three left treatises, one on the legacy of the central Europeans in their successful struggle against the communist party-state:
Jeffrey C. Goldfarb, 2007, *The Politics of Small Things: the Power of the Powerless in Dark Times*, Chicago and London: University of Chicago Press.
Ernesto Laclau, 2005, *On Populist Reason*, London and New York: Verso.
Manuel Castells, 2001, *The Internet Galaxy: Reflections on the Internet, Business, and Society*, Oxford and New York: Oxford University Press.

Last but not least, the latest cutting-edge critical contributions to theory of management from Sage:
Barry, Daved and Hans Hansen (eds), 2008, *Sage Handbook of New Approaches in Management and Organization*, London and Thousand Oaks: Sage.

Sessions

Approximately 3 sessions with ca. 9 papers, selected from ca. 20–25. All submissions accepted after double blind peer review will be distributed to all before the conference, so that at the conference there will be more to debate than papers presented 'in person' and debates will be supplemented by a film workshop and a meeting with a multimedia political organizer as a keynote speaker.

Suggested Co-organizers

Mats Alvesson, Lund University
Hugh Willmott, Cardiff University
Martin Harris, Essex University

Notes

1. Introduction: Can Values and Meanings be Outsourced and if so, to Whom?

1. Kusturica, Emir, *Underground*, Ciby 2000/Pandora/Novo Film, 1995.
2. The term 'cultural logic of selfhood' was introduced by Kavolis (1980).
3. At least in the not too discriminating eyes of the Cold War ideologues. Today we would never place Hopper with the socialist realists and no curator would have lumped him together with them at an exhibition or in a collection.
4. 'Cultural propaganda gained in subtlety and diversified its targets. Avant-garde works were sent to Paris and Berlin while more traditional paintings were shipped to Italy, where the public found the work of a painter like Ben Shahn more to its taste. At home avant-garde art was liberals' favorite' (Guilbaut, 1983, p. 248).
5. The study of the 'losers' is also far from systematic. The reconstruction of covert liaisons and projects originating in the Cold War could not only help us understand why some periodicals, universities or think-tanks performed a networking function for future professional elites, but would give us also a clue as to the subtle subversion of professionals behind the iron curtain. I recall, for instance, three or four 'book funds' and foundations (including the Polish Kościuszko Foundation from NYC), which sent me free books when I was studying for my MA and PhD in Poznań, Poland in 1968–76. Their sponsorship meant that without the need for hard currency we were receiving, for instance, theoretical studies of the rise and nature of totalitarianism and it was possible for us to compare liberal and socialist visions of modernization. Work was occasionally disrupted by the secret police confiscating some of the books (duly acknowledged with special receipts). I will probably never discover why the English version of Adorno et al.'s *Authoritarian Personality* got to me without problems, while a German version of the same was stopped as subversive two years later. Nevertheless, we did understand that this censoring of the books was the communist elite's response to the western 'softening' of future intellectuals.
6. There is no vacuum, though. In the absence of theory, mythology and common sense come to the fore. The recent outbreak of prophesies about the coming domination of 'Chindia' in world economics and politics is a case in point.
7. Ossie, or the acronym for 'Ost – Deutschen'. It stands for the former citizens of the German Democratic Republic, who had often been called 'East Germans', and it has a negative, derogatory, contemptuous, patronizing ring.
8. Hitchens duly notes that Nafisi (2003) mentions Paul Wolfowitz in her 'Acknowledgements' (she thanks him for pointing out Leo Strauss's essay 'Persecutiuon and the Art of Writing'), which, together with Hilton Kramer and Christopher Hitchens, provides an interesting context for studying Miłosz's influence on selected intellectuals (see Hitchens, 2004).
9. The volume, *Criticism and the Growth of Knowledge*, edited by Imre Lakatos and Alan Musgrave, lists the following contributors: Karl Popper, Thomas Kuhn,

Paul Feyerabend, Margaret Masterman, Stephen Toulmin, John Watkins and L. Pearce Williams (Lakatos and Musgrave, 1970).

10. That criticism of the Hofstedian framework is gaining strength is clearly visible at international conferences, where it is voiced by researchers working outside Europe (mainly in Africa and Asia), those belonging to critical management studies, who mistrust the popular appeal of culture's consequences to consultants and corporate PR experts, and those who develop alternative dimensions (for example, GLOBE teams). The international conference on 'Cross-cultural life of social values' (Rotterdam, 18–19 May 2007) was a case in point, particularly because both Hofstede and McSweeney had attended it.

11. Incidentally, Hirschman does much to disperse the explanatory pretensions of dialectical materialists who claim to have a superior analytical instrument for understanding the contradictions of social growth: 'For capitalism to be both self-reinforcing and self-undermining is not any more contradictory than for a business firm to have income and outgo[ings] at the same time! Insofar as social cohesion is concerned, for example, the constant practice of commercial transactions generates feelings of trust, empathy for others and similar doux feelings; but on the other hand, as Montesquieu already knew, such practice permeates all spheres of life with the element of calculation and of instrumental reason' (Hirschman, 1992, p. 139).

12. Weick quotes approvingly my paper on his lost opportunity to develop a theory of organizational sentiments, where I note that such theory was 'hinted at but ignored' (Magala, 1997, p. 324) Considering the response time (1997–2005), the time for re-evaluation shrank from Hirschman's 100-year cycle (from positive to negative evaluation of capitalism) to 25 years for Kuhn (from positive evaluation of a historical theory of scientific revolutions to its more balanced re-adjustment) to 8–10 years for Weick (from the theory of organizational sensemaking to the theory of organizational sensemaking overshadowed by sentimental journeys and power struggles).

13. In his last autobiographical interview (see Kuhn, 2000), the author of *The Structure of Scientific Revolutions*, spoke of researchers he had met in Princeton's Institute for Advanced Studies and who spread his influence among many academic disciplines He mentioned Clifford Geertz, the anthropologist, Quentin Skinner, the political scientist, and William Sewell, the historian, and remembered that rebellious Berkeley students in the late 1960s were fans of Herbert Marcuse and of himself.

14. Erasmus would have probably been even less amused had he heard the results of the 2006 survey among the inhabitants of Rotterdam crossing the ultra-modern bridge over the river Maas named after him. More than half of the interviewees thought that Erasmus was the name of the engineer who had designed the bridge.

2. The Past Tense of Meaning (Lost and Gained in Historical Translations)

1. The term 'meaning of meaning' comes from the title of an influential study by Ogden and Richards from 1923; an analytical definition of meaning had also been presented by many logicians, linguists and philosophers (compare

Tarski, 1936; Korzybski, 1958; Austin, 1986; Wierzbicka, 1997) The most influential philosophical discussion of meaning in a natural language has been provided by Wittgenstein (2001). The first edition of the Ogden and Richards study includes two supplementary essays, namely by Bronislaw Malinowski and F.G. Crookshank.

2. I am grateful to Yiannis Gabriel who asked me to provide an entry to a dictionary, in fact a 'creative thesaurus of key words in social and organizational theories', which he was preparing in 2007, thus helping me revise and rethink some of my intuitions about the management of meaning. Needless to say, my entry was entitled the 'management of meaning'.

3. While it would be an exaggeration to claim that the British, German and French social sciences and humanities remained isolated from one another, and influenced each other after a delay of decades rather than years, there is a distinct possibility that Sartre and Levinas reading Heidegger in German POW camps during the Second World War were the first to prepare a significant cross-national transfer of phenomenological ontology, somewhat echoing the Franco-German unification of Europe after the war.

4. This has been observed by many authors interested in interpretations and writing on semiotics, for instance, Umberto Eco. One of his studies bears the title *The Role of the Reader*, which shifts the attention from a privileged 'author' to a newly empowered 'reader'.

5. The term 'postmodern' has been subjected to a number of critiques, and is sometimes associated with a general relaxation of standards and an extreme 'Balkanization' of the social sciences and the humanities. It makes sense, however, as a general term for the anti-modernist and anti-neopositivist theoretical schools that emerged in academic institutions and the elitist media after the Cold War.

6. Commenting on attempts to develop a systematic theoretical justification I have used the phrase 'logic of religion'. This refers to a series of lectures by Jozef Maria Bochenski at New York University in 1963 (and later also in Freiburg, Basel, Amsterdam and Utrecht). Bochenski's *The Logic of Religion* appeared in English in 1965 and was only translated into the author's native Polish in 1990. I remember these dates since random historical coincidence gave me the opportunity to translate it (Bochenski, 1965, trans. 1990).

7. Reason was at first spelled with capital 'R', and temples devoted to the goddess of reason were opened during the French revolution. Education and research became state priorities. The underlying idea was that there is sufficient coherence and compatibility between different research communities to justify the use of a single 'ideal type' of scientifically supported rationality.

8. The subtitle of David Brin's book on *The Transparent Society* is: 'Will technology force us to choose between privacy and freedom?' (Brin, 1998).

9. Ranciere thinks that in reducing the space of politics governments open up another battlefield and that communities of birth and kinship will resurface as religious communities ('God's own people'). His observation might refer both to fundamentalist Muslims and to the Christian proponents of 'intelligent design'.

10. Stein was denounced as a Jewess when she was living as a nun in a convent in occupied Belgium and was murdered by the Nazis in a concentration camp. Apparently for the Nazis her racial genealogy mattered more than

either her intellectual development or her moral identity. Her philosophical development, recently analysed by Alasdair McIntyre (2006) offers an excellent example of an attempt to reconcile the religious and scientific-rational patterns of sensemaking in a single life of a thinking individual.

11. Some contemporary sociologists think that 'cosmopolitan ideas have not yet had the opportunity to exhaust their utopian potential' (Beck, 2006, p. 44). Tsoukas opens a chapter on 'Chaos, Complexity and Organization Theory' with the question 'The new Cosmopolis?' (Tsoukas, 2005, p. 210).

12. This critical assessment of the 'critical potential' of the Habermasian theory of communicative action points out that the representatives of the Frankfurt School became firmly embedded in the mainstream academic communities. It was not always so: but the decisive turn was a 'softening' of the *Dialectic of Enlightenment* from the 1944 to 1947 edition: 'The word "capitalism" was changed to "existing conditions"; "capital" was changed to "economic system"; "capitalist bloodsuckers" became "knights of industry"; "class society" became "domination" or "order"; "ruling class" became "rulers"' (Wiggershaus, 1995, 401).

13. This is the motto opening Ulrich Beck's latest political work *The Cosmopolitan Vision* (Beck, 2006) in which he also claims that 'The European Union is not a club for Christians, a transcendental community of common descent' (ibid., p. 164) and that 'Cosmopolitan Europe is taking leave of postmodernity. Simply put: nationalistic Europe, postmodernity, cosmopolitan Europe' (ibid., p. 168).

14. He did so in 'Freud: the Mind of a Moralist' (1959), 'The Triumph of the Therapeutic' (1965) and 'Fellow Teachers' (1973). None of them makes for an easy read, and all of them remain 'insider jobs', that is, elegant essays on the philosophy of the humanities and the role of a public intellectual.

15. Rieff writes *expressis verbis*: 'The entire teaching elite, the rabbinates and priesthoods, and the professoriats derived from them, have themselves engaged in a long withdrawing roar of criticism on the land of law against the ground on which they themselves could once always make their stand against rebellions. Now those priesthoods and rabbinates are themselves so enculturated in the critical intellect that they are themselves hostile to the commanding truths that are theirs to teach and reteach' (Rieff, 2006, p. 206).

3. Cases in Point

1. http://en.wikipedia.org/wiki/Brent_Spar.
2. A female social psychologist from Rotterdam School of Management.
3. Heather Hopfl, professor of business management at the university of Essex, mentioned a hidden injury of a gender inequality she had observed when visiting her colleague in Italy. As visiting professor, she had been offered a flat near the university and invited her husband to accompany her. They settled down and her husband spontaneously opened his laptop on the only table in the entire apartment. Heather sat down on a bed with hers in her lap, but noticed that even her partner-like husband did not bother to offer her a choice, quietly and almost automatically assuming that his work came first, even though it

was his wife who had been invited there (private communication at the international conference 'Novel and organization', Essex University, Colchester, 10–12 May 2007).

4. It would be interesting to note that feminist initiatives are quite successful in drawing media attention to single incidents, but that political mobilization of support turns out to be much more difficult, in spite of the fact that women have already managed to win competition for the highest positions in political establishments. Even more difficult is the shift of social preferences, which could render currently 'invisible' gendered work more 'visible' and therefore negotiable.

4. The Present Tense of Meaning (Underground Passages between Hierarchies, the Cunning of Calculating Reason and the Return of Utopian Virtues)

1. Incidentally, having first met Guillet de Monthoux during the second EURAM conference in Stockholm, I ran into him again a few years ago at a small academic conference in Bielefeld, where we discovered our passionate mutual interest in the oeuvre of Georg Simmel, one of the first European thinkers to notice the unofficial traffic in ideas across various domains of culture and society. Most of the participants at this conference were French, German, Italian and Polish PhD students and it had been organized by Otthein Rammstedt, the editor of Simmel Studies. Simmel is certainly the forgotten patron saint of postmodern thinking *avant la lettre* and should be considered an indispensable companion to Weber, correcting the latter's systemic excesses.

2. Honneth, whose book is based on his postdoctoral (Habilitation) study, tries to ground the critical theory of the post-Habermasian generation in a marriage of Hegel with Foucault (to make it critical) and to Herbert George Mead (to make it more empirical). Having started his academic career under Habermas, Honneth is right in trying to ground the latter's liberal ideology of communicative action in the critical removal of tacit exclusions from 'coercion-free' dialogue presumably led by enlightened media and informed and empowered citizens (reading the present footnote).

3. Or sugar-coating: in January 2008 all employees of the university were issued a round table of chocolate composed of four pieces in different colours fitting together as elements of a jigsaw puzzle. The chocolate had the university logo on it and an attached leaflet said 'Diversity: badly needed!' in English and Dutch.

4. Sen's arguments were forged in the course of a comparative analysis of poverty reduction and birth control in China and India in the 1950s, 1960s and 1970s, that is, under a non-market and non-democratic regime on the one hand and a market democracy on the other.

5. 'The absence of market mechanisms doomed Soviet style economies to waste and inefficiency. Socialism as a power system had sought to establish its own channels of control, thereby in effect continuing Tsarist distrust of independent civil society' (Malesevic and Hall, 2005, p. 573). This statement is a version of a standard mantra of contemporary sociologists, economists and political scientists. Only recently have critical economists started to consider

the Chinese case as a challenge to the western-centered matrix of the market organization of society (see Arrighi, 2007).

6. Italian psychoanalyst and philosopher, Armando Verdiglione, founder of an international cultural foundation and head of the Spirali publishing house, owner of the international conference and exhibition centre, Villa Carlo Borromeo in Milan-Senago and the author of the ongoing interdisciplinary project 'The Second Renaissance', has openly called for striving towards the 'reinvention' of a contemporary renaissance in interdisciplinary meetings of cultural elites and cross-cultural brainstorming of professionals from various walks of life.

7. The third cluster is much more difficult to define and its patron saints are thus also less obvious. One would think that, for instance, Foucault or Bourdieu or Said Amir Arjomand could compete for the title as well, and Edward Said's classic 'Orientalism Reconsidered' would also be a case of an attempted re-engineering of 'oriental' studies from the point of a 'revolutionary renaissance' as an ideal (see Said, 2000). The great patron saints in the Marxian tradition would have to include Antonio Gramsci, who introduced the concept of a 'collective prince' (after Machiavelli) in order to design revolutionary party policies and who also studied the ways in which ideological hegemony can be functionally maintained in spite of the lack of a single dominant content-based doctrine. If contemporary left intellectuals dream of a new theoretical synthesis, they usually envision a fertile cloning of two marginalized intellectuals from the first half of the twentieth century – Antonio Gramsci and Walter Benjamin.

8. Paraphrasing Lenin's dictum that 'communism = power of the soviets + electrification' one is tempted to sum this exhortation by Castells up as 'postcapitalism = empowered individuals + the internet'.

9. As Illouz, who continues much earlier analyses of Rieff (1966) rightly observes: 'whereas Victorian emotional culture had divided men and women through the axis of the public and private spheres, the twentieth century therapeutic culture slowly eroded and reshuffled these boundaries by making emotional life central to the workplace' (Illouz, 2007, p. 16).

10. This inclusion of a reinterpreted past in the sensemaking frames of the present used to be slow and gradual – *The Civilization of the Renaissance in Italy* (1860) by Burckhardt or *The Decline and Fall of the Roman Empire* (1776–88) by Gibbon are separated by almost a hundred years from *The Last Byzantine Renaissance* (1970) by Runciman or *The Vanished Library* (1987) (about the burning of the library of Alexandria) by Canfora – but the process of searching and including has accelerated and acquired the institutionalized shape of a professionally run rewriting of the past for present or future users (see, for instance, Lowenthal, 1998; Burke, 2001). We will return to this point when talking about mediated history and the manufacturing of virtual pasts in the context of the third mode of patterning of sensemaking processes.

11. 'Therapies' used to be for the patients, nowadays they are for 'top achievers' as well; coaches used to be for the record breakers in sports, nowadays they are for all employees; intimate relations used to be the domain of a sovereign individual, nowadays individuals are serviced by a variety of counsellors and coaches, consultants and advisers, therapists and designers.

12. In 2004 a few years after Fortuyn's death, he came top in a poll carried out by Dutch TV channel KRO to determine the most important Dutchman of all times, leaving Rembrandt, Spinoza, van Gogh, Gullit and Cruyff behind.

13. For an analysis of the role of the internalized 'supervisor' in disciplining contemporary professionals (within postmodern human resource management), based on a novel reading of Lacan, see Hoedemaekers (2008).

14. Objectors to this conclusion point out a number of studies of IT software and systems specialists, for instance, Barley and Kunda's (2004) study of staffing agencies, *Gurus, Hired Guns, and Warm Bodies: Itinerant Experts in a Knowledge Economy*. However, the overall impact of such studies has been much reduced by placing them in an academic niche of an 'ICT bubble', thus defusing the criticism with an ideological suggestion that in most other walks of professional life things are quite different.

15. Campbell Jones and Damian O'Doherty (2005, pp. 1–3) are even more explicit: 'business school extorts fees from the middle and upper classes so that it can stamp their offspring with a passport into corporate sleaze, mortgage slavery, burn-out, stress, overwork, and repression ... Education is not about training or development: it is not about league tables and excellence. It is not about measurement and attainment.'

16. The classic argument of the military bureaucrats as presented by Joseph Heller in his novel *Catch-22* still merits attention. US military pilots can be released from their duties and avoid dangerous missions if they are considered mentally impaired. However, once they write a request to be released as partly insane, they are refused permission to leave, because an attempt to quit dangerous missions is considered a perfectly rational (that is, not insane) behaviour of any normal human being. Bureaucrats can thus still order their human resources around and if those resources want to escape their control, attempts are made to legitimize escape prevention.

17. Derber et al. (1990, p. 24) quote an anti-utopia about an expert meritocracy, written by Michael Young (a kind of a *1984* with intellectuals): 'We have an elite selected according to brains and educated according to experts ... we frankly realize that democracy can be no more than aspiration and have rule not so much by the people as by the cleverest people, not an aristocracy of birth, not a plutocracy of wealth, but a true meritocracy of talent' (Young, 1961, p. 21). They also add, ironically, 'In the 1990s, Communist planner[s] may be supplanted by Western-trained economists, engineers, and other experts widely viewed as the key to the renaissance of a transformed Eastern Europe' (Derber et al., 1990, p. 24).

18. 'Nation-states have become too big for the small problems (e.g. urban congestion) and too small for big problems (e.g. global warming), in other words, the Westphalian state-centric system of sovereign states is facing serious constraints' (Tehranian, 2007, p. 90).

19. Over-psychologizing is ubiquitous: 'The same four relational structures are evident in many diverse and historically unrelated cultures, at all levels of social organization. Once we recognize that the same basic structures organize so many domains of social thought and action, the only plausible explanation is psychological: people must always be using the same elementary models to generate, understand, coordinate and judge most social relationships' (Fiske, 1991, p. 407).

20. In explaining what determines intolerance, the author claims, in a summary printed inside the jacket, that one should reduce the explanation to 'innate psychological predispositions to intolerance' and to 'changing conditions of societal threat'. The latter, in turn, should be understood primarily as 'great dissention in public opinion and general loss of confidence in political leaders'.

21. Beckford still believes that criticism of rational choice theory as constructed by Margaret Archer can ultimately be used to improve the theory rather than refute it, for instance, by allowing for the role of passion, emotion and moral seriousness in decision-making by members of society and participants in social movements: 'The pursuit of moral ends for their own sake is therefore no less a constant of decision-making than is the pursuit of rational efficiency' (Beckford, 2000, p. 224). Beckford's remarks appear in a volume of 'critical realist interventions' edited by Archer and Tritter and aimed at the 'ahistorical' conceptualization of 'instrumental rationality' of *homo oeconomicus* (rational choice theory) as the dominant meta-paradigm in social sciences organized in academic institutions.

22. One is reminded of a quip 'should scientists be on top or on tap' (after Collins and Evans, 2007, p. 4).

23. Mary Jo Hatch wrote on organizational improvising making ample use of the experiences of her husband in jazz bands and exploring the metaphor of jazz improvisation in order to explain how employees can function in a team without having formally defined, bureaucratically organized roles (Hatch, 1999).

24. Critical intellectuals such as Fanon and anti-Russian communists such as Mao Zedong invested their revolutionary hopes in the third world peasants under (neo)colonial rule, where no revolution according to the Marxist blueprint happened. The rebellious students of 1968 went on a long march through academic, political and media-related bureaucracies, but rejected the intervention of the professional bureaucracies of political parties in their political activities.

25. I would like to thank Steve Linstead, Pippa Carter and Norman Jackson for details of the beginnings of SCOS, which I first attended in Milan in 1987.

26. 'The return of "the people" as a political category can be seen as the expansion of the horizons, because it helps to present other categories – such as class – for what they are: contingent and particular forms of articulating demands, not an ultimate core from which the nature of the demands themselves could be explained' (Laclau, 2005, p. 250).

27. Said's 'Orientalism Reconsidered' has rightly been quoted by most editors of anthologies on postmodernism (see Boyne and Rattansi, 1990), but his exhortations and a call for 'greater crossing of boundaries, for greater interventionism in cross-disciplinary activity, a concentrated awareness of the situation – political, methodological, social, historical' (Said, 2000, p. 215) have rarely been mentioned in academic discussions (the same happened to his call for 'a clarified political and methodological commitment to the dismantling of the system of domination', ibid.)

28. According to (an apocryphal) story, Martin Luther King supposedly wept hearing president Lyndon B. Johnson quoting his famous speech – 'We shall overcome some day'.

29. Soviet ideologues claimed that military discipline was necessary to train Russian peasants as industrial workers, otherwise the ambitious industrialization programme would collapse, because peasants used to take naps when they felt tired and left factories altogether for harvest periods. Shooting worker-peasants down for both forms of misconduct presumably accelerated their learning processes. Their arguments echo the century-older observations of Owen and his contemporaries about the natural laziness of Scottish workers unable to function as required until subjected to draconian discipline.

30. In considering the necessity for the rational choice approach in history, Peter Wagner linked its appearance to political states of emergency: 'The problem being addressed is the lack of common cultural resources – or ... of a common register of moral-political evaluation – to deal with a sociopolitical situation. Individualist rationality is then proposed as some kind of bottom-line on which everybody can agree – or at least would be willing to agree to end a dispute' (Wagner, 2000, p. 33).

31. Arjo Klamer, who, along with Phil Mirowski, Esther Mirjam Sent and Dave Colander criticizes the privileged procedures of mainstream economics, notes that it is hard to understand 'why Cambridge UK lost the battle on the so-called capital controversy to Cambridge US (even though it had superior arguments), how war agencies seemed to have influenced the course that economic theorizing took in the fifties, and what is happening in graduate school' (Klamer, 2007, p. 89). However, he speaks of the rhetoric of academic economists, not of the vulgarized vernacular slangs, which are spoken uncritically, without self-reflexive inquiry into the hidden injuries of rational choice transaction bias.

32. 'The 'therapeutic' view of love – in which a marriage should be evaluated by how well it meets the needs of the married partners as individuals – was not really what Frank and Emily wanted to hear ... This middle class couple, like most people most of the time, adopted a new cultural perspective selectively. They listened to experts, but with reservations, appropriating only what they could use and leaving the rest' (Swidler, 2001, p. 17).

33. In February 2008 a Dutch parliamentary commission published the so-called Dijsselbloem report on the state of education, which, although focusing on basic education, critically assessed the public authorities' withdrawal from and lack of supervision of the costs and quality of educational services in the country.

34. In spite of appeals, students trickle down to the lecture hall for an hour after the beginning of a lecture. A costly method of cutting down on such behaviour is to place uniformed guards at the entrance (at random, so that students never know which lecture hall entrance will be controlled), who make latecomers wait till the coffee break.

35. As debates around 'emotional intelligence' clearly indicate, emotions are considered necessary, but instrumental, subject to rational regulation and individual management.

36. This should not come as a surprise. The rankings depend on narrowly specialized journal publications and are peer assessed. Peers are academics and a broader relevance is usually irrelevant for them or at least toned down. This well known pathology of peer control has often been criticized in the

so-called science studies, but apart from Feyerabend (and to a certain extent Fuller) nobody has made a political issue out of it.

37. This belief does not quite match the real fluctuations of rankings in, let us say, the *Wall Street Journal* and the *Financial Times*, where the implementation of these policies was actually followed by a drop and not a hike (still in the first fifty, but down from thirty-first). One could argue, however, that these rankings mainly reflect the standing of RSM's MBA and executive programmes, and that they mostly account for the commercial operations of the faculty, which are not directly influenced by these policies and which are outside the direct control of public university management (since they are the commercial enclave run semi-independently of the faculty's departments).

38. It is interesting to note that in a recent debate on the rankings of top US universities one of the participants pleaded for moving business schools beyond media rankings with 'mass customization and stakeholder education' (Glick, 2008, p. 18), another for schools giving potential students access to all available rankings (educating consumers, DeNisi, 2008, p. 15), while yet another suggested that faculty should 'get over the notion that the survey's results were just another scorecard or ranking and began treating them as a set of comparative diagnostic tools. The result just might be a giant step toward creating the culture of evidence the rankings were supposed to engender in the first place' (Zemsky, 2008, p. 14). Yet, all those critical proposals for upgrading rankings and getting rid of pathologies are safely lodged in the commercial viability framework.

39. The list of declining rituals includes some collective social events, for instance, 'the sports afternoon', which should attract tennis, volleyball and football players and end in a general barbecue party for the entire faculty. One observes a diminishing interest in these boosts to the *esprit de corps*, which used to attract about half of the faculty staff a few years ago (2001) and could barely assemble one-third of the employees in 2007 and a quarter in 2008. Increasingly these large events are replaced by departmental receptions celebrating the beginning of a new year or a forthcoming summer holiday with a glass of champagne near the small departmental conference room.

40. Strictly speaking one should say either 'skills' or 'competence' instead of 'management', because the Dutch term is 'organisatie- en veranderkunde', but both 'skills' and 'competence' are less general, and so the choice is rather between 'organization and change management' or 'sciences of organization and change'. The issues of terminology and translation are not trivial: quite a number of inter-departmental turf wars are waged on behalf of a term that justifies an occupation of another research community's territory.

41. In't Veld had once become a deputy minister of education, but had to resign after barely a week in office, when his activities came under public scrutiny. Investigative journalists discovered that he was employed full time in two positions, thus doubling his salary (and using the university status to advertise the commercial services performed in time he had officially been working for the university). The scandal accelerated the negative response of the EUR to SIOO activities. Had he survived these media attacks, it would have been interesting to see whether government policies would have favoured 'escape platforms' for academic professionals (thus legitimizing SIOO-like

initiatives) or continued to strengthen university bureaucracies and control of extracurricular initiatives of academic staff (as is currently the case).

42. The president of the board of directors of Amsterdam University and the chairperson of the Dutch rector's conference had participated in discussions preceding the launching of the Academia Vitae, thus testing the support or resistance which might be expected.

43. The original plan was to create a network of ambitious upwardly mobile managers from large corporations, who would build up a sustainable base of permanent upgraders of their broader knowledge. They would be offered weekly sabbaticals from their companies to participate in elitist workshop sessions with academics – walking like Plato's disciples under the trees of some monastery garden (the original location was an old abbey in Dordrecht).

44. Strictly speaking, the former post-secondary vocational training schools are currently providing academic – bachelor – diplomas on a par with universities. However, academic staff believe that differences persist and these views colour present policies.

45. Bachelor-Master, an acronym for the standardized structure of university programmes introduced by the EU ministers of education in Bologna in 2000.

46. I am quoting Adler after Perelman, who tries to understand why some performers attain 'star' status in spite of the fact that they are neither more talented nor more creative than their competitors who fail to reach the same heights (Perelman, 2000).

47. Max Boisot was the first to notice the further consequences of Robert Parker's success in shifting the locus of power and decision-making from the producers to the consumers in the wine business (personal communication at the guest seminar held at the Erasmus University in 2006).

48. The predominance of rankings (and their ethical ambiguity) has also been criticized in another area of applied social sciences, namely in an unpublished paper analysing the relationship between IQ and job performance as a self-fulfilling prophecy, as a result of the pre-stacked cards of psychological IQ testing and the subsequent ranking of students and 'high potential' employees (Byington and Felps, 2008).

49. The term 'inner conversation' has recently been given a new lease of life by Margaret Archer, who defines it as 'the manner in which we reflexively make our way through the world. It is what makes (most of us) active agents … Being an active agent hinges on the fact that individuals develop and define their ultimate concerns; those internal goods that they care about most, the precise constellation of which makes for their concrete singularity as persons' (Archer, 2007, pp. 6–7).

50. Even the representatives of the mainstream academic philosophy of social action have noticed this disturbing aspect of Habermas: 'Accountability of social action cannot be explained as a consequence of the fact that it is linguistically coordinated, because speech acts do not generate the type of extradiscursive commitments that Habermas claims' (Heath, 2001, p. 307).

51. Interestingly enough, this process is stimulated by the ambitions of smaller cities with no academic traditions, which invite parallel academic entrepreneurship in order to upgrade their cities for tourists, investors and inhabitants. It can be seen in the origin of Academia Vitae (discussed above)

opened by Arjo Klamer of Erasmus University. Erasmus University is in Rotterdam, a city with a population of 700,000 and located within the dense 'Randstad' urban region stretching from Amsterdam to Rotterdam. Academia Vitae opened in the northeastern town of Deventer (population 100,000, isolated in a sparsely populated rural region).

52. 'The magnitudes of improvement in living standards due to aggregate economic growth simply overwhelm any putative deterioration due to increases in inequality' (Quah, 2003, p. 41).

53. I have translated a fragment of the 'Structural Report on Extraordinary Chair in the Economy of Performing Arts' written by Arjo Klamer on behalf of the commission (of which I was a member) proposing the establishment of the part-time chair. The report was written in a language typical of academic bureaucracies and the author, who is skilled in the critical analysis of economists' rhetoric, must have felt an unusual irony at the rhetorical fate that made him employ the language he had criticized so often in the past.

54. Lash and Urry were criticized for exaggerated oversimplification, but their hypothesis about the cultural turn in an economy saturated with symbolism was also acknowledged: 'Different industries, and the economic activities therein, play across a variety of symbolic registers – abstract, expressive, affective and aesthetic – and combine them in ways which stress certain kinds of symbolic usage at the expense of others' (Allen, 2002, p. 47).

55. 'The Uses of Images as Historical Evidence' is the subtitle of a study in cultural history by Peter Burke (the main title is *Eyewitnessing*, see Burke, 2001).

56. It has often been said that the placing of clocks on church and city hall towers in the European Middle Ages trained populations, disciplining them for future capitalist calculations of effort and profit. One wonders what consequences will follow the contemporary decline of significance of not only tower clocks but also of wristwatches, since time is communicated continuously by laptop screens, mobile phone displays, radio and digital urban communication devices.

57. One would like to use the term 'privatization' (as in privacy and private property), but it is not so much a matter of ownership as of a structuring of telecommunications allowing for individual, private, intimate participation.

58. This sentimental education can be subverted and redesigned by organized groups, for instance feminists who 'join efforts in breaking down the traditional hostile dichotomies that erroneously split economic transactions and intimate personal relationships into separate spheres, one antiseptically market-driven, the other cozily sentimental' (Zelizer, 2005, p. 302).

59. 'Floating' a creation such as a film requires not only a recognition of the potential target audience (as with material consumer goods marketing), not only a strategy for influencing crucial critics in taste-forming media (as in theoretical legitimation with higher cultural values), but also the management of damage or boost control (as in the PR management of a politician in all media) (Dempster, 2006, pp. 224–33).

60. When teaching at the International School for the New Media in the refurbished and gentrified docks of the former port of Lübeck in 2004, I discovered, among my students, individuals who went to Africa and helped establish and run local radio stations in order to build the infrastructure for communications needed for stimulating the growth of civil society. The school had been

started by Hubertus von Amelunxen, who is an art critic and theoretician of the new media, specializing in contemporary artistic photography.

61. See Ivins (1969; first edition 1953), McLuhan (1967; first edition 1964), Jay (1994), Debray (1996; first edition (in French) 1994).

62. The theme of connectivity and selective disconnecting has already attracted the attention of researchers trying to explain how and why some employees are able to disconnect, distancing themselves from the email stream seeing these actions as part and parcel of the political power struggle within work organizations (Brown and Lightfoot, 2002, pp. 209–29).

63. One is almost tempted to suggest a general principle 'new technology of communication equals original design plus bending its rules by users', but rules often emerge only after some uses have already been established (the making of Wikipedia is the case in point – see Baker, 2007). For more on 'bending the rules' – see Hinde (2007).

64. Axel Honneth quotes internet dating as one of the processes responsible for the self-reification (*Verdinglichung*) of individuals who have to communicate through internet dating protocols, reducing themselves to entries in preconceived, rigid registration forms (Honneth, 2005, p. 106).

65. Alternatively they tend to be distributed among many narrower specialists, for instance, marketing specialists who study 'consumer behavior in a landscape of commodified images' (Schroeder, 2002, back cover). This is especially important in view of the unfinished regulatory activities (legal and commercial) of the new multimedia communications, which make it difficult to see which domains of knowledge and skills should best be kept 'proprietory' and which should remain free virtual commons.

66. On Monday 7 April 2008, I was driven from the centre of Paris to CEDEP's INSEAD campus in Fontainebleau. We had to take a longer route, since the holy Olympic fire had just been brought from London and displayed in a Parisian stadium before being flown off to San Francisco, and street traffic was blocked by protesting groups. Ironically, as I was lecturing on cross-cultural leadership that evening, I had to think about future leaders capitalizing on the multimedia and creating new political agendas waiting for emergent champions.

67. The tacit assumption that ideologies are vague illusions prompting materially damaging actions (in itself a reflection of the tacit assumption mentioned above), and that religion is the most persistent and harmful illusion of all seems to be the source of the intensive emotional response of the British left intellectuals to religion (see Amis, 2008; Hitchens, 2007a, 2007b; Debray, 2006). For a more balanced view of religion, which does not claim a privileged status for religious authority behind moral codes but places religion within the cultural mosaic in a more objective manner, see for instance Hinde (2007) or Sen (2005).

68. I recall lunching in the Blue Star café near Vienna's Economic University one day and talking to a student who had chosen two master programmes: theology and geography. Her choice baffled me at the time, but from the point of interdisciplinary team membership she would be an interesting candidate, linking expertise on ideological flows with knowledge of material 'loci'.

69. One has to add that championing the Catalan cause, Castells revived the concept of the 'Fourth World', coined in 1974 within the Indian context, and gave it a new twist with respect to sub-state communities: an interesting

case of research gain prompted by ideological emotions. He also wrote that 'wireless Internet increases the chances of personalized networking to a wide range of social situations, thus enhancing the capacity of individuals to rebuild structures of sociability from the bottom up' (Castells, 2001, p. 132).

70. While one should not exaggerate in attributing too many theoretical choices or professional career hurdles to a political and generational pedigree, one should perhaps note that Castells, born in 1942, had been formed by generational experiences of May 1968 in student Paris and is currently a professor at the University of Southern California in Los Angeles and the Open University of Catalonia in Barcelona.

71. An interesting chronicle of this 'cultural turn' in studies of visual culture within the US academic context is offered by Dikovitskaya (2006) published, not surprisingly, by the MIT Press.

72. Having said that, Crary goes on to study aesthetic aspects of training individuals and telling them how to focus attention on spectacles offered by new and old media (thus Cezanne and Freud, Blake and William James rather than political and economic embedding).

73. Others do not harbour such doubts: 'In American society today – where "image management" has become both a lucrative business and a matter-of-fact necessity in commerce, industry, politics and interpersonal relations – style has ripened into an intrinsic and influential form of information. In countless aspects of life, the powers of appearance have come to overshadow, or to shape, the way we comprehend matters of substance' (Ewen, 1988, p. 259).

74. Hitchens is a personal enemy of God, academically trained professionals are negatively stereotyping Christian fundamentalists; both these phenomena are linked to the lingering suspicion that without tackling the religious articulation of moral values one cannot influence a change of 'habits of heart' and successfully implement leftist projects of designing a 'better society'. The old saying that religion is opium for the people while Marxism is opium for intellectuals should be thus modified: anti-Christian fundamentalism has replaced historical materialism as the opium of media intellectuals.

75. In discussing the oeuvre of Bill Viola, an artist working with billboard-sized video installations, one critic claimed that Viola 'moves beyond the cinematographic grammatization that ... forms the basis for contemporary real-time media (the global television system) and for the age of digital television to come: what Viola shows is that media, far from being the vehicle for reproduction (writing, grammatization) of life, is a mechanism for exposing the fundamental correlation of life with ... the preindividual, the domain of a nonlived that is strictly contemporaneous with the living and that forms the conditions of possibility for its continued viability in the future' (Hansen, 2004, pp. 265–6).

76. Broughton (2008); Baker (2008, p. 10) draws attention to the 2007 wave of deletions of 'companies, urban places, Web sites, lists, people, categories, and ideas – all deemed to be trivial, NN(nonnotable), "stubby", undersourced, or otherwise unencyclopaedic' and suggests creating a 'Wikimorgue' where deleted entries could still be accessed, proposing to call it 'Deletopedia'.

77. 'For instance, the US telephone industry (providing connectivity rather than content) had revenues of $256.1 billion in 1997. In comparison, the whole of

the US motion picture industry had revenues of $63 billion' (Joinson, 2003, p. 187).

78. Stiegler, in conversation with Derrida, developed an idea of liberating reflexivity in the 'domains of the visible and of movement' in order to develop a 'culture of reception': 'It is not possible to read without knowing how to write. And soon it will not be possible to see an image analytically: "television" ("l'ecran") and "text" ("l'ecrit") are not simply opposed' (Derrida and Stiegler, 2002, p. 163).

79. Cohn-Bendit wrote about children petting him and him returning caresses in the 1970s. When his confession was publicized in 2007 he claimed that these were his sexual phantasies, hinting at the publicity value of shocking confessions (there is no indication in the article that he was describing fantasies, not real experiences). However, positive associations with highbrow cultural consumption, for example, Nabokov's *Lolita*, or the morally ambiguous paintings of adolescent girls by Balthus, diluted the moral responses of the general public. One German and one Norwegian newspaper responded with endorsements: 'gay kindergartens at last', while French newspapers reminded their readers that Jean Paul Sartre and Simone de Beauvoir had repeatedly tried to legalize paedophilia in kindergartens, making it one of the leftist *causes celebres*.

80. At times this attitude produces bizarre media behaviour: on 8 April 2008, the Dutch media argued that the prime minister should intervene with the government of Indonesia, where a Dutch producer and seller of ecstasy on an industrial scale had been sentenced to death. Apparently the Indonesian victims of his criminal activities and the Indonesian system of justice had to give way before the rights of a member of a superior race who wanted to make life more pleasant for those experimenting with new lifestyles. None of the Dutch journalists and media professionals was even dimly aware of his or her own bias, righteously if tacitly certain that 'saving one of our own' (Dutch citizen) from the hands of subhuman barbarians (inhabitants of a former Dutch colony) comes first.

81. Ad van der Berg was one of the founders of the political party, 'Love Thy Neighbour, Freedom and Diversity' (NVD) based on a programme of lowering the age of consent for children engaging in sex with adults (*Algemein Dagblad*, 30 May 2006). The party was narrowly defeated when trying to register for the Dutch parliamentary elections of 2007. The very fact that he had tried to register this programme clearly indicates that he had hoped to band-wagon on the anti-Christian prejudices of the left, which sees religious organizations as the main obstacles in the way of 'liberating' human sexuality from as many constraints as possible.

82. Brown states simply: 'Spin is the rhetoric of an information age' (Brown, 2003, p. 155).

83. Debrix praises Wodiczko for offering urban communities 'vectors of speech, new methods of signification and presentation of themselves. Outside the dominant code, different forms of meaning may be accessed. Perhaps, through new mediations of meaning, new social interactions and cultural practices may be developed' (Debrix, 2003, p. xxxviii).

84. Note the classic window of opportunity for a new oligarchy or alternative elite: speaking up for the underdogs and attracting recognition. At the same

time this begins to restrict the underdogs' access to him/herself as 'artistic (or literary) representative', the only legitimate and true mouthpiece of the oppressed. One is reminded of the Polish novelist, Jerzy Andrzejewski's definition of cognac: 'a favorite alcohol of the working class, drunk through the mouths of its representatives'.

85. Benjamin wrote, in a letter to Adorno, that 'the crisis of storytelling was related to the general decline of the aura in other arts as well' (Jay, 2005, p. 333). One should add that in spite of the general popularity of this concept, many research programmes in managerial and organizational sciences, on leadership, for instance, are conducted in total ignorance of the Weberian input (the so-called servant leadership for instance is based on a rigorously behaviouristic approach and I am surprised, talking to behaviourist researchers of the subject, how little they think they need to know about critical theoretical insights that are more than five years old and were not published in the top ten journals which matter for their publication record).

86. If we value first and start noticing next, then the valuation act would have to resemble more a leap of faith than a rational decision after a systematic and 'objectively regulated' analysis of possibilities and alternatives.

87. Those are the titles of his two collections of philosophical essays on the political economy of attention and the political economy of 'spirit' respectively. Interestingly enough Franck does not quote either Appadurai (whose mediascapes could be of interest to him) nor Debray (mediology and mediaspheres). German, English and French academic bureaucracies and intellectual elites do not seem to share, exchange or overlap in knowledge production as much as they claim, exceptional cases of close collaboration notwithstanding (Borradori, 2003).

88. Eduardo Kac is a Brazilian-born and Chicago-based visual artist best known for his 'transgenic' and 'teleporting' art, questioning his audiences on the possibility of genetically manipulated futures (Alba project with a cloned rabbit) and mediated choices (for a competent interpretation of Kac's art see Ziarek, 2004).

89. Spielberg is morally irresponsible: *Schindler's List* works only if one forgets that the poor Jews saved by working hard for the Third Reich survived through helping the Germans to exterminate their brethren and continue the war. For the most aesthetically and ethically responsible view of this dilemma (touched upon in Styron's *Sophie's Choice*) see Tadeusz Borowski's Auschwitz stories – *Farewell to Maria* or *This Way for the Gas, Ladies and Gentlemen* (Borowski, 1992). Borowski and his Jewish mates from Sonderkommando survived the camp by working at the ovens cremating the bodies of the victims of the gas chambers. Borowski went on to become a celebrated writer in communist Poland and committed suicide when close affinities between Nazism and Stalinism became unbearable to his moral and artistic conscience.

5. Case in Point: Scaffolding for a Critical Turn in the Sciences of Management

1. Since Mintzberg's anti-MBA turn it is not unusual to find papers with titles such as 'The MBA Curricula of Top-Ranked U.S. Business Schools: a Study

in Failure?' (This particular one was published by Peter Navarro from the University of California in Irvine in the Academy of Management's *Learning & Education*, 7(1), March 2008: 109–23).

2. It is interesting in this context that the market for personal sensemaking of political realities and of peering behind the media image generated by spin doctors more recently facilitated the emergence of some intriguing portraits of top politicians written from the point of view of a professional who is a public intellectual, but does not have particular political loyalties (see Yasmina Reza (2007) on Nicolas Sarkozy, and Martin Amis (2008) on Tony Blair).

3. One should also mention the fact that apart from Erasmus University's Trust Fund, we managed to secure the generous support of the German Goethe Institute (led at the time by Ms Ute Kirchhelle) in the final act of atonement for the destruction of Rotterdam in 1940, when the entire city centre was destroyed in a Luftwaffe carpet-bombing raid. The return of the German Frankfurt School to the first academic Dutch school of management in Rotterdam had thus an ironic historical underpinning. However, this was probably the last chance to surf on this ironic context, since when I approached the new head of the Goethe Institute in Rotterdam in 2007, hoping to stage a comeback of the conference in 2013, I received no reply.

4. The Netherlands Institute for Advanced Studies in Wassenaar, near The Hague.

5. Ironically enough, he was shot by an animal rights activist in the parking lot of a television studio in Hilversum, after what was to be his last public interview, that is, by an extreme alternativist in a media park.

6. By a fellow Humboldtian I mean a former post-doctoral (Habilitation) researcher who had received a scholarship from the Alexander von Humboldt Foundation in Bad Godesberg. Zoran Djindjic had written his PhD thesis under Habermas's supervision and had spent some time at the university of Konstanz, where we had met as I was touring Germany with other Humboldt scholars in late spring 1981.

7. The last two are from Northwestern in Evanston and SUNY at Stony Brook, respectively. They have a niche position among academic philosophers in the USA, with McCarthy translating and championing Habermas and Howard relying on French critical philosophers to analyse 'democracy in America'.

8. Although to a certain extent the Academy of Management is being shadowed, since every annual meeting is preceded by the CMS seminar, which attracts not only core CMS participants but also many PhD students

9. Willmott quotes an associate editor of the *Academy of Management Journal*, Dov Eden, who expects to find a 'hotbed of dissent, sedition, and insurrection' at CMS gatherings, but finds instead 'that these are Academy members with a minority viewpoint that ought to be heard' (Eden, 2003, p. 309). I am grateful to Hugh Willmott for providing me with his recent assessment of the CMS movement and for the permission to quote from his unpublished paper.

10. At this point some credit can be claimed for the pioneering role of the Rotterdam conference, since the idea of marrying critical theory with a business school was relatively new at the time. I remember the rector of Erasmus University, a medical doctor by profession, asking me if it was not too risky politically to devote a serious conference in a serious university to

the critics of capitalism (apparently the critique of capitalism was not sufficiently serious or respectable in his view). I had to reassure him that Adorno
and Horkheimer were not 'red enemies' to be afraid of, though I didn't tell
him that they had changed 'capitalist exploiters' into 'captains of industry' in their *Dialectics of Enlightenment* to facilitate the book's reception in
the USA.

11. Another founding father of critical management studies, Mats Alvesson, went
further than the self-ironic 'father' in front of my name would suggest. He
wrote in an email replying to my query about his memories of the 'roots' of
CMS: 'Before the event 1988 you invited me to give a presentation on critical theory and management studies. Feeling some modesty, I asked Hugh
Willmott to co-author and present the piece. We then felt inspired to go further and more seriously try to mobilize the troops and encourage a much
stronger interest in this interesting cross-section. This led to a small workshop and then to the edited volume *Critical Management Studies* (Sage 1992)
which some people see as the event which launched this label as an important identity marker and organizing idea. To some limited extent it may have
influenced the framing of the field. (So, in one sense, you're the grandfather
to CMS!)' (Alvesson, 2008).

12. One might argue that discourse analysis (see Potter, 2004) and critical discourse analysis (see Wodak and Chilton, 2005) are close research relatives of
narrative studies of organization, as some CDA researchers explicitly quote
Helmut Dubiel and Douglas Kellner (see Fairclough, 2005), but elective affinities do not overlap. Thus narrative researchers may share some common
ancestors – for instance Derrida, Foucault and Garfinkel – with discourse analysts (who are also social constructivists) but not others, for example, Latour,
Knorr-Cetina, Wolgar or Haraway. CMS researchers may share Bakhtin or
Dubiel or Kellner with their CDA counterparts, but not necessarily Lakoff,
Fodor or Sperber.

13. 'Ethnographical approaches ... can be interpreted as providing alternative
methodological means of accessing the embedded nature of organizational
practices. The use of narratives (Czarniawska, 1998) is one aspect of this
methodology that can be used in conjunction with other ethnographic
methods' (Soin and Scheytt, 2006, p. 63).

14. Re-enchantment activities continue, but so far remain limited to niches.
Thus Rieff's posthumously published writings refer to the futile but ongoing
attempts at a rejuvenation of 'the officer class' (academics, artists, writers,
columnists, philosophers and intellectuals able to defend the authority and
values behind the cultural theatre of daily life; see Rieff, 2007), while Chicago
economists focusing on the rhetoric of their discipline praise the return of the
'bourgeois virtues' (McCloskey, 2006 – the author presented her book-in-the-
making on PhD seminars at Erasmus University in Rotterdam in 2006 and
2007), as if suggesting that their return might fill the black hole left by the
radical destruction of core authorities in western culture.

15. The classic example of the 'established left with academic credentials' remains
the vision of 'participatory economics = parecon' (see Albert, 2004).

16. The category of hidden persuaders can include 'the experts', whose status and
ideologies may become transformed by the new media, for instance, the web
(see Walsh, 2003).

6. The Future Tense of Meaning (Cultural Revolutions, Social Transformations and Media Rituals)

1. Since the play was written before 1918, Jarry was correct in a legal sense: until the signing of the Versailles Treaty, Poland was still partitioned between Russians, Prussians and Austrians as had been the case throughout the nineteenth century. But that is not what he meant. At the time the idea of a country a thousand kilometres from Paris seemed distant, exotic and unreal. Today, Borat has to invent a fictive Kazakhstan to persuade us that distance is exotic.

2. 'Many scholars engaged in the field of organization theory argue that an organization is human or at least similar to humans. The "error" of attributing uniquely human characteristics to other types of units is called anthropomorphism and is widespread in organization literature' (Andersen, 2008, p. 174).

3. For a brief summary of this debate, better known as the Popper-Kuhn debate and canonized in Lakatos and Musgrave's *Criticism and the Growth of Knowledge*, see Magala (2005, pp. 15–16).

4. Lenin's lack of a sense of humour and his suspicions of sophisticated intellectuals influenced world academic communities in unexpected ways, for instance, when he sent the first two shiploads of Russia's intellectual elite into German and French exile in 1922. Apart from the Berdayevs and the Khodasevitches, Pitrim Sorokin (who went on to shape US sociology, establishing a department at Harvard) was on board. Bakhtin wasn't, but his sentence of imprisonment in a concentration camp in Siberia was mercifully changed to deportation to Kazakhstan.

5. De Duve is wrong, as may be empirically demonstrated: Bonnard is recycled by contemporary art galleries, museums and exhibition halls as (or more) frequently than Rodchenko. De Duve erred in freezing the dichotomies of the early twentieth century. Today, in the early twenty-first century, Lucien Freud's figurative paintings are viewed as highly (and as often) as the work of his more abstract peer, Francis Bacon. It appears that Bonnard is being resuscitated on and off by curators of large museums (in the Museum of Modern Art in New York in 1998, in Paris in 2006), while Rodchenko remains part of the Russian formalist avant-garde school, which is studied more by critics and theoreticians than it is viewed by the general public. But de Duve is a critic and thus represents a 'professional bias' in this respect.

6. Researchers are beginning to take note of the problem – see for instance, titles like *The Hyperlinked Society* (Turow and Tsiu, 2008)

7. 'The aristocrats of intelligence believe that there are truths that are not good to tell to the people. For me, as a revolutionary socialist and sworn enemy of all aristocracies and all tutelage, I believe on the contrary that the people must be told everything. There is no other way of restoring their complete freedom' (Bourdieu, 2008, p. 384; first delivered as a lecture in 2000 and published in French in 2002).

8. At the 1988 Rotterdam Congress on critical theory, Helmut Dubiel, who had been leading the research institute linked to the archives of the Institute for Social Research in Frankfurt, presented a paper on 'Domination or Emancipation: Struggle for Critical Theory's Heritage' (Dubiel, 1990). In 2006

he published the autobiographical story of another struggle – that against Parkinson's disease, 'Deep Inside the Brain', demonstrating a critical attitude and offering a humanist critique of the medical profession from the position of an almost daily patient over thirteen years (Dubiel, 2006).

9. Nobody could have predicted the appearance of existentialism nor its close links to the lifestyle of urban professionals, nor the role that Camus' literary talent or Parisian postwar jazz clubs played in the making of a new 'popular philosophy' employed as a matrix for the management of meaning in all walks of life, if all one knew was that the French philosophers were drafted, kept isolated as prisoners of war, and given access to Heidegger.

10. And does nothing to solve real problems, for instance, the conflict between traditional and conservative tribal norms of killing a woman who divorces or who marries outside her community and the legal systems of most western societies.

11. Former minister of foreign affairs, Bernard Bot, used the slogan 'proud to be European' in his public Mandeville lecture, Rotterdam, 21 May 2008. Even quality newspapers did not report this, probably classifying it as the domestic affair of a university – an elitist alternative to the populist slogan apparently was a non-issue for the media professionals.

12. Fisher quotes Bill Readings (1996).

13. Furedi quotes Bauman and adds quotations from Said, Lipset and C. Wright Mills in order to make the point that traditional (that is, as they would have been understood in the nineteenth and twentieth centuries) public intellectuals 'assume their role through representing the standpoint of a constituency or of a wider public' (Furedi, 2004, p. 36).

14. An economist, a former colleague of mine and predecessor as the head of the department, contributes to an editorial in the Saturday edition of a large Dutch quality newspaper *NRC Handelsblad,* aiding the shift of public opinion away from neoliberal market idolatry, and thus assuming this role of a public intellectual (see Nooteboom, 2008, p. 14). But he does so only once in 3 or 4 years, and even if all the editorial pages in all the weekend editions had been filled by the most critical academic intellectuals, it would still mean a relatively limited influence upon 'public opinion' forming.

15. Needless to say, de Swaan is well aware of the fact that: 'The danger of global uniformity is not in the language. It is in the power relations that prevail in the global constellation, where English is the hypercentral language' (ibid.)

16. 'The result is that the ULMC (ULMC stands for University of Leicester Management Centre) has shown a clear commitment and desire to become the major worldwide location for scholarly, creative and iconoclastic thought that challenges common assumptions about the means and ends of organizing in particular, and rethinking management, business and organization more generally' (Williams, 2005, p. xii).

17. In response to this call, I submitted the track proposal 'Limits of Inequality: Citizens and Academics' (see Appendix 1).

18. The inevitability and ubiquity of commercialization of all social exchanges are being questioned by economists who point out that 'there persists large amount of non-exchange work in the form of what is variously called "domestic work" or "housework", non-monetized exchange in the form of

volunteering continues to take place, and not-for-profit monetized exchange in either the public sector or not-for-profit sector is far from eradicated' (Williams, 2005, p. 26).
19. For instance, the invention of a biotechnological solution to the reduction of carbon dioxide emissions without slowing economic growth.
20. Dyson does not reject the environmentalist ideology (although he objects to environmentalist dogmas, which he calls a new secular religion), but pleads for paying more attention to more immediate threats to the planet – 'nuclear weaponry, environmental degradation and social injustice' (Dyson, 2008, p. 45).

7. Instead of Conclusions: the Revenge of Populism and the Transformation of Angry Mobs into Mobilized Alternative Social Networks

1. In legal terms India is a democratic federation of states, while China is a communist dictatorship. Calling for more local democracy could be seen as superfluous in India and subversive in China although it makes sense in both, because democracy is as unfinished a project in India as everywhere else and because Chinese communism has already evolved towards the 'market' part of market democracies and may face problems with the 'democracy' part in future (for an excellent analysis of this evolution see Boisot's model of information space; Boisot, 1995, 1998).
2. Butsch notices, very perceptively, that the development of survey research was boosted by commercial audience measurement and overlapping personal links (between, for instance, Cantril, Gallup and Lazarsfeld) and that both in marketing and political polling 'interactions among individuals were irrelevant. Also, in the psychometric theory that is the basis of survey research, the individual's answer is conceived as a fixed response to a fixed stimulus, the question; individuals are passive reactors, not active agents' (Butsch, 2008, p. 122).

Literature

Academia Vitae, 2007, www.Academiavitae.nl.

Adler, Moshe, 1985, 'Stardom and Talent', *American Economic Review*, 75(1) (March): 208–12.

Adler, Nancy J., 2008, 'The Art of Global Leadership: Designing Options Worthy of Choosing', in Daved Barry and Hans Hansen (eds), *The Sage Handbook of New Approaches in Management and Organization*, Los Angeles, London, New Delhi and Singapore: Sage.

Adorno, Theodor W. and Max Horkheimer, 1999, *The Dialectic of Enlightenment*, London: Verso (first edition 1944).

Adorno, Theodor W., Else Frenkel-Brunswick and Daniel Levinson, 1991, *The Authoritarian Personality: Studies in Prejudice*, New York: Norton.

Agger, Ben, 2004, *Speeding Up Fast Capitalism: Cultures, Jobs, Families, Schools, Bodies*, Boulder, CO: Paradigm.

Albert, Michael, 2004, *PARECON: Life after Capitalism*, London and New York: Verso.

Allen, John, 2002, 'Symbolic Economies: the "Culturalization" of Economic Knowledge', in Paul Du Gay and Michael Pryke (eds), *Cultural Economy: Cultural Analysis and Commercial Life*, London: Sage.

Alvesson, Mats, 2008, 'Re: CMS', personal e-mail communication, 14 April.

Alvesson, Mats and Maxine Robertson, 2006, 'The Best and the Brightest: the Construction, Significance and Effects of Elite Identities in Consulting Firms', *Organization*, 13(2): 195–224.

Alvesson, Mats and Hugh Willmott, 1990, 'Critical Theory and the Sciences of Management', in F. Engeldorp-Gastelaars, S. Magala and O. Preuss (eds), *Critical Theory and the Science of Management*, The Hague: Universitaire Pers Rotterdam.

Alvesson, Mats and Hugh Willmott (eds), 1992, *Critical Management Studies*, London and Thousand Oaks: Sage.

Alvesson, Mats and Hugh Willmott (eds), 2003, *Studying Management Critically*, London, Sage.

Amadae, S.M., 2003, *Rationalizing Capitalist Democracy: the Cold War Origins of Rational Choice Liberalism*, Chicago: University of Chicago Press.

Amis, Martin, 2002, *Koba, the Dread. Laughter and the Twenty Million*, London: Jonathan Cape.

Amis, Martin, 2008, *The Second Plane: September 11: 2001–2007*, London, Jonathan Cape.

Andersen, Jon Aarum, 2008, 'An Organization Called Hary', *Journal of Organizational Change Management*, 21(2): 174–87.

Appadurai, Arjun, 1996, *Modernity at Large*, Minneapolis and London: University of Minnesota Press.

Appadurai, Arjun, 2001, *Globalization*, Durham and London: Duke University Press.

Archer, Margaret S., 2000, 'Homo economicus, Homo sociologicus and Homo sentiens', in Margaret S. Archer and Jonathan Q. Tritter (eds), *Rational Choice Theory: Resisting Colonization*, London and New York: Routledge.

Archer, Margaret S., 2007, *Making Our Way through the World: Human Reflexivity and Social Mobility*, Cambridge: Cambridge University Press.

Archer, Margaret S. and Jonathan Q. Tritter (eds), 2000, *Rational Choice Theory: Resisting Colonization*, London and New York: Routledge.

Arrighi, Giovanni, 2006, 'Spatial and Other "Fixes" of Historical Capitalism', in Christopher Chase-Dunn and Salvatore J. Babones, *Global Social Change: Historical and Comparative Perspectives*, Baltimore: Johns Hopkins University Press.

Arrighi, Giovanni, 2007, *Adam Smith in Beijing. Lineages of the Twenty-First Century*, London and New York: Verso.

Austin, J.L., 1986, *How to do Things with Words*, Oxford: Oxford University Press (first edition 1962).

Baert, Patrick, 2005, *Philosophy of the Social Sciences: Towards Pragmatism*, Cambridge: Polity Press.

Baker, Nicholson, 2008, 'The Charms of Wikipedia', *New York Review of Books*, 55(4), 20 March.

Baldassari, Anne, 1997, *Picasso and Photography: the Dark Mirror*, Houston: Flammarion and the Museum of Fine Arts Houston.

Barley, Stephen R. and Gideon Kunda, 2004, *Gurus, Hired Guns, and Warm Bodies: Itinerant Experts in a Knowledge Economy*, Princeton and Oxford, Princeton University Press.

Bauman, Zygmunt, 1987, *Legislators and Interpreters: On Modernity, Post-Modernity and Intellectuals*, Cambridge: Polity Press.

Beck, Ulrich, 2006, *The Cosmopolitan Vision*, Cambridge: Polity Press.

Beckford, James A., 2000, 'When the Battle is Lost and Won', in Margaret S. Archer and Jonathan Q. Tritter (eds), *Rational Choice Theory: Resisting Colonization*, London and New York: Routledge.

Beebee, Thomas O., 2002, 'The Öffentlichkeit of Jurgen Habermas', in Jeffrey Nealon and Caren Irr (eds), *Rethinking the Frankfurt School: Alternative Legacies of Cultural Critique*, Albany: State University of New York Press.

Beer, Michael and Nitin Nohria, 2000, *Breaking the Code of Change*, Cambridge, MA: Harvard Business School Press.

Benjamin, Walter, 1969, 'The Work of Art in the Age of Mechanical Reproduction', in *Illuminations*, ed. Hanna Arendt, New York: Schocken.

Bennett, Jane, 2001, *The Enchantment of Modern Life: Attachments, Crossings, and Ethics*, Princeton and London: Princeton University Press.

Berger, Peter, 1963, *Invitation to Sociology*, Harmondsworth: Penguin.

Berger, Peter and Thomas Luckmann, 1966, *The Social Construction of Reality: a Treatise in the Sociology of Knowledge*, London: Allen Lane.

Bernstein, Elisabeth, 2007, *Temporarily Yours: Intimacy, Authenticity, and the Commerce of Sex*, Chicago and London: University of Chicago Press.

Bochenski, Jozef M., 1965, *The Logic of Religion*, New York: New York University Press [Polish translation by S. Magala, 1990, *Logika religii*, Warsaw: Pax].

Böhm, Steffen, 2005, 'Zero', in Campbell Jones and Damian O'Doherty (eds), *Manifestos for the Business Schools of Tomorrow*, Stanford, CA: Dvalin Books (Creative Commons).

Boisot, Max, 1995, *Information Space: a Framework for Learning in Organizations, Institutions and Culture*, London: Routledge.

Boisot, Max, 1998, *Knowledge Assets: Securing Competitive Advantage in the Information Economy*, Oxford: Oxford University Press.

Boje, David, 2007, 'Storytelling Organization', http://Storytelling-Organization.com.

Bolce, Louis and Gerald De Maio 2008, 'A Prejudice for the Thinking Classes: Media Exposure, Political Sophistication, and the Anti-Christian Fundamentalist', *American Politics Research*, 36: 155–85.

Boltanski, Luc and Laurent Thévenot, 2006, *On Justification: Economies of Worth*, Princeton, NJ and Oxford: Princeton University Press.

Booth, Wayne C., 1987, *The Idea of a University as Seen by a Rhetorician*, the 1987 Ryerson Lecture, Chicago: University of Chicago Press.

Borowski, Tadeusz, 1992, *This Way for the Gas, Ladies and Gentlemen*, Harmondsworth and New York: Penguin.

Borradoti, Giovanna (ed.), 2003, *Philosophy in a Time of Terror: Dialogues with Jürgen Habermas and Jacques Derrida*, Chicago and London: University of Chicago Press.

Bourdieu, Pierre, 2008, *Political Interventions: Social Science and Political Action*, London and New York: Verso.

Bourriaud, Nicolas, 2007, 'Relational Aesthetics: Art of the 1990s', in Margriet Schavemaker and Mischa Rakier (eds), *Right About Now: Art and Theory since the 1990s*, Amsterdam: Valiz Publishers.

Boyne, Roy and Ali Rattansi (eds), 1990, *Postmodernism and Society (Communications and Culture)*, London and New York: Palgrave Macmillan.

Brin, David, 1998, *The Transparent Society: Will Technology Force Us to Choose Between Privacy and Freedom?* Reading, MA: Perseus Books.

Broughton, John, 2008, *Wikipedia: the Missing Manual*, Cambridge, MA: Pogue Press/O'Reilly.

Brown, Robin, 2003, 'Spinning the World: Spin Doctors, Mediation, and Foreign Policy', in François Debrix and Cynthia Weber (eds), *Rituals of Mediation: International Politics and Social Meaning*, Minneapolis and London: University of Minnesota Press.

Brown, Steven D. and Geoffrey Lightfoot, 2002, 'Presence, Absence and Accountability: E-mail and the Mediation of Organizational Memory', in Steve Woolgar (ed.), *Virtual Society? Technology, Cyberbole, Reality*, Oxford and New York: Oxford University Press.

Burawoy, Michael, 1985, *The Politics of Production: Factory Regimes under Capitalism and Socialism*, London: Verso.

Burawoy, Michael, 2005, 'Conclusion: Provincializing the Social Sciences', in George Steinmetz (ed.), *The Politics of Method in the Human Sciences: Positivism and its Epistemological Others*, Durham, NC and London: Duke University Press.

Burke, Peter, 2001, *Eyewitnessing: the Uses of Images as Historical Evidence*, London: Reaktion Books.

Byington, Eliza and Will Felps, 2008, 'One Measure to Rule Them All? The Social Production of the IQ–Job Performance Relationship', paper presented at the annual meeting of the Academy of Management, Organizational Management Theory Division, Anaheim, CA,

Byrne, Richard A. and Andrew Whiten, 1989, *Machiavellian Intelligence: Social Expertise and the Evolution of Intellect in Monkeys, Apes and Humans*, Oxford: Oxford University Press.

Carroll, Noel, 2008, *The Philosophy of Motion Pictures*, Oxford and Malden, MA: Blackwell.

Castells, Manuel, 2001, *The Internet Galaxy: Reflections on the Internet, Business, and Society*, Oxford and New York: Oxford University Press.

Castells, Manuel, 2007, 'Communication, Power and Counterpower in the Network Society', *International Journal of Communication*, 1: 238–66 (http://ijoc.org).

Castells, Manuel and Martin Ince, 2003, *Conversations with Manuel Castells*, Cambridge: Polity Press.

Caute, David, 2003, *The Dancer Effects: the Struggle for Cultural Supremacy during the Cold War*, Oxford: Oxford University Press.

Chandler, Alfred D., 1977, *The Visible Hand*, Cambridge, MA: Harvard University Press.

Ciborra, Claudio, 2002, *The Labyrinths of Information: Challenging the Wisdom of Systems*, Oxford: Oxford University Press.

Clegg, Stuart, Martin Kornberger and Tyrone Pitsis, 2005, *Managing and Organizations: an Introduction to Theory and Practice*, London, Thousand Oaks and New Delhi: Sage.

Collins, Harry and Robert Evans, 2007, *Rethinking Expertise*, Chicago and London: Chicago University Press.

Crary, Jonathan, 2001, *Suspensions of Perception: Attention, Spectacle, and Modern Culture*, Cambridge, MA and London: MIT Press.

Critchley, Simon, 2007, *Infinitely Demanding: Ethics of Commitment, Politics of Resistance*, London and New York: Verso.

Critical Management Studies, Wikipedia, http://en.wikipedia.org/wiki/Critical_management_studies, 22 March 2008.

Czarniawska-Joerges, Barbara, 1988, *Ideological Control in Non-Ideological Organizations*, New York: Praeger.

Czarniawska-Joerges, Barbara, 1990, 'Rationality as an Organizational Product: on Multiple Rationalities and Organizational Learning', in F. Engeldorp-Gastelaars, S. Magala and O. Preuss (eds), *Critical Theory and the Science of Management*, The Hague: Universitaire Pers Rotterdam.

Czarniawska-Joerges, Barbara, 1992, *Exploring Complex Organizations*, Beverly Hills, CA: Sage.

Czarniawska-Joerges, Barbara, 1994, 'Narratives of Individual and Organizational Identities', in Stanley Deetz (ed.), *Communication Yearbook*, vol. 17, Newbury Park: Sage.

Czarniawska, Barbara, 1997, *Narrating the Organization. Dramas of Institutional Identity*, Chicago: University of Chicago Press.

Czarniawska, Barbara, 1998, *A Narrative Approach to Organization Studies*, London: Sage.

Czarniawska, Barbara, 1999, *Writing Management: Organization Theory as a Literary Genre*, Oxford and New York: Oxford University Press.

D'Iribarne, Philippe, 1989, *La logique de l'honneur: Gestion des enreprises et traditions nationales*, Paris: Seuil.

De Duve, Thierry, 1998, *Kant after Duchamp*, Cambridge MA and London: MIT Press (an October book).

De Swann, Abram, 2001, *Words of the World: the Global Language System*, Cambridge, Oxford and Malden, MA: Polity.

Debray, Regis, 1996, *Media Manifestos. On the Technological Transmission of Cultural Forms*, London and New York: Verso.

Debray, Regis, 2006, *Aveuglantes lumieres: Journal en clair-obscur*, Paris: Gallimard.

Debrix, François, 2003, 'Introduction', in François Debrix and Cynthia Weber (eds), *Rituals of Mediation. International Politics and Social Meaning*, Minneapolis and London: University of Minnesota Press.

Debrix, François and Cynthia Weber (eds), 2003, *Rituals of Mediation. International Politics and Social Meaning*, Minneapolis and London: University of Minnesota Press.

Dempster, Anna, 2006, 'Managing Uncertainty in Creative Industries: Lessons from Jerry Springer the Opera', *Creativity and Innovation Management*, 15(3): 224–33.

DeNisi, Angelo S., 2008, 'Rain, Snow, and Sleet are just Different Types of Precipitation', *Academy of Management Perspectives*, 22(1): 15–17.

Derber, Charles, William Schwartz and Yale Magrass, 1990, *Power in the Highest Degree: Professionals and the Rise of a New Mandarin Order*, New York and Oxford: Oxford University Press.

Derrida, Jacques and Bernard Stiegler, 2002, *Ethnographies of Television: Filmed Interviews*, Cambridge: Polity Press.

Dikovitskaya, Margaret, 2006, *Visual Culture: the Study of the Visual after the Cultural Turn*, Cambridge, MA and London: MIT Press.

DiMaggio, Paul and Walter W. Powell, 1983, 'The Iron Cage Revisited: Institutional Isomorphism and Collective Rationality in Organizational Fields', *American Sociological Review*, 48: 147–60

Djilas, Milovan, 1957, *The New Class: an Analysis of the Communist System*, New York: Praeger.

Dotti, Jorge E., 1999, 'From Karl to Carl: Schmitt as a Reader of Marx', in Chantal Mouffe (ed.), *The Challenge of Carl Schmitt*, London and New York: Verso.

Dubiel, Helmut, 1990, 'Herrschaft oder Emanzipation? Der Streit um die Erbschaft der Kritischen Theorie', in Ph. v. Engeldorp-Gastelaars, S. Magala and O. Preuss (eds), *Wirkungen kritische Theorie und kritisches Denken*, Rotterdam: Universitaire Pers Rotterdam.

Dubiel, Helmut, 2006, *Tief im Hirn*, Munich: Verlag Antje Kunstman.

Dubord, Guy, 1992, *La Societé du Spectacle*, Paris: Gallimard.

Dufresne, Todd, 2003, *Killing Freud: Twentieth Century Culture and the Death of Psychoanalysis*, London: Continuum Books.

Dyson, Freman, 2008, 'The Question of Global Warming', *New York Review of Books*, LV(10): 43–5.

Eagleton, Terry, 2007, *The Meaning of Life*, Oxford: Oxford University Press.

Eco, Umberto, 1979, *The Role of the Reader: Exploration in the Semiotics of Texts*, Bloomington: Indiana University Press.

Eden, D., 2003, 'Critical Management Studies and the Academy of Management Journal: Challenge and Counterchallenge', *Academy of Management Journal*, 46(4): 390–4.

Ehrenreich, Barbara, 2002, *Nickel and Dimed: Undercover in Low-Wage USA*, London: Granta Books.

Engeldorp-Gastelaars, Frits van, Slawomir Magala and Otmar Preuss (eds), 1990, *Critical Theory Today. The Frankfurt School: How Relevant Is It Today?* The Hague, Universitaire Pers Rotterdam.

Erasaari, Risto, 1990, 'Network Society as a New Critical Concept?', in F. Engeldorp-Gastelaars, S. Magala and O. Preuss (eds), *Critical Theory and the Science of Management*, The Hague: Universitaire Pers Rotterdam.

Erasmus University Rotterdam, 2008, 'Een carrière in de wetenschap? Vrouwenlijke hoogleraren over hun vak en hun leven', Rotterdam, Europoint Media.

Essers, Juup, 2007, 'Incommensurability and Organization: the Reconstruction of an Academic Stalemate', PhD thesis, Rotterdam, Erasmus Research Institute of Management.

EURAM 2009 – Call for Track Proposals, 22 May 2009, Brussels, http://www.euram2009.org/r/default.asp?iId=EDKLMF.

Ewen, Stuart, 1988, *All Consuming Images: the Politics of Style in Contemporary Culture*, New York: Basic Books.

Fairclough, Norman, 2005, 'Critical Discourse Analysis in Transdisciplinary Research', in Ruth Wodak and Paul Chilton (eds), *A New Agenda in (Critical) Discourse Analysis: Theory, Methodology and Interdisciplinarity*, Amsterdam/Philadelphia: John Benjamins Publishing Company.

Ferguson, Harvie, 2006, *Phenomenological Sociology: Experience and Insight in Modern Society*, London: Sage.

Feyerabend, Paul, 1967, 'On the Improvement in the Sciences and the Arts and the Possible Identity of the Two', in Robert E. Cohen and Marx W. Wartofsky (eds), *Boston Studies in the Philosophy of Science, Volume III*, Dordrecht: Reidel, pp. 387–415.

Feyerabend, Paul, 1975, *Against Method*, London: Verso.

Feyerabend, Paul, 1999, *Conquest of Abundance: a Tale of Abstraction versus the Richness of Being*, Chicago: University of Chicago Press.

Fischer, Michael M.J., 2003, *Emergent Forms of Life and the Anthropological Voice*, Durham and London: Duke University Press.

Fiske, Alan Page, 1991, *Structures of Social Life: the Four Elementary Forms of Human Relations*, New York: The Free Press.

Franck, Georg, 2005, *Mentaler Kapitalismus. Eine politische Oekonomie des Geistes*, Vienna: Carl Hanser Verlag.

Fromm, Erich, 1994, *Escape from Freedom*, New York: Holt (first edition 1941).

Fuller, Steve, 2000, *Thomas Kuhn: a Philosophical History for our Times*, Chicago and London: University of Chicago Press.

Furedi, Frank, 2004, *Where Have All the Intellectuals Gone? Confronting 21st Century Philistinism*, London and New York: Continuum.

Gabriel, Yiannis, 1999, *Organizations in Depth: the Psychoanalysis of Organizations*, London: Sage.

Gabriel, Yiannis, 2002, 'On Paragrammatic Uses of Organizational Theory: a Provocation', *Organization Studies*, 23: 133–51.

Gabriel, Yiannis, 2004, *Myths, Stories and Organizations: Premodern Narratives for our Times*, Oxford: Oxford University Press.

Gabriel, Yiannis, 2008, 'Against the Tyranny of PowerPoint: Technology-in-Use and Technology Abuse', *Organization Studies*, 29: 255–76.

'General Electric: Jack Welch's Second Wave', 1992, video, Harvard Business Club.

Ghoshal, Sumantra and Nitin Nohria, 1997, *The Differentiated Network: Organizational Knowledge Flows in Multinational Corporations*, San Francisco: Jossey-Bass.

Giacalone, Robert A., Carole L. Jurkiewicz, and John R. Deckop, 2008, 'On Ethics and Social Responsibility: the Impact of Materialism, Postmaterialism and Hope', *Human Relations*, 61(4): 483–514.

Glick, William H., 2008, 'Rain Man or Piped Piper? Moving Business Schools beyond Media Rankings with Mass Customization and Stakeholder Education, *Academy of Management Perspectives*, 22(1): 18–23.

Goldfarb, Jeffrey C., 2006, *The Politics of Small Things: the Power of the Powerless in Dark Times*, Chicago and London: Chicago University Press.

Gomez, Lavinia, 2005, *The Freud Wars: an Introduction to the Philosophy of Psychoanalysis*, London: Routledge.

Gore, Al, 2006, *An Inconvenient Truth: the Planetary Emergence of Global Warming and What We Can Do about It*, New York: Rodale Books.

Grey, C. and Hugh Willmott, 2005, *Critical Management Studies: a Reader*, Oxford and New York: Oxford University Press.

Guilbaut, Serge, 1983, *How New York Stole the Idea of Modern Art: Abstract Impressionism, Freedom and the Cold War*, Chicago: University of Chicago Press.

Guillet de Monthoux, Pierre, 2004, *The Art Firm: Aesthetic Management and Metaphysical Marketing*, Stanford, CA: Stanford University Press.

Habermas, Jurgen, 1972, *Knowledge and Human Interests*, Boston: Beacon Press.

Habermas, Jurgen, 1984, *The Theory of Communicative Action*, vol. I, Boston: Beacon Press.

Habermas, Jurgen, 1987, *The Theory of Communicative Action*, vol. II, Boston: Beacon Press.

Hansen, Mark B.N., 2004, *New Philosophy for New Media*, Cambridge, MA and London: MIT Press.

Harrison, Bennett, 2003, 'Lean and Mean: the Changing Landscape of Corporate Power in the Age of Flexibility', in Michael J. Handel (ed.), *The Sociology of Organizations: Classic, Contemporary and Critical Readings*, Thousand Oaks, CA: Sage.

Hatch, Mary Jo, 1999, 'Exploring the Empty Spaces of Organizing: How Improvisational Jazz Helps Redescribe Organization Studies', *Organization Studies*, 1(1): 75–100.

Heath, Joseph, 2001, *Communicative Action and Rational Choice*, Cambridge, MA and London: MIT Press.

Hinde, Robert A., 2007, *Bending the Rules: Morality in the Modern World from Relationships to Politics and War*, Oxford and New York: Oxford University Press.

Hirschman, Albert O., 1992, *Rival Views of Market Society and Other Recent Essays*, Cambridge, MA: Harvard University Press.

Hitchens, Christopher, 2004, 'The Captive Mind Now: What Czeslaw Milosz Understood about Islam', http://www.slate.com/id/2105821/.

Hitchens, Christopher, 2007a, *God Is Not Great: How Religion Poisons Everything*, New York: Twelve Books.

Hitchens, Christopher, 2007b, *The Portable Atheist: Essential Readings for the Nonbeliever*, Cambridge, MA: Da Capo Press.

Hite, Shere, 2004, *A National Study of Female Sexuality*, New York: Seven Stories Press (first edition 1976).

Hoedemaekers, Casper, 2008, 'Performance Pinned Down: a Lacanian Analysis of Subjectivity at Work', Erasmus Research Institute of Management, Rotterdam.

Hofstede, Geert, 1980, *Culture's Consequences: International Differences in Work-related Values*, Newbury Park, London and New Delhi: Sage.

Honneth, Axel, 1994, *Kampf um Anerkennung. Zur moralischen Grammatik sozialer Konflikte*, Frankfurt am Main: Suhrkamp.

Honneth, Axel, 2005, *Verdinglichung*, Frankfurt am Main: Suhrkamp.

House of Commons Treasury Committee, 2008, Stern Report, http://www.hm-treasury.gov.uk/stern_review_climate_change.htm.

Huntington, Samuel, 2005, *Who Are We? The Challenges to America's National Identity*, New York: Simon and Schuster.

Hyde, Lewis, 1983, *The Gift: Imagination and the Erotic Life of Property*, New York: Vintage Books.

Illouz, Eva, 2007, *Cold Intimacies: the Making of Emotional Capitalism*, Cambridge: Polity Press.

Irwin, P. and R. Lynn, 2005, 'Sex Differences in Means and Variability on the Progressive Matrices in University Students', *British Journal of Psychology*, 96(4), November: 505–24.

Ivins, William M. Jr, 1969, *Prints and Visual Communication*, Cambridge, MA: MIT Press.

Jay, Martin, 1973, *Dialectical Imagination: a History of the Frankfurt School and Institute of Social Research 1923–1950*, London: Little, Brown & Co.

Jay, Martin, 1990, 'Urban Flights: the Institute of Social Research between Frankfurt and New York', in F. Engeldorp-Gastelaars, S. Magala and O. Preuss (eds), *Critical Theory Today. The Frankfurt School: How Relevant is it Today?* The Hague: Universitaire Pers Rotterdam.

Jay, Martin, 1994, *Downcast Eyes: the Denigration of Vision in Twentieth-Century French Thought*, Berkeley, Los Angeles and London: University of California Press.

Jay, Martin, 2005, *Songs of Experience: Modern American and European Variations on a Universal Theme*, Berkeley, Los Angeles and London: University of California Press.

Jones, Campbell and Damian O'Doherty (eds), *Manifestos for the Business Schools of Tomorrow*, Stanford, CA: Dvalin Books (Creative Commons).

Joinson, Adam N., 2003, *Understanding the Psychology of Internet Behavior*, Basingstoke and New York: Palgrave.

Kavolis, V., 1980, 'Logics of Selfhood and Modes of Order: Civilizational Structures for Individual Identities', in R. Robertson and B. Holzner (eds), *Identity and Authority*, Oxford: Blackwell.

Kets de Vries, Manfred F.R., 2001, *Struggling with the Demon: Perspectives on Individual and Organizational Irrationality*, Madison, CT: Psychosocial Press.

Kets de Vries, Manfred F.R. and D. Miller, 1984, *The Neurotic Organization: Diagnosing and Changing Counterproductive Styles of Management*, San Francisco: Jossey Bass.

Kinsey, Alfred, Wardell Pomeroy and Martin Clyde, 1975, *Sexual Behavior in the Human Male*, Bloomington: Indiana University Press (first edition 1948).

Kiser, Edgar and Justin Baer, 2005, 'The Bureaucratization of States: Towards an Analytical Weberianism', in Julia Adams, Elisabeth S. Clemens and Shola Orloff, (eds), *Remaking Modernity: Politics, History, and Sociology*, Durham, Duke University Press

Klamer, Arjo, 2007, *Speaking of Economics: How to get in the Conversation*, London: Routledge.

Klamer, Arjo, 2008, 'Structuurrapport voor de bijzondere leerstoel Economie van de Podiumkunsten' [Structural Report on Extraordinary Chair in the Economy of the Performing Arts], unpublished typescript, Erasmus University Rotterdam.

Klein, Naomi, 2002, *No Logo: No Space, No Choice, No Jobs*, New York: Picador.

Konrad, Gyeorgi and Ivan Szelenyi, 1979, *The Intellectuals on the Road to Class Power*, New York: Harcourt Brace Jovanovitch.

Korzybski, Alfred, 1958, *Science and Sanity: an Introduction to Non-Aristotelian Systems and General Semantics*, Lakeville, CT: International Non-Aristotelian Publishing Company.

Kramer, Hilton, 2004, 'The 'Memory' of Czeslaw Miłosz, 1911–2004', *New Criterion*, 23 (October): 79.

Krugman, Paul and Robin Wells, 2006, 'The Health Service Crisis and what to do about it', *New York Review of Books*, 53(5), March.

Kuhn, Thomas S., 1996, *The Structure of Scientific Revolutions*, 3rd edn, Chicago: University of Chicago Press (first edition 1962).

Kuhn, Thomas, 2000, *The Road Since Structure: Philosophical Essays 1970–1993 with an Autobiographical Interview*, ed. James Conant and John Haugeland, Chicago: Chicago University Press.

Kusturica, Emir, 1995, *Underground*, a CIBY 2000 (Paris), Pandora Film (Frankfurt), Novo Film (Budapest) co-production.

Laclau, Ernesto, 2005, *On Populist Reason*, London and New York: Verso.

Lakatos, Imre and Alan Musgrave (eds), 1970, *Criticism and the Growth of Knowledge*, Cambridge: Cambridge University Press.

Lakoff, George, 1987, *Women, Fire and Dangerous Things*, Chicago: University of Chicago Press.

Lamberts, Steven, 2005, 'De "gender paradox" in de studentenpopulatie van de Erasmus Universiteit Rotterdam', http://www.eur. nl/universitaire_plechtigheden/diesnatalis/2005/lamberts/print.html.

Larkin, Philip, 1974, *High Windows*, London: Faber and Faber.

Larson, Magali Sarfatti, 1993, *Behind the Postmodern Façade: Architectural Change in Late Twentieth Century America*, Berkeley: University of California Press.

Lash, Scott and John Urry, 1994, *Economies of Sign and Space*, London: Sage.

Latour, Bruno, 2005, *Reassembling the Social: an Introduction to Actor-Network Theory*, Oxford: Oxford University Press.

Leeuven, T.N. van and A.F.J. van Raan, 2007, 'Bibliometric Profiles of Management Research at the Erasmus University 1999–2003', Leiden, CWTS Report to ERIM, May.

Leinberger, Paul and Bruce Tucker, 1991, *The New Individualists: the Generation after the Organization Man*, New York: Harper Collins.

Linstead, Steven, 2008, personal e-mail about the origins of SCOS.

Lowenthal, David, 1998, *The Heritage Crusade and the Spoils of History*, Cambridge: Cambridge University Press.

Luckmann, Thomas, 2008, 'On Social Interaction and the Communicative Construction of Personal Identity, Knowledge and Reality', *Organization Studies*, 29(02): 277–90.

Lynch, Allen, 2005, *How Russia is not Ruled: Reflections on Russian Political Development*, Cambridge: Cambridge University Press.

Magala, Slawomir, 1997, 'The Making and Unmaking of Sense', *Organization Studies*, 18(2): 317–38.

Magala, Slawomir, 2005, *Cross-Cultural Competence*, London: Routledge.

Majakowski, Vladimir, 1925, *Vladimir Ilich Lenin: a Poem'*, Leningrad: Gosudarstvennoe Izdatielstvo, p. 25 (verses 1300–8) (in Russian).

Malesevic, Sinisa and John A. Hall, 2005, 'Citizenship, Ethnicity and Nation-States', in Craig Calhoun, Chris Rojek and Bryan Turner (eds), *The Sage Handbook of Sociology*, London, Thousand Oaks and New Delhi: Sage.

Malinowski, Bronislaw, 1969, 'The Problem of Meaning in Primitive Languages', in C.K. Ogden, and I.A. Richards, *The Meaning of Meaning*, London: Routledge (first edition 1923).

Marciniak, Katarzyna, 2006, *Alienhood: Citizenship, Exile, and the Logic of Difference*, Minneapolis and London: University of Minnesota Press.

Marcuse, Herbert, 1974, *Eros and Civilization: Philosophical Enquiry into Freud*, Boston: Beacon Press.

Marcuse, Herbert, 1999, *Reason and Revolution: Hegel and the Rise of Social Theory*, Amherst, NY: Humanity Books (first edition 1941).

Marcuse, Herbert, 2006, *One-Dimensional Man*, London: Routledge (first edition 1964).

McCarthy, Thomas, 1990, 'After the Linguistic Turn: Critical Theory Versus the New Pragmatism', in F. Engeldorp-Gastelaars, S. Magala and O. Preuss (eds), *Critical Theory Today. The Frankfurt School: How Relevant is it Today?* The Hague: Universitaire Pers Rotterdam.

McCloskey, Deirdre, 2006, *The Bourgeois Virtues: Ethics for an Age of Commerce*, Chicago: University of Chicago Press.

McCoy, Elin, 2006, *The Emperor of Wine: the Remarkable Story of the Rise and Reign of Robert Parker*, London: Grub Street.

McIntyre, Alasdair, 2006, *Edith Stein: a Philosophical Prologue*, London: Continuum Books.

McLuhan, Marshall, 1962, *The Gutenberg Galaxy*, Toronto: University of Toronto Press.

McLuhan, Marshall, 1967, *Understanding Media: the Extensions of Man*, London: Sphere Books.

McSweeney, Brendan, 2007, 'Predictive Failure and Construction Flaws: Testing and Unpacking Hofstede's Claim to Have Demonstrated Validity', paper for the IACCM Conference, Erasmus University, Rotterdam, 18–19 May.

Mead, Margaret, 2001, *Coming of Age in Samoa*, New York: Harper (first edition 1928).

Miłosz, Czeslaw, 1953, *The Captive Mind*, New York: Vintage.

Mitchell, Timothy, 2005, 'Economists and the Economy in the Twentieth Century', in George Steinmetz (ed.), *The Politics of Method in the Human Sciences: Positivism and its Epistemological Others*, Durham and London: Duke University Press.

Mitchell, W.J.T., 2005, *What do Pictures want? The Lives and Loves of Images*, Chicago and London: University of Chicago Press.

Mosquera, Patricia M. Rodriguez, Agneta H. Fischer and Anthony S.R. Manstead, 2004, 'Inside the Heart of Emotion: on Culture and Relational Concerns', in Larissa Z. Tiedens and Colin Wayne Leach (eds), *The Social Life of Emotions*, Cambridge: Cambridge University Press.

Mouffe, Chantal (ed.), 1999, *The Challenge of Carl Schmitt*, London and New York: Verso.

Mouzelis, Nicos, 1995, *Sociological Theory: What Went Wrong?* London: Routledge.

Musil, Robert, 1996, *A Man without Qualities*, New York: Vintage.

Myers, Fred, 2002, *Painting Culture*, Durham: Duke University Press.

Nafisi, Azar, 2003, *Reading Lolita in Tehran*, New York: Random House.

Noble David F., 1986, *Forces of Production: the Social History of Industrial Automation*, Oxford and New York: Oxford University Press.

Noble, David F., 2005, *Digital Diploma Mills: the Automation of Higher Education*, New York: Monthly Review Press.

Nooteboom, Bart, 2008, 'We denken veel te simple over marktwerking', *NRC Handlesblad, Opinie & Debat section*, 24 May: 14.

Nordhaus, William, 2008, *A Question of Balance: Weighing the Options on Global Warming Policies*, New Haven and London: Yale University Press.

Norris, Pippa, 2002, *Democratic Phoenix: Reinventing Political Activism*, Cambridge: Cambridge University Press.

Nussbaum, Martha, 2001, *Upheavals of Thought: the Intelligence of Emotions*, Cambridge, Cambridge University Press.

Oakes, Guy, 2004, *The Imaginary War: Civil Defense and American Cold War Culture*, New York and Oxford: Oxford University Press.

Ogden, C.K. and I.A. Richards, 1969, *The Meaning of Meaning: a Study of the Influence of Language upon Thought and of the Science of Symbolism*, London: Routledge (first edition 1923).

Ong, Aihwa, 2006, *Neoliberalism as Exception. Mutations in Citizenship and Sovereignty*, Durham and London: Duke University Press.

Perelman, Michael, 2000, *The Invention of Capitalism: Classical Political Economy and the Secret History of Primitive Accumulation*, Durham and London: Duke University Press.

Pfeffer, Jeffrey, 1997, *New Directions for Organization Theory: Problems and Prospects*, Oxford: Oxford University Press.

Piore, M.J., 1995, *Beyond Individualism*, Boston: Harvard University Press.

Pomper, Philip, 2002, 'Darwinizing History: the Evolution of Power in Russia', in Philip Pomper and David Gary Shaw (eds), *The Return of Science: Evolution, History and Theory*, Lanham, Boulder, New York and Oxford: Rowman and Littlefield.

Popper, Karl, 1959, *Logic of Scientific Discovery*, New York: Basic Books.

Popper, Karl, 1966, *The Open Society and its Enemies*, Princeton, NJ: Princeton University Press.

Popper, Karl, 1972, *Objective Knowledge: an Evolutionary Approach*, Oxford: Clarendon Press.

Popper, Karl, 2002, *The Poverty of Historicism*, London: Routledge (first edition 1957).

Potter, Jonathan, 2004, *Representing Reality: Discourse, Rhetoric and Social Construction*, London, Thousand Oaks and New Delhi: Sage (first published 1996).

Powell, Walter W., 2003, 'Neither Market nor Hierarchy: Network Form of Organization', in Michael J. Handel (ed.), *The Sociology of Organizations: Classic, Contemporary and Critical Readings*, Thousand Oaks, CA: Sage (first published 1990, *Research in Organizational Behavior*, 12: 295–336).

Quah, Danny, 2003, 'One Third of the World's Growth and Inequality', in Theo S. Eicher and Stephen J. Turnovsky (eds), *Inequality and Growth: Theory and Policy Implications*, Cambridge, MA and London: MIT Press.

Ranciere, Jacques, 2004, *The Politics of Aesthetics: the Distribution of the Sensible*, London and New York: Continuum Books.

Ranciere, Jacques, 2004, *The Politics of Aesthetics*, London and New York: Continuum Books.

Ranciere, Jacques, 2006, *Hatred of Democracy*, London: Verso.

Readings, Bill, 1996, *The University in Ruins*, Cambridge, MA: Harvard University Press.

Reich, Wilhelm, 1973, *The Functions of Orgasm: Discovery of the Orgon*, New York: Farrar, Straus and Giroux (first edition 1968).

Reza, Yasmina, 2007, *L'aube le soir ou la nuit*, Paris: Flammarion/Albin Michel.

Rieff, Philip, 1966, *The Triumph of the Therapeutic: Uses of Faith after Freud*, London, Chatto and Windus.

Rieff, Philip, 2006, *My Life among the Deathworks: Illustrations of the Aesthetics of Authority*, Charlottesville: University of Virginia Press.

Rieff, Philip, 2007, *The Crisis of the Office Class: the Decline of the Tragic Sensibility*, Charlottesville and London, University of Virginia Press.

Ritzer, George (2004), *The McDonaldization of Society*, revised edn, Thousand Oaks, CA: Sage.

Rorty, Richard, 1989, *Contingency, Irony and Solidarity*, Cambridge: Cambridge University Press.

Said, Edward W., 2000, *Reflections on Exile and Other Essays*, Cambridge, MA: Harvard University Press.

Sarkar, Bhaskar, 2008, 'The Melodramas of Globalization', *Cultural Dynamics*, 20(1): 31–51.

Schmidt, Peter, 2008, 'Values and Support for Immigration: a Cross-Country Comparison', seminar paper, http://www.uu.nl/uupublish/onderzoek/onderzoekcentra/ercomer/seminars/abstract/46955.

Schmitt, Carl, 1979, *Politische Theologie. Vier Kapitel zue Lehre von de Souveranitat*, Berlin: Duncker and Humblot (first edition 1922/1933).

Schroeder, Jonathan E., 2002, *Visual Consumption*, London and New York: Routledge.

Sen, Amartya, 1999, *Development as Freedom*, New York: Knopf.

Sen, Amartya, 2005, *The Argumentative Indian: Writings on Indian History, Culture and Identity*, New York: Farrar, Straus and Giroux.

Sennett, Richard, 2006, *The Culture of the New Capitalism*, New Haven and London: Yale University Press.

Sewell, William H., Jr, 2005, *Logics of History: Social Theory and Social Transformation*, Chicago: University of Chicago Press.

Simmel, Georg, 1978, *The Philosophy of Money*, Boston and London: Routledge and Kegan Paul (first German edition 1907).

Soin, Kim and Tobias Scheytt, 2006, 'Making the Case for Narrative Methods in Cross-Cultural Organizational Research', *Organizational Research Methods*, 9: 55–77.

Sojak, Radoslaw and Daniel Wicenty, 2005, *Zagubiona rzeczywistość. O społecznym konstruowaniu niewiedzy* [Lost Reality: on Social Construction of Ignorance], Warsaw: Oficyna naukowa.

Sokal, Alan, 1996, 'Transgressing the Boundaries: Towards a Transformative Hermeneutics of Quantum Gravity', *Social Text*, 46/47, spring/summer: 217–52.

Sokal, Alan, 2008, *Beyond the Hoax: Science, Philosophy and Culture*, Oxford and New York: Oxford University Press.

Sokal, Alan and Jean Bricmont, 1999, *Fashionable Nonsense: Postmodern Intellectuals' Abuse of Science*, New York: Picador.

Sontag, Susan, 1977, *On Photography*, New York: Penguin [Polish translation by S. Magala (1986), *O fotografii*, Warsaw: Wydawnictwa Artystyczne i Filmowe].

Sontag, Susan, 2003, *Regarding the Pain of Others*, New York: Farrar, Straus and Giroux.

Śpiewak, Paweł, 2005, *Pamięć po komunizmie* [*Memory after Communism*], Gdańsk: słowo/obraz terytoria.

Staniszkis, Jadwiga, 1984, *Poland's Self-limiting Revolution*, Princeton, NJ: Princeton University Press.

Staniszkis, Jadwiga, 1992, *The Ontology of Socialism*, Oxford and New York: Oxford University Press.

Starski, Stanislaw (penname of Slawomir Magala), 1981, *Class Struggle in Classless Poland*, Boston, MA: South End Press.

Steinmetz, George (ed.), 2005, *The Politics of Method in the Human Sciences: Positivism and its Epistemological Others*, Durham and London: Duke University Press.

Stenner, Karen, 2005, *The Authoritarian Dynamic*, Cambridge: Cambridge University Press.

Swidler, Ann, 2001, *Talk of Love: How Culture Matters*, Chicago and London: University of Chicago Press.

Syberberg, Hans-Jurgen, 1981, *Die freudlose Gesellschaft: Notizen aus dem letzten Jahren*, Munich and Vienna: Hanser.

Tarski, Alfred, 1946, *Introduction to Logic and to the Methodology of Deductive Sciences*, New York: University Press (first edition 1936).

Taylor, Charles, 2004, *Modern Social Imaginaries*, Durham and London: Duke University Press.

Taylor, Charles, 2007, *A Secular Age*, Cambridge, MA and London: The Belknap Press of Harvard University Press.

Tehranian, Majid, 2007, *Rethinking Civilization: Resolving Conflict in the Human Family*, London and New York: Routledge.

Terkel, Studs, 2003, *Hope Dies Last: Keeping the Faith in Difficult Times*, London: New Press.

Thrift, Nigel, 2002, 'Performing Cultures in the New Economy', in Paul du Gay and Michael Pryke (eds), *Cultural Economy: Cultural Analysis and Commercial Life*, London: Sage.

Thrift, Nigel, 2005, *Knowing Capitalism*, London, Thousand Oaks and New Delhi: Sage.

Tsoukas, Haridimos, 2005, *Complex Knowledge: Studies in Organizational Epistemology*, Oxford: Oxford University Press.

Tubella, Imma, 2004, 'Television, the Internet, and the Construction of Identity', in Manuel Castells (ed.), *The Network Society: a Cross-Cultural Perspective*, Cheltenham, UK and Northampton, MA, USA: Edward Elgar.

Turow, Joseph and Lokman Tsui (eds), 2008, *The Hyperlinked Society: Questioning Connections in the Digital Age*, Ann Arbor: University of Michigan Press.

The United States District Court for the Middle District of Pennsylvania, Case 4:04-cv-02688-JEJ, Document 342, filed 12/20/2005.

Veblen, Thorstein, 1953, *The Theory of the Leisure Class*, New York: Mentor (first edition 1988).

Wagner, Peter, 2000, 'The Bird in Hand: Rational Choice – the Default Mode of Social Theorizing', in Margaret S. Archer and Jonathan Q. Tritter (eds), *Rational Choice Theory: Resisting Colonization*, London and New York: Routledge.

Wallerstein, Immanuel, 2004, 'Cultures in Conflict: Who are We? Who are the Others?' in Samir Dasgupta (ed.), *The Changing Face of Globalization*, New Delhi, Thousand Oaks and London: Sage.

Walsh, Peter, 2003, 'That Withered Paradigm: the Web, the Expert and the Information Highway', in Henry Jenkins and David Thorburn (eds), *Democracy and the New Media*, Cambridge, MA and London: MIT Press.

Weick, Karl, 1995, *Sensemaking in Organizations*, Thousand Oaks, CA: Sage.

Weick, Karl, 1998, 'Improvisation as a Mindset for Organizational Analysis', *Organization Science*, 9: 543–55.

Weick, Karl, 2001, *Making Sense of Organizations*, Oxford: Blackwell.

Weick, Karl, Kathleen Sutcliffe and David Obstfeld, 2005, 'Organizing and the Process of Sensemaking', *Organization Science*, 16(4), July–August: 409–21.

White, Stephen, 2000, *Affirmation in Political Theory: the Strengths of Weak Ontology*, Princeton and Oxford: Princeton University Press.

Whitehead, Alfred N., 1925, *Science and the Modern World*, Lowell Lectures, London: Macmillan.

Wierzbicka, Anna, 1997, *Understanding Cultures through their Key Words: English, Russian, Polish, German and Japanese*, Oxford: Oxford University Press.

Wiggershaus, Rolf, 1995, *The Frankfurt School: its History, Theories and Political Significance*, Cambridge, MA: MIT Press.

Williams, Colin C., 2005, *A Commodified World? Mapping the Limits of Capitalism*, London and New York: Zed Books.

Williamson, O.E., 1975, *Markets and Hierarchies: Analysis and Antitrust Implications*, New York: Free Press.

Willmott, Hugh, 2008, a personal communication (e-mail of 20 March) with fragments of an unpublished paper on critical management studies.

Wilson, Andrew, 2005, *Virtual Politics: Faking Democracy in the Post-Soviet World*, New Haven and London: Yale University Press.

Wittgenstein, Ludwig, 2001, *Philosophical Investigations. Philosophische Untersuchungen*, Malden, MA: Blackwell (first edition 1953).

Wodak, Ruth and Paul Chilton, 2005, *A New Agenda in Critical Discourse Analysis: Theory, Methodology and Interdisciplinarity*, Discourse Approaches to Politics, Society and Culture, New York: John Benjamin.

Wodiczko, Krzysztof, 1992, *Public Adresses: Krzysztof Wodiczko*, Minneapolis: Walker Art Center.

Young, Michael, 1961, *The Rise of Meritocracy*, Harmondsworth, Penguin.

Zelizer, Viviana, 2005, *The Purchase of Intimacy*, Princeton and Oxford: Princeton University Press.

Zemsky, Robert, 2008, 'The Rain Man Cometh – Again', *Academy of Management Perspectives*, 22(1): 5–14.

Ziarek, Krzysztof, 2004, *The Force of Art*, Stanford, CA: Stanford University Press.

Žižek, Slavoj, 1994, *The Metastases of Enjoyment: Six Essays on Women and Causality*, London and New York: Verso.

Žižek, Slavoj, 2003, *The Puppet and the Dwarf: the Perverse Core of Christianity*, Cambridge, MA: MIT Press.

Žižek, Slawoj, 2008, *In Defense of Lost Causes*, London and New York: Verso.

Name Index